NOLS CANOEING

Alexander Martin

STACKPOLE BOOKS

0 11557 01172 2

Published by
STACKPOLE BOOKS
5067 Ritter Road
Mechanicsburg, PA 17055
www.stackpolebooks.com

Printed in the United States

First edition

10 9 8 7 6 5 4 3 2 1

Cover photo by Zand B. Martin
Interior photos & illustrations by Zand B. Martin

FSC
www.fsc.org
MIX
Paper from
responsible sources
FSC® C005010

Library of Congress Cataloging-in-Publication Data

Martin, Zander, 1980-
  NOLS canoeing / Alexander (Zand) Martin.
    pages cm
  Includes index.
  ISBN-13: 978-0-8117-1172-2 (pbk.)
  ISBN-10: 0-8117-1172-2 (pbk.)
  1. Canoes and canoeing—Handbooks, manuals, etc. 2. Recreation leadership. 3. Adventure and adventurers. I. Title. II. Title: National Outdoor Leadership School expedition canoeing.
  GV783.M32 2013
  797.122—dc23
                                                            2013004452

Contents

Introduction

The founder of NOLS, Paul Petzoldt, famously emphasized the danger of teaching novices skills without helping them develop the judgment to use these skills safely. This book is intended as a reference as well as a collection of ideas from the world of expeditionary canoe travel. It mines the wealth of knowledge accumulated by NOLS students and instructors over many years as they navigated inland waterways in small, open boats. The goal of the text is to clearly present NOLS best practices in a fluid and flexible, judgment-based framework. It also suggests practices and tips that are part of the wider canoe world and would be useful to the expert or aspiring expedition canoeist.

This book is only a tool. It must be accompanied with and followed by experience. A NOLS course is an excellent way to gain this experience and accelerate your growth. As your skill and judgment mature, this text supports the next steps with instruction on leading and executing personal and institutional canoe expeditions, along with training in wilderness medicine and river rescue.

This book will not teach you how to paddle, though it gives tips you can refer to while practicing, training, planning, and even on expeditions. You will not find comprehensive explanations here about how to camp, set up a tent, or cook, as they are covered elsewhere in the NOLS Library.

So use this book as a tool and a reference—one of many—as well as a motivating impetus for getting the maps out.

What Is Expedition Canoeing?

Canoeing is the act of traveling in a simple open boat, usually fairly narrow, propelled by human power applied with a single-bladed paddle. For the purposes of this book, we are talking about the North American type of canoe. NOLS and most dictionaries define an *expedition* as a journey or effort undertaken by a small, dedicated team to achieve a specific goal—to do research, teach skills, or travel to a certain place and point, among others.

So expedition canoeing, then, is any travel by canoe undertaken by a small, dedicated group or individual to achieve a specific goal. In most cases, it implies carrying your gear and traveling along a planned route with more movement than leisure.

One of the things I love about the canoe is its pure accessibility: it can be used by an octogenarian paddling about on the local millpond with as much pleasure as the dry-suit-clad team traversing arctic Canada. The world of canoeing is diverse, and this text focuses on expedition canoeing—travel by canoe, on moving water as well as on lakes and oceans—rather than racing, pure recreation, whitewater day runs, or playboating.

It is important to consider what expedition canoeing is not. The scope of canoeing is broad and vast and takes on many faces around the world. In the Pacific Northwest and across the Pacific in Hawaii and New Zealand, canoeing is a pillar of cultural pride and revival, while on the Mekong, Congo, and Amazon Rivers, it remains central to subsistence trade, travel, and food gathering. Canoeists race at the Olympics and on 500-mile (805-kilometer) wilderness courses; they travel under sail on the ocean, cross continents, and paddle through the rapids of the Grand Canyon; and they poke around the local ponds and go fishing. The focus of this book is on North American style expedition canoeing, however, and in that sense, canoeing is a sport, a means of travel, and potentially a platform for research and education.

The modern canoe has been used on long expeditions on every continent with liquid water, and most bodies of water have been paddled in open canoes, for trade, exploration, migration, and adventure. Expeditions are undertaken solo and by teams, fielded by institutions, and begun purely to provide classrooms for experiential and transformative education, such as at NOLS.

In a certain sense, the canoe is the perfect vehicle. With relatively little wear to the human body, it runs for thousands of miles carrying loads several hundred pounds in weight and requires no more fuel than a bit of sweat. It does not need roads and can go a thousand miles in a month. Its only real limit is how quickly its passengers eat their way though their food, a period that can extend over thirty days. The canoe travels upriver and down, through mountains and to the sea. It follows the landscape without aggression or dominance.

Henry David Thoreau declared that "in wildness is the preservation of the world," but he has often been misquoted as saying "wilderness." People often think of expedition canoeing as taking place only in the wildernesses of the world, but that is a limiting definition. Rather, expedition canoeists seek out wildness—not really a place at all, but an intangible feeling in the paddlers' hearts that they have moved out of the mundane and into the natural world. This is the essence of exploration and is a wonderful component to many expeditions. The canoe is a simple conveyance that can foster this feeling perhaps better than any other means of travel yet devised.

NOLS and Its Canoe Program

The National Outdoor Leadership School (NOLS) was founded in 1965 in Lander, Wyoming, to train leaders in the skills of wilderness travel. Paul Petzoldt founded the school specifically to educate people who would go on to lead others in the wilderness, so the emphasis from the beginning was on teaching and coaching in strong technical and leadership skills, as well as helping students develop judgment in using them. The school has grown in its forty-seven years to include operations on six continents and courses ranging from 3 to 140 days. Skill types include mountaineering, climbing, backpacking, backcountry skiing, sailing, whitewater rafting and kayaking, sea kayaking, and expedition canoeing. These skills are still used primarily as platforms to teach leadership, technical skills, environmental science and ethics, risk management, judgment, and decision-making.

For four decades, NOLS has offered a canoe program. It is based on a style of river travel that grew out of a western mountain and canyon white-water environment, allowing it to cross-pollinate with rafting and kayaking while staying true to the roots of canoeing in eastern North America. NOLS field faculty working in the canoe program have a broad base, with diverse skills such as whitewater and sea kayaking, rafting, mountaineering, and backpacking. The canoe faculty have come from a broad spectrum of camps, guiding companies, and paddling schools, where they were teachers, leaders, participants, or a combination of the three. The variety of styles they brought to NOLS, the quantity and quality of expeditions they fielded, and the diverse environments they traveled through have resulted in solid program values and techniques, some of which are mentioned in this text.

Today the school fields canoe courses, or courses that include significant canoe elements, in Alaska, Utah, Idaho, Texas, Colorado, the Brazilian Amazon, North Australia, New Zealand, and Canada's Yukon Territory, with occasional forays into the Northwest Territories and Nunavut.

A History of the Expedition Canoe

The modern expedition canoe is the product of many thousands of years of development. Open canoes are used all over the world for sport, trade, and travel; before the modern era, canoes carried Polynesian colonists across thousands of miles of open ocean to seek new homes, just as they supported northern European trade networks and bore explorers and fur traders in the first western drives in the wilderness of North America.

The word *canoe* was derived from the Spanish *canoa*, meaning a small, open, human-powered craft. At his first meeting with the Arawak natives of San Salvador, Christopher Columbus pointed to the craft they had paddled up in and asked its name. They replied by shouting *kanua*, which made some of the sailors think of the Portuguese word for water trough, *canoa*. Within a few generations, the native peoples of the Caribbean were gone, but they had passed their word meaning into European languages.

The modern North American expedition boat is about 16 feet (4.8 meters) long, nearly 3 feet (.92 meters) wide, and designed for extended travel in rough conditions, moving people and goods long distances. The story of its origin begins in the mixed deciduous and coniferous forest of the Northeast: southern Ontario and Quebec, New York, and New England. This region contains a symphony of natural materials ideally suited to canoe building, as well as a deeply interwoven network of rivers and lakes that makes waterborne travel easy.

The ancestors of the Algonquin and Iroquois arrived in this region thousands of years ago, possibly first migrating into the area by water on seasonal hunting expeditions. The dense forest both thwarted significant overland travel and provided material for boat construction. Native stories support the idea that the first canoes built there were modeled after the rib cage of a large ruminant, with the ribs and skin translating into the structure of the hull.

Each tribe or band had its own designs that suited its local environment. Form followed function to produce a dizzying array of shapes. Canoes that were sometimes used in the ocean were very large and seaworthy, like those of the Passamaquoddy; those used mostly on rivers were small and heavily rockered (angled up at the bow and stern) so as to be light and nimble in moving water, like some eastern Cree hulls.

The Wabanaki peoples of Quebec, New Hampshire, Maine, and New Brunswick, part of the larger Algonquin-language group, developed a highly versatile hull made from cedar ribs and a birchbark skin. The seams were sealed with bear grease and conifer pitch. To construct their canoes, they drilled holes with stone, friction, and fire and sewed the pieces together with soaked spruce root. The resulting craft were durable and easily repaired with the materials at hand. They used these craft for hunting, fishing, seasonal migration, and raiding. Many other peoples built such craft of one material or another, but it was the Wabanaki builders and their design that most influenced the creation of the modern expedition canoe.

When Europeans first began to explore, trade, and colonize the Northeast, they quickly realized that travel was possible in what they viewed as the wilderness only if they traveled from watershed to watershed in small boats as the Algonquin, Iroquois, and Wabanaki did. They took native guides and purchased native craft, and by the eighteenth century, huge trade networks stretching thousands of miles and supported by trading posts and headquarters, called factories, had come into existence through the use of the canoe. The appropriation of this Native American and First Nations object marks the transition from subsistence to commercial and imperial use and is the major link in our understanding of the history of this aspect of North American material culture.

Birchbark was not the only skin material used, but it was by far the best, and by the middle of the nineteenth century, much of the bark of useful size had been stripped from the trees to feed the need for craft by fur traders as well as explorers and natives. The slow collapse of the fur trade was just beginning, and although logging was taking up some of the slack, an entirely new use for canoes was tentatively on the horizon—recreation.

By the latter half of the nineteenth century, a significant canoe building industry had grown along the Penobscot River, incorporating native design with American commercial production. In a workshop in Bangor, Maine, in 1875, birchbark was replaced with tightly woven duck canvas and then painted, creating the first wood-and-canvas canoe.

Within twenty years, companies across Maine, New Brunswick, and Ontario were building canoes this way, and the utility and durability of the new craft were apparent to all. These canoes were used by traders, loggers, and native peoples across the continent, and also increasingly by recreational users on the tail end of the first American ideological shift toward viewing wilderness as a place to relax rather than a place of fear and discomfort.

After World War II, the American warplane industry lost a huge percentage of its production demand, and the enormous aluminum infrastructure that supported it was in danger of falling into disuse. The factories were retooled to produce, among other things, aluminum canoes for the explosion in recreational needs in 1950s America. The aluminum canoes were durable and cheap, and they took their lines from the canvas canoes of the previous generation, just as those boats had taken the lines of the Penobscot and Passamoquoddy birchbark canoes. The wider use in the 1950s and 1960s fueled the creation of new companies and new materials; hulls were being produced in fiberglass, Kevlar, and myriad plastics and plastic composites. In the 1960s, a sandwich of vinyl, ABS plastic, and foam called Royalex was released by Uniroyal and was quickly appropriated as a canoe hull material. These space-age materials were infinitely stronger and more durable than aluminum or wood. With these materials and increased leisure time, people started canoeing in ways that had been unthinkable before, such as racing, expedition canoeing, and paddling whitewater.

Setting safety for a small chute on the Hyland River, Yukon Territory.

BUILDING COMPETENCE

Of all the revelations I have had in the outdoors, one of the loudest and most memorable was when a co-instructor twice my age and with thirty times my experience asked my opinion about how to do a forward stroke and then practiced my method. He might never use it again, and while his openness and willingness to listen had a big impact on me, the more dramatic realization I had was that there is a spectrum of growth that has no real end. In watching older professionals, it is easy to forget that on a day not so long ago, they were at a similar place as you, and that the very best still view themselves as learners.

In going into the wilderness and treating it as a classroom, a NOLS canoe course has a goal of teaching leadership in conjunction with—and usually through—technical expedition skills. One of my favorite outcomes I hear students talk about is that they have learned *how* to learn. Sometimes this is taught formally, but more often they simply develop the *confidence* to try things that are new for them, *patience* with the process of learning, and *leadership* to take control by setting goals and pursuing growth. Everyone learns differently, but we all need to develop these qualities, as well as obtain the support of more experienced paddlers.

The real professionals are the ones who continue to work on improving how they do things. Building competence does not stop at any particular level—there is no end goal, only moments of confidence in oneself that, clarified by self-awareness, can be the motivating force for a big trip.

Strong role models, good instruction, and practical experience in new environments are all elements that support growth, but they must be supplemented by an honest sense of reflection and constant striving to improve your systems and skills. The style you grow up with becomes ingrained, and if you are not careful, you will start to think it is the only way things can be done. The keys are to gain experience and keep an open mind so as to build the judgment that allows for flexible critical thinking.

One way to grow as a canoeist is to take a course. Whether it is expedition based, like those offered by NOLS, or a day- or weekend-long purely technical development course, like those offered by the American Canoe Association, Paddle Canada, or British Canoe Union, taking a course can jump-start your competence and confidence. Talk to the organization ahead of time about your desired experience and outcomes to find the course that's the best fit for you. All paddling schools and organizing bodies have courses for beginners. Less formal and less expensive skill development is often available from local paddling clubs and university outing clubs.

Before you can perform skillfully in a challenging environment, you should practice in that environment at the necessary level of skill under controlled conditions. In certain environments that are easily managed for risk, challenging yourself to the point of failure can be a valuable learning tool. Aggressively attempting certain skills can help hone your knowledge of every aspect of the maneuver as well as build your knowledge of water.

Paddling with new people or organizations can help you develop a higher skill level and exposes you to new ways of doing things. Another way to grow is to try a new design or style of canoe, such as a playboat or racing canoe. Traveling in other craft, such as a kayak or raft, will teach you to see water in different ways and make you a better canoeist.

Teaching or leading novices at a low level is another great learning opportunity. Coaching and explaining techniques to another paddler is a wonderful exercise in structuring your thoughts and skills. Peer teaching can be another powerful way of sharing knowledge and honing your skills, with experienced paddlers giving each other pointers on technique or form or asking the others for feedback.

CHAPTER 1 | EXPEDITION PLANNING

Helpful guidelines and tips on planning a canoe expedition

> Had I done it alone by canoe I might have boasted a little.
> —F. S. Farrar, RCMP, third mate of the RCMPV St. Roch,
> the first vessel to circumnavigate North America

The nervous excitement and grinning anxiety of planning a long trip are all encompassing: laying out sheet after sheet of maps with wending blue lines and dark, sharp shores; making endless phone calls and sending countless emails; writing lists; putting together all the necessary items like flour, pasta, and tiny stove pieces; smelling varnish and epoxy in the air; and realizing that before long you will depart from your familiar world and put blade to water in some far-off, distant place, becoming immersed in wildness. Planning is an exciting time. *NOLS Expedition Planning* is a great place to start when thinking about your first long trip.

From the perspective of how they are organized, canoe expeditions can come in many flavors; it is these differences that often dictate how they are planned, supplied, and executed. A team expedition is organized by equal partners around a destination or an existing personal relationship. A leader is sometimes designated, elected, or generated de facto by group needs. Although goals beyond the logistical are sometimes not discussed, over-arching goals, if not part of the genesis of the expedition, should be agreed on to provide structure and support the leadership.

For the majority of paddlers, their love of canoeing began on an institutional expedition, a trip led by experienced, paid leaders and supported by an institution such as a school, summer camp, tripping company, youth travel outfitter, or guide service. The institution organizes these types of expeditions and in most cases also equips, funds, and fields them. It usually sets the goals and arranges the details ahead of time, with little or no participant input, and there is a clear distinction between the instructors, leaders, or guides, and participants. Risk management is often more regulated here, with the institution requiring or at least preferring certain practices and systems. These expeditions can be wonderful for building experience both

3

An advanced hydrology class on a NOLS course on the San Juan River, Utah.

as a participant and as a leader, depending on the quality of leadership and support by the institution.

However the group comes together, the team members need to bond over a common set of goals and structures, which will help inform the planning process. Seasoned experts can plan a monthlong wilderness canoe expedition in just a few hectic days, if the team has worked together before or has strong leadership and the gear is all readily available and in good shape. It will take longer to put together multimonth, remote, or international expeditions, as well as those with a high percentage of beginners. Having clear goals, structures, and expectations will help streamline the process, as will having all the team members clearly express their needs and strengths in their individual processes of preparation. It is often helpful to do some things a few weeks or months ahead of time, such as researching routes, assembling maps and permits, and checking the readiness of the gear, so that when the planning really starts, all the ingredients will be ready.

Putting Together a Team

On an institutional expedition, the base staff or admissions department usually puts together the team, matching participants with experienced leaders. Building a team outside of an institutional framework can be much harder. The most logical place to start is with friends and family, with the caveat that people with whom you have positive and functional relationships back home might end up being your worst enemies when under significant stress in the backcountry.

Sometimes the best partner is not a close friend or loved one. Great places to look for potential partners are through extended social networks associated with camps or schools, at local paddling clubs, and on message boards, forums, and social media like Facebook or Twitter. I met my partner for a ninety-day trans-Europe canoe expedition for the first time at the airport two hours before our flight to France. It is not ideal or advised to go on an expedition after spending so little time together, but it worked out okay for us. You cannot predict how well you will function with another person or group while under stress in the backcountry, so it is best to put together your team ahead of time, structure the leadership, set group goals, and perhaps go on a few short but challenging trips together beforehand.

Setting Goals

Once you've put together your team, the first step in planning an expedition is to set goals as individuals and then bring the goals of all the team members into harmony with one another. The difference between a trip and an expedition is much more than just length: an expedition is guided by overarching goals and values, whereas a trip may not be. Choosing and identifying goals will focus the planning and help structure every single decision, from what paddle to take, to how the team communicates, to selecting a destination and route, all the way to putting the gear away at the end. It also is a good first challenge for the group—many talented teams on big expeditions have failed because the members had different goals. Everyone need not have all the same specific goals, but team members must not be in conflict over the goals of the group.

The team members' skills, needs, and experience help dictate what appropriate goals might be. For example, a group of advanced paddlers might set a primary goal of exploring a remote watershed by flying or portaging in, with a secondary goal of paddling whitewater. The goals of the expedition will inform all the other decisions made in planning and execution: the route needs to be structured to support the goals, along with the gear, training, transport, food, and so on.

Destination and Route Planning

Trip planning often revolves around the destination. The canoe is a vehicle for accessing inland waterways, and it can take you into some astounding environments and landscapes. Let your imagination run wild, with the only limitations being your team members' skills and resources. Reading canoeing books, looking through photo albums and coffee-table books, reading travel and outdoor blogs, and simply spinning the globe or poring over an old map are wonderful activities that can provide a multitude of ideas for journeys. Opening Google Earth and viewing the thin lines of rivers and compound shapes of lakes can be mesmerizing. Turn on the Panoramio option and tiny icons pop up all around the water systems; clicking on them shows photos of the landscape and the environment of the river or lake system.

Once all the team members have agreed on the general destination for the expedition, the next step is to plan a route. If your destination is a commonly paddled stretch, like the Colorado River through the Grand Canyon, then the route is already pretty well set, though even the Grand, the Allagash Wilderness Waterway, or a lake route in Algonquin or the Adirondacks will require some thought. Most route planning involves a bit more time, research, and energy, however.

It's important to keep the goals of the expedition in mind while planning the route. If, for example, you are planning a weeklong lake loop with the primary goals of family bonding and catching fish, you might want to avoid huge distances and long portages. Route planning should be a creative process that is supported by research and stays in touch with desired outcomes. Routes that involve ascending streams, tackling open lakes, paddling whitewater, and connecting these elements with long portages require specialized skills. Stringing lakes and ponds together with fast-flowing rivers, passes, heights of land, and beautiful, remote country is a worthy goal, but only if the group is ready for the challenges of a route like this.

Portaging hundreds of miles over snowy mountain passes, being dropped off by helicopter, shipping canoes around the world—these things and more are part of expedition canoeing, and the more research and experience you accumulate, the more possibilities are opened up. The sky is the limit here: you can dream up an exciting expedition, and then build the skills and experience necessary to eventually make this dream a reality.

Until recently, planning routes was a rather challenging part of canoe trip planning. Today, with focused use of technology and available resources, you can sketch out these details with efficiency and ease. The place to start is on the Internet, but route planning always ends with paper on a table, as it has for hundreds of years. Begin with free satellite map-

NOLS students lounging on the banks of the North Branch of the Big Salmon River, Yukon Territory.

ping programs like Google Earth and FlashEarth, tracing and connecting watersheds and judging the feasibility of new routes, and correlate these maps with topographic databases and river guides. Google Maps is useful for determining put-ins, take-outs, and travel distances. Use Google or another search engine to look for other trips on similar, related, or identical routes. Wikipedia can provide general river information and watershed maps. Finally, visit a good library and look at large-scale maps and atlases, matching these with your online research.

River guides and outfitters who paddle your destination are invaluable sources, not only for hard-to-find information on remote rivers, but also for advice on paddling the creek down the street. Search the Internet for local outfitters or guides, and call them to chat about what resources they can offer. They know the area better than anyone and can provide you with information and offer logistical help.

Maps

The ideal map set for a canoe expedition consists of 1:50,000 scale maps of the entire route, with 1:250,000 scale maps as an overview. Depending on the destination, this level of detail could be unnecessary or vital. For huge, winding, flat rivers, 1:250,000 could be adequate, but for large complex

Sources of Maps

United States

For maps of U.S. locations, the United States Geological Survey website (www.usgs.gov) is the place to go. The USGS Store Map Locator and Downloader provides free downloads of high-resolution topographic maps in the 7.5-minute series (1:24,000) and up, in PDF format. With this series, you can open the maps in Adobe Reader and turn map data layers on or off. USGS's National Map (nationalmap.gov) also provides a huge number of maps and customizable mapping resources.

Canada

Topographic maps in any scale for Canadian locations can be downloaded for free from Natural Resources Canada's GeoGratis website (www.geogratis.ca). The website has myriad mapping products; canoeists should look for CanTopo Digital Topographic Maps in 1:50,000 to 1:250,000 scale or a similar series. In Canada, 1:250,000 scale maps are named with a one- to three-digit number, a capital letter, and a name: 105K Quiet Lake, for example. That map is then broken down into sixteen 1:50,000 scale maps.

International

Most of Asia and Eastern Europe are covered by the now-outdated Soviet Army Survey maps, which are available from multiple sources on the Internet, usually for paid download but sometimes for free. Some of the files can be quite large but are easily printed at a local copy shop. The price of printing dozens of color maps on good paper can quickly become prohibitive, however, and printing maps in gray scale risks losing detail. Sometimes buying them directly from the government or a retailer is a better idea. In print, they are available from Omni Resources in North Carolina (www.omnimap.com), which has the largest selection of international maps, including some weird and random sheets of far-off places in surprising quality. For off-the-beaten-path destinations, it's also a good idea to call outfitters or guides that operate in those areas.

lakes, whitewater rivers, or hard-to-find portages, 1:50,000 is best, while 1:100,000 might be the most efficient option in the United States and 1:75,000 in Europe.

This can result in a huge amount of paper to carry if you are planning a longer route. You can cut this down somewhat by identifying which sections require a high level of detail and which do not, as well as comparing different scales and types of maps of the given area. It is possible to paddle across continents using nothing but road atlases and tourist maps; in fact, it can be easy and it has been done. However, on a foggy day on a huge lake studded with islands and narrow, reed-filled bays, the navigator will need the best map available, weight be damned.

Several types of maps can be found on the Internet and in bookstores and libraries. Road atlases and gazetteers are available for each state and province in North America, as well as for many other countries and regions. They are an inexpensive and effective way to plan and cover longer routes, as they rarely cost more than $20 and have lots of condensed information. They can often be used for navigation, but the scales can change from page to page and the difficulty of navigation can change from lake to lake, so you might end up in situations where you wish you had a map with a larger scale. Road atlases tend to use a much smaller scale in areas with fewer roads, which are often just where canoeists want to go.

Commonly paddled routes often have local canoe area maps or river maps. Canoe area maps come in various scales and focus on popular routes or areas, like the Boundary Waters in Minnesota, Bowron Lakes in British Columbia, Allagash River in Maine, or St. Regis area in New York. River maps are usually bound in a book or with a spiral ring and are either hand-drawn or cut-down topographic maps. These save a huge amount of paper on popular routes and also provide a great deal of useful information on rapids, water sources, and natural and human history. River maps are best paired with at least one set of overview topos, especially necessary in case of an evacuation or lost-person search because they provide information about the surrounding area.

Cycle touring guides often follow routes along rivers, as the fluvial right-of-way is usually used for bike paths and infrastructure. Therefore, bike maps are a great option for long rivers close to civilization, as you can carry hundreds of miles of river information in one small map booklet.

Maps are not sacred texts; they can be wrong, and they can be written on. In empty spaces, write in pertinent information from guidebooks or satellite surveys. On long, featureless stretches, consider adding tick marks so that you can easily gauge distances and determine your travel speed.

Permits and Visas

The number of federal, state, tribal, and provincial permits needed for some trips can be dizzying. Some agencies have specific launch dates, usage days, and permit regulations, while others have simple "iron rangers" at certain gateways. Some take registration only over the phone, but others allow you to register online. The details are many, but you need to take care of them well ahead of time—in some cases, six months to a year before your expedition.

Fishing, hunting, and gun permits add another level of complexity. Fishing licenses are often easy to obtain at gas stations or tackle shops—though checking ahead is a good idea—whereas hunting, especially large game, requires more complicated permits. Guns are not required or encouraged for travel in bear country.

If your expedition will take you to another country, visas are a whole other issue. The rules for some countries, especially in Asia and Africa, change monthly, and you can expect to pay a lot of money for the right to enter the country. Countries in Europe and North America, as well as Australia and New Zealand, are usually much easier to enter. You will also need a valid passport. Do research on what the country requires well in advance on the Internet (the U.S. State Department's Citizens Abroad site, the Lonely Planet country pages, and Thorn Tree forum are excellent places to start). You may also want to call the embassy in any country you plan to visit.

Equipment

Judicious choices in equipment can prevent much hardship and inefficiency on the expedition (see chapter 2 for detailed discussions of many gear items). Plan ahead to save money and avoid scrambling at the last minute. Fix, repair, and test everything ahead of time, and lay out your gear in neat lines on the floor of a clean, uncluttered room or garage. Make lists (see appendix A).

It is best not to bring a piece of gear on an expedition for group use if you are not willing to risk its being lost or permanently broken. When you offer it up, it becomes group gear for group use. If a number of people are supplying expensive group gear for the voyage, consider giving them discounts in other areas, such as on gas or food costs. This can get complicated fast. Team members all need to be honest up front about their expected budgets and feelings about money and gear use. The time to figure this out is before the trip, not during or after. Accounts should be kept, as even the appearance of a lack of balance could cause turmoil within the group.

A key step in determining your gear needs is figuring out whether you are planning a camping trip or a paddling trip. Both activities will occur, but in different ratios depending on where your team's focus lies. Some people like to spend more time in camp, fishing, baking, going for day hikes, and living outdoors. Other people focus more on travel and might not take camp shoes or clothes at all, let alone a camp chair or fancy kitchen gear. After they tie up their boats, they'll still be wearing river gear while they attack a bowl of mac and cheese, finally crawling into a bivy sack under a tarp after dark. Many expeditions try to balance both camping and paddling. Agreeing on your group's focus ahead of time will help provide structure for the trip and determine a lot of your gear choices.

Packing Systems

Expeditioning for recreation, research, or education has come a long way from the days of rolled-up plastic and canvas tarps in army-surplus duffels and the associated daily hang-up of every piece of wet gear. Today, with the right equipment and skills, if things in your pack get wet, you have either done something wrong or gotten woefully and historically unlucky. Good packing systems for canoeing have just a few basic principles: they should be simple, organized, and use reliable packs that are waterproof and durable.

CANOE PACKS

All canoeists have their favorite packs, and some use a variety of packs for different purposes, route types, and environments. Packs are often needed for food and kitchens, as well as for group and personal gear.

Blue Barrels

The ideal pack for any canoe expedition—especially those with routes involving river travel—is not really a pack at all, but a repurposed food and industrial container sometimes called an olive or pickle barrel. These high-density plastic barrels are amazingly durable containers, and when fitted with pack harnesses, they become the perfect canoe packs. The barrel, usually blue, has an aluminum clamp on one end that secures a plastic lid with a rubberized gasket, forming a

Each pack option has its uses on this trip on the Boundary Waters in Minnesota: the purple rucksack as a day bag, the orange dry bag for food and kitchen gear, the blue barrel for personal and camp gear, and the black duffel for small group gear that can get wet but is hard to portage on its own.

waterproof seal; most come with two black handles near the lid that are helpful in moving them around. Sizes range from 1,830 cubic inches to 13,425 cubic inches (30 to 220 liters), with 3,661 cubic inches (60 liters) being by far the most common and useful size. Barrels and the harnesses used to carry them are available from many paddlesports-specific stores, such as Rutabaga and NRS. If you buy used barrels from a restaurant supply store or food importer, confirm that they were not used to store chemicals, especially if you plan to use them to hold food. Olive barrels are another option; these have screw-on lids and are available used from some delis. With these and any other used barrels, check that they don't have a strong smell.

Blue barrels are highly effective for packing food and kitchens as well as personal gear. One 3,661-cubic-inch (60-liter) barrel can easily hold one person's clothing and gear for any length expedition, or a full kitchen, ten days' food for two people, and a wet tent and tarp. Dedicated solely to food, it can hold enough to feed two people, working hard in warm weather, for twenty days. A barrel of this size densely packed with food

On the Rio Grande in Texas, barrels provide storage for the kitchen gear and food as well as personal gear.

weighs about 80 pounds (36.3 kilograms) and is just about the limit that can be safely carried by an adult for long periods, both for personal health and because of the harness stitching.

The aluminum clamp that holds the lid on is the only really fragile part of the barrel and should not be taken off for any reason. Keep the gasket clean and free of debris, and occasionally renew it with RTV sealant, available at auto repair stores. If the clamp develops a tendency to pop open, a cotter pin inserted in the lock space will hold it closed.

When bought new, a barrel and harness are only slightly more expensive than a dry bag or Duluth Pack, about $120 in the United States, but can outlast many of them. Barrels are also more effective as flotation when securely rigged in. A good harness is well padded with stiff shoulder straps and an adjustable hip belt. If you are tall or have a long torso, however, you might find that a barrel is too short to really engage the hip belt, which makes it uncomfortable to carry over long portages.

Soft Packs

Nonrigid packs of cotton or synthetic canvas (Cordura), such as the classic Duluth Pack and its modern derivatives, come in many sizes and fit well inside a canoe; they are durable and lightweight and will collapse down to a very small size when the food is gone, freeing up space for other items. The challenges with these packs are in waterproofing and in protecting delicate objects, problems usually solved by putting one or two dry bags inside the soft pack; two 2,440-cubic-inch (40-liter) dry bags work well for this. The pack protects the dry bag from wear, and the dry bag keeps contents dry.

Using pack liners inside soft packs works to a point, but submersion for any length of time will soak the contents of the liner. Liners of coated nylon with a roll top and clip closure system are better and can be waterproof, but these are often fragile and can be punctured or ripped. And setting down a pack roughly can split individual food bags inside them or push sharper objects against the walls of the liner.

Dry Bags

Large PVC, vinyl, or thick urethane-coated nylon dry bags are commonly used as packs for food and personal gear. When new and properly closed, they are waterproof, but if handled roughly, they will puncture or abrade, so you need to treat them carefully and avoid packing them with hard edges or sharp items near the sides. They are often large—over 6,102 cubic inches (100 liters) is not uncommon—and floppy, making them harder to pack than a barrel. Their volume and waterproofing are strong selling points, as are the integrated backpack-style shoulder straps and hip belt that are common on larger versions. Large dry bags can be lined with a plastic bag or coated nylon pack liner when used for personal gear; all vital items, like sleeping bags, should be packed inside lined stuff sacks as well.

Duffel Bags

Large, simple nylon duffel bags with two handles and a full-length zipper are good packing options as an addition to other systems. They are inexpensive, have a huge capacity, and can carry or store light, bulky items in the boat and on the trail, and then basically disappear into another pack when empty. While portaging, you can place a large, floppy duffel bag—holding all the small bits of gear you otherwise would have carried in your arms, like water bottles, map cases, PFDs, helmets, daypacks, throw bags, and bailers—on top of a barrel or pack and comfortably carry it some distance. In camp, the duffel helps you keep things organized and out of the sand and dirt.

Boxes

Large, rectangular boxes are functional storage options for food and kitchen equipment. One type, often called *wannigans* after the Algonquin word for an underground, stone-lined food cache, is commonly made of plywood and used by summer camps as a cheap and durable option for food and kitchens. The primary disadvantage of the wooden wannigan is that it is

rarely built to be waterproof, relying instead on a slight overlap in the plywood lid and a strap or rope to hold it on. However, for protected flatwater travel where a capsize is unlikely, wannigans are a functional and cheap option. They also make excellent seats.

Other, more modern storage box options abound, including fully waterproof dry boxes made of plastic or aluminum. While expensive, these have all of the organizational benefits of the wannigan and are a better option for use in whitewater. However, they have the same

A simple plywood wannigan like the one used here on Mooselookmeguntic Lake in Maine is a cheap and durable option for flatwater travel.

The ABCs of Good Packing

Good packing is simple, if you remember the ABCs:

Accessible. Pack so that the most important and often used things are the easiest to find and get.

Balanced. The heaviest things should be distributed from top to bottom and from side to side. If long portages are planned, concentrate the weight close to your back.

Compact. Compress large items like sleeping bags and pads, and fill all the little gaps and air pockets with items to make the load as dense and small as possible.

Dry. Use a waterproof pack and line it with a second waterproof layer. Add yet another layer of waterproofing around all vital or hard-to-dry items, like sleeping bags, puffy jackets, and books.

Everything inside. Nothing should be sticking out of a pack or attached to the outside.

weakness as all boxes: they are awkward to carry any distance without a tumpline, a load-bearing device requiring a bit of strength and training.

Organizing the Canoe Packs

Each tandem expedition canoe should be able to hold four barrels, boxes, or packs—also called pieces—two personal and two with food or gear. Having four barrels is a common and effective practice; the only downside is that when a barrel is used as a food pack and is finally emptied, it cannot be collapsed and stuffed into another pack.

Inside the packs, some semblance of organization is helpful. The less frequently used items tend to drift to the bottom, so they might as well start there. Sleeping systems can be placed at the bottom with soft clothing packed around them; a Therm-a-Rest pad, deflated and rolled up, spoons well around a sleeping-bag compression stuff sack with a thick plastic bag liner.

A densely packed stuff sack tends to add bulk by creating air pockets around it, and this is amplified if you use several sacks. One solution is to pack things loose or in half-full stuff sacks; another is to use a thin, medium-size duffel bag. The goal is the same: organizing your things to avoid losing something small, like a sock, in the nether regions of a pack, especially a problem with a soft pack.

Barrels have the advantage here, as they prevent you from overpacking, and they require little energy to pack well because they are hard-sided and things can just be stuffed in. A small, light nylon bag left at the top of the pack or barrel works well for storing camp shoes and will keep out the sand, dirt, and water that often accompany them.

Packing Food and Kitchen Gear

Packing the food for an extended canoe expedition can take as little as a single day and does not require any special equipment or preparation. It's a fairly simple process that involves planning ahead and making lists of what you'll need, buying and repackaging the food in plastic bags, and then packing it all in an organized manner for the trip. This can be done by the whole team or assigned to an individual member.

Refer to books like *NOLS Cookery* and *NOLS Expedition Planning* to determine your food needs. For a trip shorter than about five days, plan a daily menu where each meal is predetermined; for a trip longer than five days, plan a bulk food pantry with staple ingredients that can then be combined to make individual meals. For expeditions in warm weather or easy travel, 1.3 to 1.5 pounds (590 to 680 grams) dry weight of food per person per day is typical; for adolescents, big eaters, or people working hard in cold weather, 2 to 2.2 pounds (907 to 998 grams) per person

per day may be necessary. Adding some variety is a bonus on long trips. Identify team members' food preferences and sensitivities, make a list of all the food items you'll need (you may want to use a spreadsheet to simplify things), and then go shopping.

You can find everything you need for a nutritious, lightweight menu at any large supermarket. However, you can save money by shopping around at discount or bulk food stores, and some specialty items are available only at health food stores or online. If you have a food dehydrator, you can dry your own food. The possibilities are endless for fruit leathers, sauces, vegetable mixes, and jerkies, and these

A simple kitchen for a solo trip on Georgian Bay, Lake Huron, Ontario.

are often worth the cost of the dehydrator and the significant amount of time involved.

Prepackaged, dehydrated, or canned meals, such as those sold at many outdoor stores, can be a good first step, but they can be two or three times as expensive as the ingredients themselves, and they are often high in sodium and not all that appetizing after the first few meals. That said, the more complicated and numerous the bulk ingredients you take along, the more cooking time and skill will be required later. Paddling records have been set by canoeists eating only simple foods like macaroni and cheese and granola, and with a little creativity, they can be quite healthy. Do not count on wild foods when judging rationing needs ahead of time, as such sources are extremely fickle.

After purchasing everything you'll need, clear a large, flat, clean space in your home for packing and organizing. Wash the surfaces and all hands that will be touching food. A small scale and a large spoon or scoop can be helpful for dividing large quantities of bulk food into smaller units.

Start by getting rid of all the original packaging and pouring or scooping everything into thick plastic bags. The ideal bag is taller than it is wide, and thick enough to withstand a few weeks of being handled. The bags that U.S. convenience stores use for ice are ideal for 1-pound (454-gram) units, and they will often part with hundreds of them for a few dollars. They can also be ordered online by searching "ice storage bags," or washed and reused from previous trips. I have gotten countless Golden Arches branded ice bags at my local McDonald's, perfect for food packing; the kind manager gives them up for a small fee whenever asked, saying she is supporting adventure in the world. Most Ziploc and similar bags, as well as very thin or wide bags, are best avoided; few of the bags for sale in supermarkets are good for use on expeditions. The newer heavy-duty Ziploc bags are useful for many items, but I wouldn't trust them for something like flour. For expeditions that will be very long or in hot or humid conditions, vacuum sealers can be used to great effect in preserving things like cheese and jerky.

As you fill the bags, organize them by lining them up by food type (you can mark off areas on the floor with masking tape and marking pen) or putting them into labeled or color-coded duffel bags, stuff sacks, or larger plastic bags. Check off everything against your list as you go.

Dry food, as packed following the recommendations in *NOLS Cookery*, takes up the least space when 1-pound (454-gram) bags are packed loosely and one at a time into a hard-sided container, like a blue barrel. Using this method, the food barrel is packed to the gills and unorganized. You can organize the food in each barrel by packing it first in three or four medium-size duffel bags, even going so far as to use a different color bag for each barrel or food type, but the zip bags make it harder to fit as much food in each barrel. The same technique works if you are using dry bags for food storage.

Kitchen items like the pots and stove fit well near the top of the barrel or pack, although they may be too sharp or hard for a soft pack. Fuel bottles should be stored in a small dry bag or pack that has no other purpose, as fuel can contaminate food easily and permanently. A good method is to rig fuel jugs in the canoes, and then use these to fill up stove fuel bottles to lessen the need for the smaller bottles. Tents and tarps can be stored in the kitchen packs, instead of group gear packs or personal packs; when wet and sandy, the impact on a kitchen barrel is vastly lower than it would be on a personal pack, so it may be best to plan on storing them there to begin with.

Transport

During the planning phase, you also need to think about how best to get all your team members, gear, and boats to the starting point of the expedition. This can sometimes be an adventure in itself. Driving to the put-in and home from the take-out can actually be more dangerous than the canoe trip.

Unless your route ends at the same spot where it begins, you will need to make arrangements for a shuttle or transportation. Short river and lake trips are often supported by leaving a vehicle parked at the take-out, and shuttling people and gear between there and the put-in, or by arranging for an outfitter or very kind friend to drive the vehicles to the take-out. Outfitted or institutional trips commonly provide an arranged drop-off and pickup.

If the team members are handling the transportation themselves, plan on a station wagon or large car being able to carry one tandem boat, two paddlers, and all their gear and food for thirty days. For a shorter trip, it is possible to transport four paddlers, two canoes, and personal gear, but overloading a light-use vehicle is easy, and on an uneven road surface, this can be disastrous. Including a medium- or full-size pickup truck in the mix is helpful, as all of the packs can be carried in the bed and two canoes on the lumber rack, while the car or station wagon behind does what it does best: moves people. A pickup truck can also tow a canoe trailer, vastly increasing the transport options. Towing a trailer with a loaded twelve-passenger van is possible and frequently done, but some organizations are moving away from it for insurance and safety reasons.

Once the roads run out, transport options may include trains or bush planes. Quebec, Ontario, and Manitoba have famous railroads that pass through remote wilderness, where the trains often stop at a bridge or pond to drop off or pick up an entire expedition with boats and gear. In Europe and northern Asia, this is also possible but less common. If you need to

A de Havilland DHC-3 Otter bush plane with floats is loaded on the Stewart River in Mayo, Yukon Territory.

book a bush plane call a number of pilots or services for price quotes. Have your mileage and destination in mind ahead of time, as well as your starting point; the number of people, boats, and pieces of gear; and the total weight. Each plane has different capacities and restrictions, and each pilot will have more on top of that. Most pilots do this sort of thing regularly and know how they like things to be done; find this out ahead of time.

If you are taking a common carrier flight to your destination, find out the airline's weight and size restrictions, and expect to pay $50 to $100 extra per person. Packing all the maps, books, and electronics in a carry-on bag will lighten the checked packs significantly. Several paddles packed in a long, tubular ski bag padded with tents can be checked, as can most packs and barrels. The various straps on a barrel harness can get caught in baggage conveyor belts, however, and the pressure changes in the cargo hold of a jetliner can cause a barrel to deform. One trick is to pack the barrel tightly with loose, soft, or fragile gear, and then leave the lid on but not clamped. Place your pack in a larger thin nylon duffel bag, and fill the remaining space with big, bulky items like PFDs, pads, and throw bags. Zipped up, it will come in under the weight and size limits.

Flying with food is usually foolish. If you are landing at an airport, there will be a grocery store nearby. In other countries, the food available might be more expensive or unfamiliar, but you can usually research this ahead of time. A canoe cannot be flown on a passenger flight, and sending it by air freight is astronomically expensive or impossible. Shipping it by a ground method will cost several hundred dollars and is slow, with a noteworthy chance of damage. Shipping internationally usually requires a massive wooden crate around the boat and costs thousands of dollars, and then you pray that you will see it again, weeks later in a hard-to-find harbor shipping office abroad. It may be easier to rent some gear at the destination or take a folding canoe.

CHAPTER 2 | CHOOSING AND OUTFITTING A CANOE

The form and function of open canoes, gear for expedition canoeing, and craft design and repair

> *[I] always try to find a simple solution, rather than*
> *a techno-fix, to everything that I do.*
> —Yvon Chouinard

Good gear can help support safe, efficient, and comfortable journeys, and the gear you take on an expedition is a detail that needs to be addressed with care and thought beforehand, during the planning stage. Although some folks like to talk shop and have strong opinions about certain brands and styles of canoeing gear, the truth is that most of them work well for the experienced paddlers who use them. Paddlers can go on long expeditions in wood-and-canvas canoes or space-age flatwater boats, use ash or carbon paddles, race upriver or down, focus on flatwater speed or whitewater skill. There is no right or wrong approach to canoeing, and you can always learn from others by looking closely at their gear and styles. This is a good way to further develop your own skills.

The saying "the more you carry in your head, the less you carry on your back" also holds true in canoeing, but while skill holds a vital place, canoeing is gear-intensive even at its most basic, and the gear is often expensive. Buy quality items, learn how to use them, take care of them and repair them, and either sell or retire them when they are no long useful. Carry simple, durable gear that is as light as possible, including single things that serve many purposes, and build a kit that can be repaired easily with a few simple tools. Outfitting parties before or after trips can be great fun.

The Canoe

A canoe is the largest and probably the most expensive piece of your expedition gear, and because there are so many options, it would be easy to head out on the water with a less-than-ideal boat. Note that there is no such thing as a perfect canoe. There are only bad, good, and better canoes for a given use, as all canoe designs are a compromise. When you know whether you will be on rivers, lakes, or a mix, and what kind of water you expect to paddle, you can begin to experiment with what forms suit those functions. But before deciding on which of the various expedition canoe hull styles will best suit your purposes, you need to know the basic canoe parts and canoeing terminology.

CANOE PARTS AND TERMINOLOGY

The world of canoe hull design and expedition outfitting has its own jargon. An expedition canoe is a specialized boat in terms of function, and its design, manufacture, materials, and outfitting differ from those of other types of canoes. Function on an expedition, both technical and interpersonal, is vastly improved when everyone knows and is speaking the same language. For clarity in communication, it is important that everyone involved in an expedition uses the same words or terms. Some of the definitions are accompanied by descriptions of the effect of the particular component or characteristic on performance or of outfitting preferences.

Length. The length of the canoe can be measured as waterline length, overall length (stem to stem), and sometimes loaded waterline length. The greater a boat's length, the higher its idealized hull speed. This is a potential speed under neutral conditions that cannot be exceeded without significant wave drag from bow and stern waves. Increased length is also a factor in increased wind drag. Greater length increases a canoe's tracking ability, carrying capacity, and stability, while decreasing maneuverability.

Bow. The front of the canoe. This term can be used to modify other components of a canoe, such as bow seat and bow thwart.

Stern. The rear of the canoe. This term also can be used to modify other parts, such as stern seat and stern thwart.

Amidships. The center section of the canoe.

Stem. The sharp edges at the bow and stern of a canoe hull that extend vertically from the deck to the bottom of the canoe. It can be rounded or more square in profile. Rounded stems tend to rise up on waves and avoid crosscurrents, while square stems cut through them. Stems work with entry lines and fullness to determine hull speed and seaworthiness. A sharp, square stem that transitions into a sleek, gradually widening bow has far less drag and is much faster than a rounded, blunt stem that widens quickly. The stem is a major wear point and is often protected with a skid plate.

Fullness. How quickly the hull achieves its maximum width from bow or stern to the center. A hull that quickly widens out is often referred to as *blunt*, and this feature allows it to ride up on waves in conjunction with *rocker*, at the cost of speed; it also creates more carrying capacity and stability. A hull that widens gradually usually has a sleeker look and is faster, but at the cost of seaworthiness and stability.

Pivot point. The imaginary point on the bottom of the hull around which an empty or well-loaded canoe will turn or pivot. This center point, or fulcrum, is a vital concept for understanding steering forces and canoe handling.

Rocker. The amount of curve in the hull from bow to stern when viewed from the side. On dry land, a hull with no rocker has its entire length on the ground; a hull with 1 inch (2.54 centimeters) of rocker has the bow and stern both 1 inch (2.54 centimeters) above the ground, while the pivot point and much of the center of the hull rest on the ground. Rocker is a vital characteristic in a canoe's maneuverability: a highly rockered hull responds to steering forces much better, with less resistance, than a hull

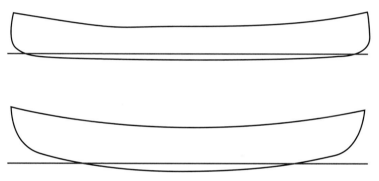

The bottom boat is significantly more rockered—has more curve in the hull from bow to stern—than the top boat.

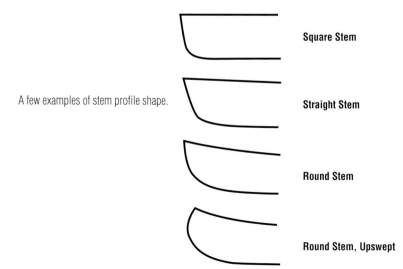

A few examples of stem profile shape.

Square Stem

Straight Stem

Round Stem

Round Stem, Upswept

with little to no rocker. A canoe with no rocker will track better than a rockered canoe, however, meaning that it will travel in a straight line with fewer correction strokes. Some hulls are designed with differential rocker; these canoes have no rocker in the center section of the hull and moderate to high rocker in the ends.

Keel. A thin raised ridge that runs from bow to stern along the bottom of the hull. Keels are used in some hulls as a strengthening device for the bottom or an aid in tracking. The keel helps a canoe track better and works to keep it from being blown sideways. Keeled canoes are less suitable for river travel, however, as the keel significantly reduces maneuverability and is subject to increased wear. Keels are more common in older canoe designs, like aluminum Grummans and certain fiberglass boats. The keel is not the same thing as the *centerline*, which refers to an imaginary line that runs along the bottom of the hull from stem to stem. All keels have a centerline, but only some canoes have a keel. In keeled canoes, the centerline usually runs along the keel.

Beam. The width of the canoe at its widest point. The beam is often measured at the waterline, or the gunwales, depending on the hull type. The beam of a canoe hull affects its stability, speed, and capacity—but only in relation to its length. A wide, or "beamy," canoe is generally more stable, slower, and has a higher load capacity. A canoe with a narrower beam is generally less stable, faster, and has less room for gear. These characteristics are in relation to the length of the canoe. An 18-foot (5.5-meter) hull with a 3-foot (0.9-meter) beam is fairly normal. A cheap fishing canoe might have a low width-to-length ratio of around 1:5, and a fine racing canoe might have a high ratio of around 1:7, but most expedition hulls, either whitewater or flatwater specific, have a ratio between 1:5.3 and 1:6.

Symmetry. Most hulls are symmetrical, meaning that the widest point is exactly amidships; that is, the widest point, yoke, and pivot point are all exactly halfway between bow and stern. Some flatwater canoes, especially racing hulls, are asymmetrical, with the widest point astern of amidships. This design is more efficient in calm water.

Chine. The transition from bottom to sides of the canoe. These "corners" in the cross section of the hull can be "soft," meaning rounded with a smooth gradual transition, and a large radius, or "hard," meaning sharp with an abruptly rounded transition with a very small radius. The primary impacts these features have on boat handling are in stability and whitewater performance. Soft chines have the effect of making the canoe more forgiving when transitioning from flat to tilted. They also reduce the effect of upstream river currents on a canoe, such as when completing an eddy turn. Softer chined canoes are well suited to expedition, tripping, and whitewater canoeing, and they are easier for novices to control and have success in.

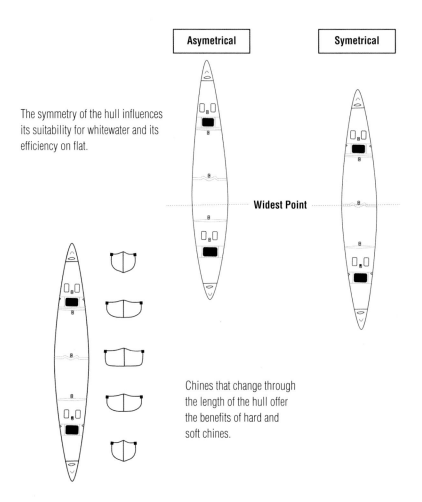

Asymetrical

Symetrical

The symmetry of the hull influences its suitability for whitewater and its efficiency on flat.

Widest Point

Chines that change through the length of the hull offer the benefits of hard and soft chines.

Hard chines make the canoe less forgiving; it is more common for a hard-chined canoe to tip and capsize. This is often referred to as being "edgy." Canoes with hard chines are usually high-performance craft. In whitewater, they track better, perform crisper eddy turns and ferries, and carve better. However, they require excellent balance and edge control to paddle effectively. Some canoes, mostly solo craft, have a double chine, which combines the benefits of both soft and hard chines. Some have a hard chine amidships and a soft chine toward the bow and stern. For a focused river boat, this can be the best of both worlds. Many solo canoes employ a tucked gunwale, which provides volume high on the side for more secondary stability. Most expedition canoes have decent secondary stability, whether they are for flat or moving water.

Depth. The depth of a canoe hull is the distance from the bottom of the hull to the top of the gunwale. This measurement often changes along the length of the canoe. Depth is a factor in determining volume, seaworthiness, and to an extent, wind profile. Basically, the deeper the hull, the larger the load it can carry and the higher the gunwales will be out of the water; this makes it less likely to take on water in open water or whitewater, with the cost of increased wind resistance. Various depths are sometimes given or can be measured, such as the bow, stern, or center depth; waterline depth; freeboard; or draft. Some hulls are deeper due to highly curved or upswept ends; this increases the wind profile, often with little or no added benefit. Bark and cedar canoes often had ends like this, but this style is less common in modern canoes.

Tumblehome and flare. These terms refer to the shape of the sides of the canoe as viewed in a cross section of the middle of the boat. Tumblehome refers to the sides of the canoe curving inward to the gunwales—the opposing sides of the canoe are closest at the gunwales—from the point of maximum width, while flare refers to the point of maximum width being close to or at the gunwales. Tumblehome provides a benefit in that the gunwales are closer to the paddler and therefore are slightly out of the way of the paddler's knuckles for some strokes and paddling styles, and it can help with reach and paddle position. It also allows a canoe to be tilted farther before water pours in. Flare helps deflect waves in larger open water and increases final stability. Many hulls have vertical sides, meaning they have no tumblehome or flare, and some have elements of both at different points.

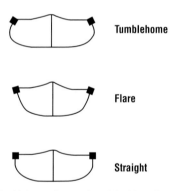

Tumblehome, flare, and straight sides affect the dryness of the hull, among other things.

Entry lines. A design element that combines rocker, fullness, depth, chines, and the shape of the stem. Entry lines are often described as either sharp or blunt, and determine how the ends of the boat enter the water. Canoes with sharp entry lines tend to have a squarer stem, less rocker and depth, and a hull that widens gradually from stem to center. This combination creates a faster, sleeker hull that tends to track well and punch through waves; it is ideal for flat water. Blunt entry lines tend to include a more rounded stem, more rocker and depth, and a hull that widens very close to the stem. This combination creates a slightly slower, more maneuverable hull that rides up and over waves and is ideal for whitewater.

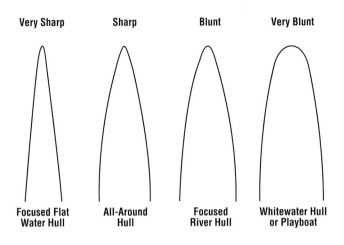

Very Sharp	Sharp	Blunt	Very Blunt
Focused Flat Water Hull	All-Around Hull	Focused River Hull	Whitewater Hull or Playboat

Entry lines help determine the speed, tracking, and maneuverability of a canoe hull.

Port and Starboard/Left and Right. The terms *port* (meaning left) and *starboard* (right) are typically used with all types of watercraft to designate the sides of the vessel when looking toward the bow. However, because of the vital importance of clear communication in canoe handling, expedition canoeists more often use *left* and *right*, as they eliminate the need for a few seconds of processing and interpretation.

Deck. The hard plastic triangle, often with an integrated handle, that strengthens and covers each end of the canoe and is fixed to gunwales at bow and stern. Some canoes have much larger decks, but the common expedition boat deck is rarely more than 16 inches (40.6 centimeters) long.

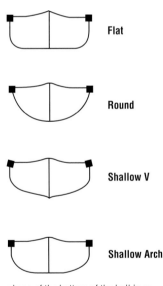

Flat

Round

Shallow V

Shallow Arch

The shape of the bottom of the hull is an important factor in a canoe's performance.

Gunwales, or gunnels. The plastic, vinyl, aluminum, or wooden pieces that run the length of the canoe along the upper edges of the canoe sides. The term comes from "gun wall," the strengthening rail and wall of a sailing ship's upper decks that braced against the recoil of cannons. On a canoe,

Hull Shape and Stability

The shape of the bottom of the hull below waterline can be flat, round, shallow arch, or shallow V. Hull shape has a great influence on stability and handling. Stability is usually described in two stages: initial, or primary; and final, or secondary. Initial stability refers to how stable or tippy the canoe is when it is flat on the water. Final stability refers to how stable the canoe is when it is being tilted over on its side, either intentionally, to perform a carve or maneuver, or unintentionally in currents or rough water.

Flat bottom. A canoe with a flat-bottom hull feels stable in calm flat water and has high initial stability, making it ideal for families, fishermen, and paddlers engaging in light recreational use in protected conditions. It is slower because of a relatively large wetted surface area and thus higher friction.

Round bottom. A canoe with a round-bottom hull feels unstable in calm flat water due to its relatively low initial stability, but it can be quite fast and require less energy to paddle because it has a lower wetted surface area than other bottom shapes. Final stability can be quite high. This shape is common in racing and other special-use canoes.

Shallow arch bottom. This hull shape has elements of the flat and round shapes and is a rough compromise between the two, delivering some speed and some stability. The canoe has good initial and final stability, tracks well in variable conditions, holds a tilt well, and delivers strong performance in moving water. Most expedition hulls have shallow arch bottoms.

Shallow V bottom. This shape also has elements of the flat and round shapes and is similar to a shallow arch bottom, though it has a bit more wetted surface area, which slows the canoe. The advantages of this shape are mainly in increased tracking ability, a potentially stiffer overall hull, and good final stability in tilts.

Whether a canoe is loaded or not has a big impact on stability. Heavy loads change the waterline and therefore engage different areas of the chines. Test a new canoe or a potential purchase with different loads.

they also have a strengthening function, since much of the hull's rigidity—a vital part of handling and efficiency—comes from the gunwales.

Thwart. The usually wooden pieces that are perpendicular to the gunwales and attached to them with metal bolts. Most canoes have at least two thwarts: a center thwart, or yoke, and a stern thwart. Some also have a bow thwart and sometimes a small thwart close to each deck plate. The term is derived from an Old English word meaning "across" or "side to side." A useful way to remember the term is that these pieces "thwart" the hull from opening up—the small amount of tension on them provides significant hull shape and rigidity.

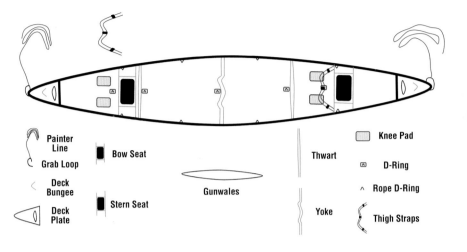

One way of outfitting a canoe for all-around expeditioning.

Yoke. All tandem canoes should have a thwart at the balance point, which is sometimes called the center thwart or yoke. *Yoke* specifically refers to a center thwart that is cut to provide a comfortable C-shaped place to rest the upturned boat on your neck and shoulders during a portage. Solo canoes sometimes have removable yokes to make them easier to transport on expedition.

Painter lines, or painters. The lines that attach to the bow and stern of the canoe. In the manufacture of a wood-and-canvas canoe, the two lines were used to suspend the boat at eye level to make painting easier, hence their name. A rope is a length of cordage, and a line is a rope put to use.

D-ring. A metal D-shaped ring that is sewn to a piece of webbing and thereby attached to a vinyl patch and glued to the interior of the hull as an attachment point for gear and flotation.

Grab-loop. A small continuous loop that passes through each stem, and to which the painter lines are tied.

Deck bungee. The U-shaped piece of bungee cord that sticks up from each deck plate in a rainbow orientation and under which the painter lines are secured.

CHOOSING A CANOE

To summarize and simplify the dozens of hull types and thousands of models in existences, this section focuses on three basic expedition canoe hulls, each of which lends itself to different uses and environments. The categories as described here represent ideal use; all three styles can function in all environments, but certain features provide significantly higher performance in particular environments and types of water.

The main qualities to consider are hull speed, maneuverability versus tracking, durability, application, and carrying capacity, with the understanding that superiority in one of these characteristics usually means lower values in another. The focused river hull emphasizes durability and maneuverability, and often carrying capacity; the focused flatwater hull emphasizes speed, tracking, and carrying capacity; and the all-around hull incorporates all of the above qualities, while not achieving excellence in any one.

A fourth type of canoe you might consider using on an expedition is a folding canoe, also described in this section. A river or lake canoe, on the other hand, may not be the right boat for the types of water you will encounter on an expedition. You may already own one of these other types of canoes, but before deciding to use it on your expedition, you need to make an honest appraisal of the planned route, and your team must be willing to portage if the boat is not able to navigate a particular set of rapids.

Focused River Hull

A focused river canoe design usually has the most rocker of the three types, between 3 and 5 inches (7 and 13 centimeters), and a blunt bow and stern to ride up on waves rather than cut through them. The chines allow for carving and maneuvering, and they feed into relatively high sides, meaning that the overall canoe has significant depth. Lengths of 16 to 17 feet (4.8 to 5.2 meters) are most common. The material is usually durable Royalex ABS, as canoes of this design are often dragged over, rammed into, and occasionally wrapped around rocks and other river obstacles, all while fully loaded. This hull type is at its best on moving water. It makes for an expedition-ready boat that is nimble and dry in big-water rapids, but these canoes require some skill and energy to paddle long stretches of flat water. Examples of canoes with this hull type are the Esquif Canyon and Mad River Legend 16.

Focused Flatwater Hull

This hull shape is characterized by low to nonexistent rocker and potentially a greater-than-average waterline length. The stem is often square and the entry is fairly sharp. Canoes designed for this use are the most likely to be slightly asymmetrical: the widest point of the canoe might be a foot or two closer to the stern than in a symmetrical hull. Lengths of 17 to 18½ feet (5.2 to 5.6 meters) are most common. Royalex ABS is common, as are various lightweight materials such as Kevlar, carbon fiber, and fiberglass.

This hull type is at its best on flat water. Hull speed and seaworthiness take precedence over maneuverability, making a canoe that is at home crossing large, open bodies of water at speed. However, it is affected by slight currents and requires large steering forces or distance to effectively turn. Examples are Bell Northwind, Wenonah Minnesota II, Clipper Mackenzie 186, and Old Town Penobscot.

All-Around Hull

This hull shape is characterized by 1 to $3\frac{1}{2}$ inches (2.5 to 9 centimeters) of rocker and lengths of $16\frac{1}{2}$ to $17\frac{1}{2}$ feet (5 to 5.3 meters), with 17 feet (5.2 meters) being most common. The hull is usually symmetrical, with medium-hard chines amidships and rounded chines near the seats and ends. Royalex ABS is the most common material, as the hull must be river-ready. This hull type is a true hybrid, as it sacrifices excellence in any one use to achieve functionality in all. It handles well in whitewater and on large, open bodies of water and is a stable expedition workhorse. These canoes are maneuverable but often require some skill and tilting to turn quickly, especially when loaded. Examples are Esquif Prospector 17, Old Town Tripper, Clipper Tripper and Prospector, and Bell Alaskan.

Folding Canoes

Yet another alternative is a folding canoe. Being able to turn a single large pack into a fully functional expedition canoe within a few hours demonstrates the exceptional utility of this type of canoe. Folding canoes are transportable across oceans, on trains, and in tiny bush planes, and they are easily assembled in the field; this allows access to distant routes where the logistics of moving a massive canoe just do not work. Folding canoes are much more durable and rigid than you might imagine and can withstand significant punishment on an expedition. They cannot match hard-hulled boats in any category, however, but they come very close, with the huge added bonus of easy portability. ALLY Canoes and PakBoats are the most common manufacturers.

MATERIALS

Common canoe hull materials include acrylonitrile butadiene styrene (ABS), aluminum, fiberglass, Kevlar, wood and bark, wood and canvas, wood and epoxy, and a host of propriety composites and high-density plastics.

Royalex ABS

Of the common hull materials, only acrylonitrile butadiene styrene (ABS) functions at a high level over time in all environments and weather. Other materials work very well in certain environments, but for all-around

A cross-section of standard thickness Royalex. The black outer skin is vinyl, the yellow ABS plastic, and the off-white is the foam core. The top layer of ABS thickens toward the bow and stern in some models for strength.

functionality, ABS is the material of choice. What is commonly called an "ABS canoe" is actually made out of Royalex, a composite plastic that is a sandwich of five layers: a layer of vinyl that is PVC mixed with rubber, a layer of ABS, a foam core, another layer of ABS, and another layer of PVC/rubber vinyl. These layers are vulcanized in huge presses to create single sheets, which are then shipped to canoe builders around North America. Royalex was developed by the Uniroyal Company and is now produced by Spartech in Indiana; very similar composites produced in the same factory include Royalite, which is lighter in weight but less dent-resistant and durable over time, and Oltonar, Old Town Canoe's version.

The sheets are heated in a massive oven until pliable, and then placed over a full-size canoe form for the intended model. A shell form is lowered onto the sheet, and a vacuum pump sucks the sheet in and sandwiches it between the male and female parts of the mold. After the formed canoe body has cooled, it is taken out and the scraps are trimmed off. The stems often need to be molded together if the hull has any curvature there. The hull is now ready for gunwales, seats, decks, and thwarts.

For the expedition paddler, Royalex ABS stands alone because of its combination of light weight, relatively low cost, and certain unique characteristics that support extended tripping: the vinyl outer layer tends to slip off rocks and resist abrasion well. The hull has a significant "plastic memory," meaning that once deformed, it will usually pop back into the shape in which it was molded giving it the highest impact resistance of any hull material. The only significant downsides to Royalex ABS are that differential curves are hard to produce, especially in the bow and stern, and repairing the material requires a large, bulky, and unattractive patch. While canoes made from this material may need repair and patching far less than other boats, they take repairs to the hull poorly. Certain components in the Royalex sandwich have a melting point around 200 degrees Fahrenheit (93 degrees Celsius) roughly 10 degrees lower than the boiling point of water; thus significant heat can melt and deform the hull. For this reason, setting up a stove in the canoe or building a fire near a boat on land is not advised. In a similar vein, ultraviolet radiation will break down Royalex over time, so keep the canoe out of the sun when in storage.

High-Density Plastics

Canoes made of a high-density plastic (HDP), most often polyethylene, are usually cheap, durable, and heavy. Common materials include high-density and ultra-high-density polyethylene, along with the cross-linked polyethylene used in the popular Old Town Discovery. Boats made from these materials are ideal for local recreational use but might not be the best choice for longer expeditions, as they are usually quite heavy and not as frequently available in good expedition hull shapes. Some dedicated solo whitewater canoes are now being built of HDPs.

Kevlar-Carbon Composites

Composite layers and weaves of Kevlar, carbon, and other superstrong space-age materials have been shaped into excellent expedition canoes almost since their invention. One of the first marketing attempts DuPont made for its new Kevlar material was to give sheets of it to Verlen Kruger to build the canoes that took him across continents in the 1970s and '80s. Kevlar and carbon fiber both boast incredible tensile strength for weight, and this equates to canoe hulls that are extremely light. Using Kevlar or carbon fiber cloth saturated in epoxy inside a mold, these hulls can be built in much more complex—and efficient—shapes than those made of Royalex.

Unfortunately, because of low abrasion resistance and minimal flexibility, many Kevlar canoes are not as well suited to river travel, and some must be babied on long flatwater expeditions. Hulls made with Kevlar, carbon fiber, or some proprietary mix are usually designed for racing or flatwater touring, with the exception of the more flexible and durable options from Hellman and Clipper.

Kevlar is rigid and strong for its weight, making it ideal for ultralight flatwater canoes.

Fiberglass and Aluminum

The workhorse of expeditions from the 1950s to 1970s, fiberglass and aluminum canoes are less commonly used today, but they are still highly effective craft for expedition travel, though mainly on flat water. Aluminum and fiberglass boats remain among the most affordable options and are the most available on the used boat market. Aluminum also has the advantage that it can be left outside year round and in all weather and will not be adversely effected, but it is loud when paddled and tends to get stuck on rocks. Older fiberglass canoes tend not to be very durable and lose their shape over time, though they are easily repaired.

Wood

The majority of wooden canoes have hulls made from thin ribs, usually of cedar, that are bent around a reusable form with ½- to 1-inch (1.2- to 2.5-centimeter) planks tacked perpendicularly to them. These hulls are then covered, sealed, and strengthened with birch tree bark, to create a birchbark canoe; canvas, to make a wood-and-canvas canoe; or epoxy resin, for a cedar strip canoe. Wooden canoes are beautiful, functional pieces of art and are the direct descendants of Native American and First Nations canoes. When made well, these boats are durable and paddle beautifully because the rigidity of the hull transfers the power of the strokes more efficiently into movement, as well as the ability of wood to hold complex angles in the hull profile.

Wooden canoes are often fabulously expensive and require a huge amount of time and skill to maintain; while somewhat durable in the short term, over time they wear much faster than other hull types and must be cared for lovingly. Expert woodworkers and outdoorspeople can repair wood canoes in the field if in specific eastern and northern forest types, provided that they have the right tools. Wood-and-canvas canoes are rarely built

Most wooden canoes are made of a cedar ribs and planking with a skin of canvas or bark.

today with extended expeditioning in mind; more often, they are intended for gentle lake use. Still, one mild broach on a rock and a wooden canoe may be lost or in need of major repair; a Royalex boat, on the other hand, will be ready to continue downriver in minutes.

Paddles

Choosing the right paddle is a complicated mix of preference, cost, durability, sizing, and intended use. Most paddles will do the job required, but some types and sizes work better for some people and certain environments. The key factors that set paddles apart are material, weight, rigidity, shape of blade and shaft, and strength and durability. Start with an inexpensive paddle you can afford, one that is sized well for you and suited to your intended use. Then borrow and demo other paddles to see if you find one that works better for you. Use any new paddle on shorter trips to test it out before taking it on a long expedition.

To choose the right size paddle, an easy measuring trick is to put the grip in your armpit like a crutch; while keeping that arm straight, grasp the shaft of the paddle with that hand and then the grip with the other. The hands will be a little more than shoulder width apart and are in proper paddling position. There should be enough shaft extending below the lower hand so that when you are kneeling in the boat, the blade will be fully in the water, the lower hand just barely about the gunwale, and the grip at or just below eye level. Every paddler's body is different and every boat and outfitting setup is different, so beware of any simple chart that tells you what size you need.

PADDLE ANATOMY

As with canoes, there is a set of terminology you should know regarding the parts of a paddle.

Blade. The thin, working end of the paddle that meets the water. Blades come in a variety of shapes, angles, and surface areas. The power face of the blade is the side that faces the stern during a simple forward stroke.

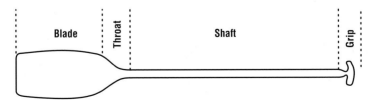

The parts of an oar.

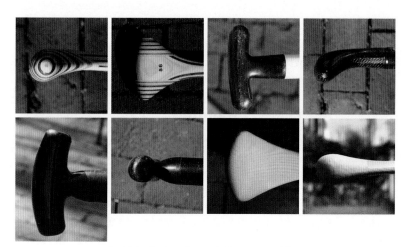

A variety of grip options exist for canoe paddles.

Grip. The handle at the opposite end of the shaft from the blade that the top hand uses to control the paddle. Grips can come in T shapes, V shapes, or rounded palm grip styles. Generally, the T grips provide more control in whitewater, with some having aggressive 6-inch (15.2-centimeter) bars, while V grips and rounded palm grips are more comfortable, ergonomic shapes for touring and distance paddling.

Shaft. The part of the paddle that runs from the grip to the blade. It can be perfectly round, oval, or some combination of the two.

Throat. The transition area between the shaft and the blade. The waterline is at the throat of a paddle during the power phase of a stroke.

TYPES OF PADDLES

Canoe paddles come in several different styles. The *straight-shaft paddle* is the most common, with a shaft that is straight from grip to tip. These paddles are the best all-around choice for mixed routes and general use. The *bent-shaft paddle* has a 10- to 15-degree angle in the throat of the paddle. This means the power face is closer to vertical for more of the length of the stroke, giving significantly more forward power per unit of energy input.

A scooped paddle, like this Werner Bandit, catches more water on each stroke.

Designed for efficiency in flatwater travel and racing, bent-shaft paddles are inappropriate for whitewater and are challenging to use well in rough conditions. The *scooped, curved,* or *spoon paddle* has a straight shaft through the throat, but the blade is slightly bow-shaped, allowing it to catch more water during each stroke. As a result, these make excellent whitewater paddles, but they can be more awkward in flat water. This is the paddle style of choice for most whitewater canoeists.

PADDLE MATERIALS

Paddles can be made from the traditional wood or a more modern material. Wood tends to be easier on the body than fiberglass, carbon, or aluminum, absorbing some of the shock with each stroke; it is also warmer in the hand. Wooden paddles also have the benefit of giving you some warning of an impending break; they usually let you know with cracks and groans over time.

Solid wood. A paddle carved from a solid piece of wood, such as ash, willow, or cherry, and then varnished can be a beautiful, functional piece of art. Harder woods like maple and ash make more durable paddles; lower-cost paddles are often made from softer woods such as yellow poplar. Traditional ottertail and beavertail paddles are still in wide use, but they are usually much more fragile than other paddle types, and because of the

From the top: a straight shaft composite wood paddle, a solid ash wood ottertail paddle, an injection molded aluminum paddle, a fiberglass scooped-blade paddle, a bent-shaft composite wood paddle, and a bent-shaft carbon-fiber paddle.

common blade shapes, they are more suited to flatwater travel. Hard expedition use favors other materials, though with care, solid wood paddles can last a very long time.

Wood laminate. The higher-quality wood laminate paddles are often augmented with a plastic tip or aluminum insert on the blade to cover the end grain of the wood and protect it from wear, as well as fiberglass and epoxy reinforcement on the blade. When made with a variety of woods, these can be quite rigid, durable, and very beautiful, but expensive.

Wood composite. Composite paddles use a wood along with other materials, such as fiberglass or carbon fiber, to create strong and highly functional tools. These paddles may be made from wood laminate blades and grips with carbon shafts, such as Bending Branches Sunburst; wooden shafts with carbon blades, like Mitchell Premier; or various other combinations.

Aluminum and plastic. The standard rental, outfitter, or camp paddle is made of aluminum with a plastic grip and blade. These paddles are cheap and exceptionally durable, and thus they make good spare paddles. Most dedicated paddlers move on from this type, however, as they can be heavy and cumbersome. Examples are Carlisle and Mohawk.

Fiberglass. Fiberglass can be used for shafts, grips, blades, or a combination of the three, resulting in paddles of widely varying shapes and qualities. The best use high-quality epoxy and cloth to shape a stiff, scooped blade or shaft. Cheaper paddles might have a fiberglass shaft and plastic blade. Both types can be very tough and rigid, but they can abrade quickly with hard use, which often results in the blade being ground away, starting at the corners and tip.

Carbon fiber. Although carbon fiber is usually expensive, these paddles can be extremely light, durable, and rigid. Carbon fiber also allows designers to easily create complex shapes in the blade, throat, and grip. One downside, in addition to cost, is that when these paddles break, they usually fail catastrophically and with no warning.

Outfitting, Rigging, and Repair

There are as many possible ways of outfitting and rigging a canoe as there are paddlers to paddle them. The simplest approach is to consider first what you will *most often* be using the canoe for, and then select outfitting and rigging options that are versatile and match your skill level and the intended environment of use. Institutional canoe fleets are often outfitted slightly differently to provide conformity in equipment, facilitate repair, and support institution goals.

Comfort, safety, and control surfaces—knee pads, seat, thigh straps—appropriate to the intended use and your skill are the keys to good outfitting, particularly for boats that will be used in moving water. Following are basic lists of what you might need for each hull type, depending on the intended use and style.

Focused River	Focused Flatwater	All-Around
Knee pads	Knee pads	Knee pads
Seat	Seat	Seat
D-rings	Grab loops	D-rings
Rope D-rings	Painters	Rope D-rings
Thigh straps	Deck bungee	Thigh straps
Grab loops		Grab loops
Painters		Painters
Deck bungee		Deck bungee
Flotation		

The outfitting must be specific to the intended use of the boat, but it can be roughly adjustable to allow people of different sizes and shapes to paddle that craft. Highly specialized whitewater and racing canoes require the outfitting to match the single paddler much more closely than your average tandem expedition canoe. Many manufacturers will sell a blank hull on special order—one without gunwales, decks, seats, or thwarts—to allow for the ultimate in customization. These are usually less expensive options, especially if you have customization in mind.

One question to consider in outfitting, rigging, or repairing a hull, new or used, is whether to do it yourself or have it done in the factory or by a professional. For the cost, having the work done in a shop is a great choice and results are usually high quality. Doing it yourself is fun and relatively easy; it also provides a nice element of customization, guarantee of fit, and a certain metaphysical bond to your craft. For most canoe outfitting, rigging, and repair techniques, you can find excellent videos online. The ideal workspace is warm and well ventilated, as many of the adhesives need temperatures between 60 and 80 degrees F (15 and 27 degrees C) to set quickly and correctly, with 72 degrees F (22 degrees C) being the average sweet spot. Most glues, cements, and epoxies emit carcinogenic compounds into the air; use an approved volatile organic compound (VOC) respirator, or do the work in a big shop with the windows open and significant ventilation or even outside.

WORKING WITH HULLS OF VARIOUS MATERIALS

Many of the methods and variations detailed in the following pages describe outfitting a Royalex ABS hull, as it is the most common expedition hull material. Royalex canoes are fairly easy to outfit with the right tools, preparation, and chemicals. You are bonding the items to the outside vinyl skin of the Royalex sandwich, and vinyl is a thermoplastic, which is notoriously difficult to bond things to. The one exception is when the thing being bonded is also made out of vinyl, in which case solvent cements can be used to melt the two together, forming a very strong bond if done correctly. D-rings, for example, should have vinyl patch surfaces if they are being bonded to a Royalex hull. Different adhesives are used for attaching different items to Royalex, as described below. Royalex is damaged by UV radiation, meaning that a boat's life will be lengthened by storing it inside and treating it with a 303 Products protectant a couple times a year.

Royalex ABS, polyethylene (HDPE, UHDPE), and some of the new hull materials such as Twintex are thermoplastics. Polyethylene hulls are usually considered to be unbondable, making them less attractive if you need to outfit a hull easily. Special adhesives for polyethylene are available but are quite expensive. Flame treating, or sintering, is an option on all thermoplastics to help them bond better. This involves using a blowtorch to lightly scorch the surface of the plastic, without charring black, and creating a surface that will bond better.

It is easier to bond to fiberglass and Kevlar hulls than to Royalex and other thermoplastics, and it is also easier to repair significant tears or holes; different methods are required, however. Two-part urethane of good quality, such as that made by 3M, works well on outfitting rough-surfaced inner hulls. High-quality contact cement works well on smooth inner hulls; it can be smoothed with high-quality epoxy and filler if needed.

ADHESIVES

Using adhesives in the field is rarely a tenable option, and a failure while on expedition can adversely affect your safety, comfort, and ease of travel. It is important to use high-quality adhesives if you want your outfitting and repairs to last the entire trip and beyond. Adhesives don't last forever, and many are ruined by freezing. Epoxy has a shelf life of about a year, depending on the brand, with quality going downhill quickly after the expiration date. An adhesive will often dry out in its packaging if left for too long; check before packing it for the trip. Most canoe outfitting suppliers, such as Northwater or NRS, have appropriate adhesives available. Following is a rundown of adhesives that work well and others to avoid.

Epoxy

For large repairs and putting on skid plates, the standard for boats is West System Epoxy, a two-part marine-grade epoxy formulated for use in damaging water environments and designed for use on a variety of materials. This company also makes an epoxy UV sealant that is good for paddles and wood gunwales. System Three also makes quality epoxies, as does Cold Cure brand. Aeropoxy is more expensive but is of a very high quality and is not as temperature sensitive when setting as other brands. For small repairs and stocking a repair kit, Permatex and J-B Weld make good epoxies that are usually available more widely.

Avoid the no-name or hardware store brand epoxies, which are of lower quality than the above name brands and will not last as long. Automotive fiberglass resin, usually sold in gallon or liter containers, is polyester resin, which is brittle, bonds poorly to thermoplastics, and won't last. You can tell it is polyester resin if the hardener is in a very small container. An intermediate step between true epoxy and polyester resin is vinyl ester resin; this is less commonly used for canoe repair but is sometimes used in Kevlar and fiberglass hull manufacture.

Contact Cement

Use contact cement to attach knee pads and D-rings. For attaching D-rings to Royalex hulls, Vyna Bond is a standard contact adhesive. It is a solvent adhesive that chemically bonds two layers of PVC or other vinyl together. If used for D-rings, the D-ring must first be sewn to a vinyl fabric patch so that it can bond correctly.

Using a solvent contact adhesive like Vyna Bond to bond foam knee pads to Royalex hulls can end in disaster, however; any aromatic solvent can melt or dissolve ABS plastic, and the vinyl layer is not an effective barrier. The result can be a mushy, spongy spot in the hull, and in the case of knee pads, this section of the hull will be wrinkled and weak. Use very thin coats, and allow the two surfaces to dry thoroughly before they touch.

For attaching foam knee pads, both 3M Super Weatherstrip Adhesive and Permatex contact cement work well and can be found at most hardware and auto-parts stores. Spray-on contact cement is handy for foam knee pads, as it applies quickly and evenly; look for a quality brand such as 3M. Quality contact cements also work well for knee pads and D-rings on fiberglass and Kevlar hulls, provided they are prepared correctly.

Avoid water-based contact cement. While good for wood veneers, it is unsuitable for plastics and wet environments. Hardware store contact cement, used for laminating countertops, will work for foam pads but lacks the strength needed for D-rings.

Other Adhesives

3M Two-Part Scotch-Weld Urethane Adhesive is expensive, but it is very strong and is good for filling holes, gluing on D-rings, and general repair. Marine Goop is easy to find and extremely versatile, making it an excellent field repair kit choice. The company makes a two-part epoxy paste and a general-duty urethane adhesive. The paste can be used to fill holes and saturate fiberglass for larger field repairs, creating a much more flexible and durable patch than normal resins. The urethane Goop is a great adhesive.

Avoid Weldbond, Elmer's Glue, and any other adhesives that are meant for paper and crafts.

DECKS AND GUNWALES

Most decks are riveted on, with a few manufacturers having switched over to screws to increase ease of repair and replacement, especially on expeditions. The deck plate is usually removed only when replacing or repairing the gunwales, but it may be popped off when a swamped canoe is swept into shallow water.

Removing or replacing decks or gunwales requires a handheld power drill with a drill bit set for removing POP rivets and a Phillips-head or flat-head bit for removing and replacing screws; POP rivets and a rivet gun of appropriate gauge for replacing rivets; masking tape; permanent marker; and ruler.

Start by using a ¼-inch or 6-millimeter drill bit to cut through the round, black ring stopper of the POP rivet. Once the bit has ground through the millimeters-thin piece of aluminum, the rivet will release and can be pushed inward. The new decks or gunwales usually do not come with predrilled holes, so you will need to match them with the existing holes in the hull. Make sure everything is cut to length and fits when fully seated on the hull—check this multiple times. Once you've drilled holes in the new decks or gunwales and they match up with the holes in the hull, insert a POP rivet with the rivet gun, which is pressured and pulls a pin through that expands a cylinder to make a nonreleasable fastener. The pin then snaps off, leaving a clean, permanent attachment.

Even drastically bent gunwales can be finessed back into shape with clamps, cam straps, spreader bars, and multiple attachment points. The hull will go back to its normal shape most of the time, but depending on the extent of damage, it might make sense to replace the gunwales entirely. Most manufacturers offer gunwales, though it is usually easiest to have them shipped along with a canoe order to a shop, as the length of the gunwales makes it difficult to have them shipped to a home address via a common carrier. Gunwales come in bare anodized aluminum, vinyl- or plastic-sheathed aluminum, wood, or plastic. Gunwales made entirely of plastic are becoming more common, while retaining the box or molding shapes common in other materials. Plastic gunwales can be quite rigid but flex to absorb impacts and pins without failure.

WOOD

Repairing, replacing, or adding new wood pieces is one of the most straightforward aspects of working on your canoe. For most expedition canoes, the wood is ash. Ash is flexible for a hardwood and tends to have a straight, continuous grain. It weathers more quickly than most hardwoods and must be finished appropriately. Mahogany and walnut are also common on higher-end lake canoes. Wood can last a long time but may need refinishing once a year and after each long use.

Refinishing scuffed or worn wood is easy. For major refinishing, remove the piece from the canoe and secure it on a workbench. For minor jobs, the piece can usually be left on the boat. Starting with 80- or 100-grit sandpaper and slowly working your way up to 220-grit sandpaper, remove the existing finish and any imperfections or debris, and then clean with mineral spirits. For a major refinish, sand until all of the old varnish is gone and the piece looks uniformly stripped. For a minor job, sticking to the small area that needs attention is fine.

Coat the area with a wood finish like tung oil or brand-name Gunwale Guard. Linseed oil is also an option, and you may have it on hand for paddle finishes, but it provides slightly less protection. Marine spar varnish or another oil-based urethane can be used, but these have the disadvantages of not soaking into the wood as well and not flexing with the movements of the piece if applied improperly. If the right varnish is applied correctly, however, it can flex. Spar varnish and urethane are more commonly used for thwarts, seats, and yokes, which flex much less than gunwales and are less exposed.

A soft, clean rag can be used to apply oils, while a brush is more useful for varnishes. Let the first coat dry before applying a second. One way to save time is to hang the piece by a string so as to apply an even coat all the way around. The bolt holes may need to be redrilled after the finish dries.

This gunwale is in need of refinishing.

THWARTS

Tandem canoes should have at least two thwarts: a center yoke and a stern thwart about 2 to 3 feet (0.6 to 0.91 meters) in front of the stern seat. Hanging thwarts is best done with long bolts with a wide Phillips head. Seat them in a large washer above the gunwale; most hanger bolts come with the right parts. Below the thwart or seat, put a washer on to prevent the bolt from working into the wood under pressure, and consider using a wingnut to increase the ease of tightening and replacement, though this comes at the cost of adding a relatively sharp point that can tear packs and skin alike. Wingnuts are often used on the gunwales, decks, thwarts, and seats of canoes that are intended to be nested together for transportation purposes and then quickly reassembled in the field.

The yoke, or center thwart, can be taken out and redrilled; having two bolts on each end spreads out the load and lessens the chance of breakage. This is helpful on boats that will be portaged often. The yoke should be placed above the pivot, or balance, point of the outfitted canoe—portaging an unbalanced boat is much more work than it is worth. Padded yokes are available, as are a variety of other comfort aids; a rolled-up shirt works well, but if portaging is a big part of your expedition style and will be necessary on your chosen routes, you may be happy to have padding. Removable pads work well for trips that start with a lot of land travel and end with river travel. Solo canoes benefit from removable yokes that clamp onto the gunwales above the pivot point, as in such canoes, the paddler sits on or just astern of the pivot point. Look for thick, well-cut yokes that have a continuous grain across them; cheap yokes might be cut across the grain of the wood, making them much more likely to split and break.

SEATS

Flat, wood-framed seats with 2-inch (5-centimeter) thick black webbing is a fairly common seat type, and perhaps the best available for extended use. Butt-shaped molded plastic seats are also common; these are fine for recreational use but have the disadvantage of being hard to kneel with, and they keep the skin wet and prevent it from breathing. Cane seats are attractive and work well but are highly susceptible to wear and UV damage. Metal tractor seats have some of the advantages and disadvantages of the above but are much better suited to racing and flatwater canoes.

Hanging a seat usually involves long hanger bolts, washers and nuts, some kind of wooden or plastic spacer, and the seat. The seat is sometimes hung so that the edge closest to the knee pads is lower, allowing for a slightly angled plane that can be more comfortable when sitting or kneeling; this depends on personal preference. The spacer used is often wood or plastic and is strongest when made of one solid arch-shaped piece for each side, rather than individual drilled-out dowels.

A seat with loose or broken webbing is easily fixed with spare 2-inch (5-centimeter) singular webbing, clamps, and a staple gun. A seat with broken wood is usually best replaced, unless you are a talented carpenter capable of joinery. Simple cracks in the wood can be stopped and strengthened by drilling a pilot hole at the advancing edge of the crack and putting in a single wood screw.

D-RINGS

Attaching a D-ring to a Royalex hull is easy with the right tools and space. Because of the chemicals involved, a dry, warm, and well-ventilated space is important. Most expedition hulls require about nine D-rings. The most common D-rings have nickel-plated metal rings attached to a circular vinyl patch. webbing, or cordelette tied through small holes in the hull, and 2-inch (5-centimeter) rings are the most useful.

For metal D-rings, start by measuring each potential placement several times, and then tape each vinyl patch lightly in place with masking tape. Measure again, and then do a mock load, loading the empty barrels, putting in thigh straps, and even getting into the boat to make sure everything fits with the possible D-ring placements.

Then trace each D-ring patch and remove the tape and patch. Clean the boat thoroughly of all dirt, grease, or wax. Use a rag to rub acetone on the hull and patches as a last cleaning step, being careful not to erase the traced lines.

To glue a D-ring to a Royalex hull, apply a thin coat of Vyna Bond vinyl cement with a foam brush to both the PVC vinyl back of the D-ring patch and the canoe hull. Let both pieces dry for fifteen to twenty minutes, more if in a humid environment. When dry, they should be tacky or sticky but have no residue.

Next, working on one D-ring at a time, heat the patch and spot on the hull where it will be attached with a large, hot hair dryer or heat gun. Reheating the cement starts the chemical process that will form the bond; the glue partially dissolves the vinyl in the patch and hull, which allows the two to bond. Then place the D-ring patch into the traced outline, and press on with a roller or other round object, starting from the inside and working out. Repeat the procedure for the next D-ring. Let the glue set for at least twelve hours.

D-rings have many applications but are most useful for attaching thigh straps and securing the rigging that holds packs in a loaded canoe. For thigh straps, one D-ring is placed as a "crotch anchor" between the legs on the centerline of the hull, 3 to 7 inches (7.6 to 18 centimeters) forward of the seat, depending on your size and shape. The closer the ring is to the seat, the higher the straps will fall on your thighs, making the straps more secure. This can be an important decision, as a dedicated expert whitewater paddler will want a more secure strap, whereas that placement might be dangerous or uncomfortable for a novice. A boat that is used by a variety of paddlers might have two D-rings on the floor or one in the middle. Finally, one D-ring patch is placed under each gunwale, just behind your hips, or between the two hanger bolts that hold each side of the seat; this makes a total of three D-rings for each paddler's thigh straps.

For the rigging attachment points, one D-ring is placed under each of the thwarts and another on the centerline of the canoe inside the hull, for a total of three. For rope D-rings, mark a spot halfway between each thwart and just under the gunwales, and drill two holes about 2 inches (5 centimeters) apart. Lace ⅜-inch (8-millimeter) cordelette through the holes and tie with a double fisherman's knot inside the gunwale, creating a loop with a diameter of about 3 to 4 inches (7.6 to 10.1 centimeters). Some paddlers like to sheath the cordelette in tubular webbing. This rope D-ring forms the link in the rigging system detailed later in the Diamond Rig section. The holes can be sealed with epoxy and drilled out, or tubing can be glued in to keep water out of the foam, as described below for the grab loop, but this is not vital.

GRAB LOOP

The ideal attachment system for the grab loop starts with a ½-inch (1.3 centimeters) PVC or surgical tubing ring fitted inside two holes drilled on the stem 1 or 2 inches (2.5 to 5 centimeters) above the loaded waterline

A grab loop on an Old Town Penobscot 186.

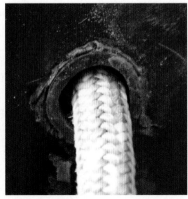

A worn example of a grab loop eyelet finished with glue and rubber tubing.

and secured with marine epoxy or Gorilla glue, followed by ³⁄₈-inch (8-millimeter) cordelette passed through and permanently tied to the ring with a double fisherman's knot inside the hull. The PVC or tubing ring often is necessary only in recreationally used expedition canoes, as over the shorter lifetime of an institutional canoe, little saturation through the hole's side-wall occurs before the canoe is retired. This ring, or grab loop, should be small enough that you cannot get a hand into it easily. The painter line is tied to this loop.

The closer the attachment point is to the waterline on both bow and stern, the less leverage will be exerted when the current and line are pulling in opposite directions. Most lining capsizes occur when the upstream end of the canoe is let too far out and the grab loop is attached too far up the stem. In addition, with the grab loop low, it is closer to the surface when the canoe is fully swamped and capsized, making rescue easier.

PAINTER LINE

The painter line is tied to the grab loop and coiled, ideally with a butterfly coil, before being tucked under the deck bungee. The most common knot used to tie the painter to the canoe is a simple bowline tied with a few inches of "tail" inside the loop. Wash the painter line knot-free periodically to prevent knots from welding and to keep the rope strong.

A standard length for each painter line is about a boat length and a half, about 25 feet (7.6 meters) for most tandem expedition canoes. A line of 25 feet (7.6 meters) allows for a full range of lining moves and will protect you when you're using it by distancing you from the water. Lines of 40 to 60 feet (12 to 18 meters) are not unusual in expedition circles, but their use is specific to a select few river environments and a small circle of lining experts; in the hands of a novice or beginner, a long line can become a tangled, dangerous waste of time with little added utility.

One effective way to secure a painter line is to tie off one end with a bowline knot and then secure the remaining coil in a stack under the bunji cord.

Tracking up Pony Creek in the Yukon Territory.

Most painter lines are of multifilament, sheathed, or kernmantle polypropylene with a thickness of ⅜ inch (9.5 millimeters). These ropes are dynamic—they are stretchy—but only to a small degree relative to simple nylon ropes or a rubber band. Static line, or line that does not stretch, works for painters but is not ideal; dynamic line will decrease strain on swimmers in a self-rescue and on liners or rescuers. A length of static line like Dyneema or Spectra, while expensive, is ideal to have around in a throw bag or a rescue kit for mechanical advantage systems, but for painters, dynamic is best.

Perhaps more important than line type is width—if the line is much smaller than ½ to ⅜ inch (12.7 to 9.5 millimeters) in width, it will be too narrow to hold on to or haul on effectively.

Whether you use a line that floats depends on personal preference and intended use. In moving water, a loose line can cause problems if it is below the surface, either entangling swimmers or catching on rocks. Floating line is easy to see and use, but it is not vital for all uses. In calm water, nonfloating line will sink after a few minutes of saturation, but few lining situations happen in calm water. Start with what is available and experiment over time with what you like, making adjustments for new situations or types of water.

DECK BUNGEE

A ⅜-inch- (1-centimeter-) thick, 12- to 15-inch- (30- to 38-centimeter-) long piece of elastic bungee cord is ideal for a deck bungee; the kind with a nylon sheath that is available at most hardware stores works well. Drill two holes about 3 to 4 inches apart in each deck plate, and place a figure-eight or other stopper knot in one end. Draw the other end up and through the deck, then back down through the other hole, forming a U-shaped "rainbow" above the surface of the deck. Knot the other end as you did the first one. Sizing the U shape of the bungee is best done with the painter coiled in place; make the loop tight enough to hold the painter snugly, but large enough to easily get it in and out. The bungee loses its stretch over a few years and should be checked and, if necessary, replaced *before* your trip.

FLOTATION SYSTEM

A flotation system consisting of large, durable airbags secured into a canoe with D-rings, straps, and gunwale-to-gunwale lacing is a big part of outfitting a frontcountry whitewater canoe, be it a playboat or river runner. The term frontcountry refers to an area that is easy to get to by vehicle and often visited just for the day. The airbags displace water if the canoe swamps or capsizes. A boat with airbags filled or partially filled with water floats much higher and is much easier to roll, drive to shore, or paddle through the rest of a set of rapids than a boat without airbags. An airbag-equipped canoe also will avoid broaching and pinning more effectively than a boat without flotation.

Expedition boats usually do not have room for traditional full boat flotation because of the large loads they often have to carry. For a canoe that will be used in moving water, a compromise is to install small airbags, sometimes called end bags, in the extreme bow and stern. Filling a spot often used to clip in day bags is only a minor annoyance, and adding this extra bit of flotation will potentially prevent deck plates from breaking or bottom pins from occurring, especially on shallow rivers. Although dry bags and barrels do provide flotation when securely tied in, the added bonus of small airbags can be significant. If running bigger whitewater, consider using bow and stern float bags, as well as potentially center float bags to fill any cargo areas not used by gear.

Even the best airbags are fragile and must be treated with care and kept inflated. The lacing and other outfitting required to secure them can pose an entrapment hazard to a swimmer, so it is important to do it right and to coach swimmers to be aware of them.

SPRAY DECKS

A spray deck is a removable nylon or synthetic canvas cover for an open canoe. It is made of one to three sections linked with Velcro, with cinching spray skirts for each paddler and any number of pockets, straps, and reinforcements. There are arguments both for and against using a spray deck.

Among their advantages, they provide a margin of safety and efficiency in large, continuous wave trains, as they tend to shed water and prevent swamping. This is particularly useful on cold northern rivers with rapids that are difficult to paddle without getting wet. In continuous rapids, it may take a long time to rescue a swamped boat, making it all the more important to avoid swamping. Many guiding companies on such rivers use spray decks on every canoe, resulting in less bailing and fewer swamps. For novice paddlers who sometimes have trouble recognizing dry lines (a dry route down a rapid) as well as experts who wish to paddle bigger water, spray decks are a helpful tool for both safety and efficiency.

This two-piece Cooke Custom Sewing spray deck was used on a solo canoe on the French River in Ontario.

This homemade two-piece spray deck was used on an Esquif Prospecteur on the Danube River in Hungary.

A less frequently heard argument in favor of spray decks is for their utility in open-water travel and in cold or wet weather. The deck drastically cuts the wind profile of a canoe, making travel in any kind of wind much more efficient. In cold or wet conditions, the lower body is protected and kept relatively warm and dry, potentially extending the paddling day.

However, any attachment to the canoe should be used with caution. A spray deck should be easy to escape from, as should thigh straps and seats, and all lines and rigging should be low-profile to prevent entanglement. Adding in a spray deck with a cinched spray skirt adds extra attachment. Many spray decks will release the canoeist in case of a roll or swamping, leaving the swimmer to self-rescue free from entanglement, but some will not release in a capsize, potentially holding the paddler in. And even if it does, the paddler now may be swimming with as much as 25 square feet (2.3 square meters) of fabric tied around the waist.

If canoeists are in a situation where they are regularly taking large amounts of cold water over the bow, spray decks should not be the first solution. And on exposed open water, paddling through cold, wind-driven waves is questionable whether the canoe has a spray deck or not. A spray deck should be viewed primarily as an efficiency and comfort item, and not wholly a risk-management item. Whether or not to use a spray deck is a judgment-based decision.

Spray decks are expensive, costing up to 40 percent as much as the canoe, and they are fragile, lasting only with great care. North Water and Cooke Custom Sewing produce good commercially available spray decks.

You can attach a spray deck to the canoe in one of two ways. Riveted snaps allow the spray deck to be taken off and put on quickly, and in a capsize, it should—though does not always—release easily. The snaps often break, however, and need frequent replacement. A more common option is riveting webbing along the sides of the canoe and then attaching the spray deck to it with webbing and friction buckles. An alternative to the second method involves riveted hooks or plastic pieces and a single piece of cord that laces the cover and hooks together.

SKID PLATES

Skid plates are small pieces of protective armor that guard the stems of a canoe. They are most often made of Kevlar cloth that has been saturated with epoxy resin and applied to the stems of a Royalex canoe that have been sanded and prepared so as to create a permanent bond. Many canoe builders offer these as factory standard, and there are good arguments for having them put on.

For skid plate application, you will need the following supplies: latex or rubber gloves, a permanent marker, Kevlar felt cut to shape, plastic sheeting or bags, electrical tape, high-quality two-part epoxy resin (see the section above on adhesives for information on appropriate epoxy types), a mixing container, an old brush or plastic spatula, and 40- to 60-grit sandpaper. Institutions can buy large rolls of Kevlar felt to save money; individuals will want to buy kits or purchase Kevlar and epoxy separately. If you have to cut your own skid plate, trace it on a piece of cardboard and cut this out as a template for future use.

Start by cleaning the stern and bow with acetone or mineral spirits to remove any grease or dirt. On

A standard Kevlar felt and epoxy resin skid plate on an Old Town Penobscot 186 protects the stem.

both bow and stern, mark a point about 3 inches (7.6 centimeters) up the stem from the loaded waterline, or 10 to 12 inches (25 to 30 centimeters) from the deck plate on the stem. Using masking tape, attach the piece of Kevlar felt, with the narrow end on the point you marked and the wider end under the stem.

Create a border around the felt with electrical or painting tape, with a ½-inch (1.3 centimeters) gap between the tape and the felt. Making the curves in tape can be done by either using a lot of short straight pieces or placing three parallel pieces alongside one another and cutting the curve out of them with a razor knife. Now remove the felt and sand the exposed part of the stem and hull, using a thorough circular motion and sanding right up to the edge of the tape without damaging it. Brush away any debris thoroughly. Using plastic sheeting or cut-up bags, tape one edge of the plastic to the existing tape to create a skirt around the exposed stem and hull; this will protect the rest of the boat from dripping epoxy.

In a well-ventilated, warm and dry workspace, mix the two-part epoxy (resin and hardener) as indicated on the packaging. If you have a set amount of epoxy to attach two skid plates, mix only half the solution, as it might start to harden before you get to the second plate.

Use a brush or spatula to saturate the felt with epoxy, and press the epoxy into the fabric with your gloved hands. Still using your hands, smooth it out, eliminating air bubbles, ripples, and globs of epoxy. Let dry until tacky and no longer liquid, about twenty minutes, and then remove tape and plastic. Repeat on the other end of the canoe.

EXTRA PIECES

A couple other small items serve vital functions. Keep them stashed in a large duffel bag while in camp or in storage, rather than on the ground or underfoot. Bailers are important for getting water out of a boat and for cleaning. The best

A clipped-in map case provides durable, waterproof access to maps while under way.

Carrying and Using Maps

Some maps come printed or sealed such that they are water resistant. Whether laminated, coated, or printed on a plastic paper, these maps might not saturate as easily as plain paper, but their ink can run and they will wear over time. A cheaper and easier solution is to use a map case, which is essentially just a thick plastic bag with a zipper lock and webbing sewn on the edges. It protects the map from the elements, keeps it flat and organized, and can be easily tied in and down, making it the best solution for keeping a map in front of the paddler.

Large cases, up to 25 inches (63.5 centimeters) on a side, provide an ideal amount of space and the potential that the case need not be opened at all while on the water. Maps should be folded and organized so that the route flows across one side of the case and onto the other, avoiding a messy, wet, and potentially map-losing changeover on the water. For large lake travel, keep a pencil in the case or handy in a hard-sided storage container. Using thin dry-erase markers on laminated maps or the outsides of cases is another option for marking lines of position and intended passages.

Where the map is stored in the boat or within the group can be a challenging question. Ideally, the group will have a map in every boat, creating a culture where there is no one navigator, but rather a navigation team that can bounce ideas around and challenge each other's assumptions. The cost of maps on a long route, however, will likely limit their availability to two or three full sets in the group, and these should usually be in the hands of the lead boat and strong navigators.

option is a 2-liter hard plastic jug—orange juice containers, milk jugs, and so on work well—with an integrated handle and a 3-foot (0.91-meter) piece of p-cord tied on. The cap can be glued in place and the bottom cut off at an angle to provide a leading edge for scooping water and getting the grit out. When worn out or cracked, they can be recycled. A plastic or vinyl map case with a secure zipper-style closure is another necessity and will keep your maps flat, dry, and accessible. Tie it in with a 2- to 3-foot piece of p-cord.

Building an Equipment Set

Outdoor clothing and equipment are expensive only when you have to acquire a lot of items in a short period of time. When you buy or make quality things, maintain them well and repair them often, and slowly accumulate a full kit, the lifetime cost is vastly lower. By purchasing clothing and gear over time, you can make smart choices after seeing what works well for you and for other people, and you can often find discounted or used items.

Certain pieces of gear, however, must be new or certified by an accredited body. Helmets, PFDs, and rescue equipment top the list. But canoes are a great item to buy used. Evaluating used boats includes checking for hasty repairs, floors or bottoms that have lost their shape, saturated foam cores, or small cracks or wrinkles from old accidents.

The choice between buying a new and a used canoe depends on the type and quality of used boats available. Purchasing a known make and model gives you an idea of what you should be getting, and taking it for a test drive never hurts. Buying a canoe without a manufacturer's name plate or other indication of the maker is a bad idea—good manufacturers and builders are proud of their high-quality canoes and label them.

If you are unsure of exactly what you want in an expedition boat, buying a series of low-cost used canoes and using them hard can tell you a lot about your preferences and how the boat's form will support the intended function. This probably isn't feasible for most people, however, and demo days at local outfitters are a great way to experiment with a variety of boats; take along a couple of packs and really test them out. Borrowing boats during local canoe club outings is another way to test out a number of different models.

Good places to look for canoes include Craigslist, local online forums such as BoaterTalk or Northeast Paddlers Message Board, and demo days at your local shop. Talking to paddlers, calling outfitters that rent boats, and emailing institutions that can provide an outfitted canoe at low cost are also good rocks to look under.

ON THE WATER

What to wear on the water, from toes to head; personal safety and rescue gear; and personal packing systems for a day on the water

Preparing for your time spent on the water includes choosing the right clothes; having the appropriate safety and rescue gear; and organizing your food, water, and small items of gear so that they will be close at hand when you need them.

Dressing for the Water

A common mistake in dressing for the water is in suiting up for how you feel while onshore, ignoring the fact that you may be fully submerged within the hour. Ideally, this should be a rare occurrence on a remote canoe expedition, but you still must be prepared for it. Some paddlers say that you must always dress based on water temperature because of the risk of a swim and rapid hypothermia. There are many other factors, however, including wind speed, air temperature, and likelihood of speedy rescue, as well as your size, personal characteristics, and how well hydrated and fed you are.

The bottom line is that you should dress for the possibility of spending extended periods of time in the water if conditions include the risk of swamping or capsize. It is vastly easier to cool down than to warm up, especially when surrounded by cold water. Experiment in safe, frontcountry conditions to see just how fast your body loses heat in wet and windy conditions; this is often an eye-opening experience.

One of the differences between canoeing and kayaking is that a canoeist is above and protected from the water, while a kayaker is at the water level and can expect to get much wetter and therefore colder. Wearing a dry-top and warm layers is almost a must for whitewater kayakers much of the year, while canoeists might need that level of protection only on dedicated whitewater river expeditions and in cold and rough open-water journeys.

What clothing options you choose depends on your personal preference and needs. Left to right: wind jacket and pants, splash jacket and rain pants, dry suit, and rain jacket and wind pants.

The paddler's dressing system should be flexible. You need to have at least a few options handy in a daypack that you can add to and subtract from your basic set. Three general layers are a wicking base layer, a thick insulating layer, and an outer layer that shields you from spray, wind, rain, and snow. The base layer consists of a shirt and leggings of thin, wicking wool or a synthetic fabric such as polypropylene or Capilene. The insulating layer can be a fleece jacket or vest and pants, neoprene pants and shirt, or a union suit or Farmer John. The outer layer is a rain shell, splash jacket, or dry-top in combination with waterproof pants, or a dry suit.

FOOTWEAR
The basic qualities to look for in expedition footwear are durability (will it survive the abuse of being wet, dragging through rocks, and hiking over

You have a lot of footwear choices for canoeing. Left to right: hybrid sandals with neoprene socks, open sandals, water-specific sneakers with neoprene socks, neoprene booties, sneakers, and sneakers with neoprene socks.

portages and scouts?), stability (does it have ankle support and a rigid enough body to protect the sides, sole, and toe box area of the foot?), profile (is it slim enough to fit under the seat of a canoe and come out again quickly?), insulation (is it warm or cool enough for expected conditions?), water resistance (does it absorb or keep out water?), and functionality if you are forced to take a swim (is it easy to swim with and will it stay on?). Knowing the terrain and temperature of the environment you are heading into, as well as having a sense of portaging needs, will help you decide what footwear to use on a particular expedition.

Simple tennis or light trail shoes have yet to be outdone by any of the various equipment manufacturers. They are inexpensive and comfortable, and the soles are thick enough to protect your feet in rocky and uneven terrain. Technical sneakers from the major gear companies also work well. It's best to wear broken-in shoes that you will not worry over, as they will be abused on a canoe expedition.

Another option, and one particularly suited to colder climates, is calf- or knee-high flexible neoprene boots, often called mukluks after the traditional Native American moosehide traveling footwear. Chota, the Original Muck Boot Company, and NRS make boots in molded plastic rubber and neoprene; these are some of the warmest and most effective boots for cold-water river trips that require frequent wading. Any boots you wear while canoeing must be soft and small enough to slide in and out from under the canoe seat while kneeling, as it is imperative to avoid foot entrapment in a capsized or broached canoe. Hiking or mountaineering boots are inappropriate for this reason.

Sandals and hybrid sandal shoes are popular among paddlers and rafters, and the best among them—Chaco, Teva, and Keen—are well made and durable. They are, however, more likely to slip off if caught or in a swim, are not warm enough for some conditions, and they expose your feet to sun, bugs, dirt, and injuries such as bruises and abrasions. Footwear that does not protect your toes from injury is not recommended.

Expedition paddlers should avoid flip-flops, footwear that easily slides off, or bare feet. It is important to keep your feet warm and healthy. Wear shoes all the time, change your socks regularly, and air your feet out every day.

Socks are a must both for warmth and for protection against the chafing that comes with scouting and portaging. While harder to find, calf- or knee-high neoprene socks can be a compromise between sneakers and mukluks. Avoid ankle-high, zip-up or slip-on neoprene booties; these are primarily meant as surfing booties, but they are commonly also sold as canoe or kayak footwear. They often lack padding in the sole, making it difficult or painful to portage, line, or walk in rough terrain. And during a swim, the moving water can unzip the zippers and pull the booties off. If you still want to use ankle-high booties, look for types with Velcro, buckles, or laces.

If you will be encountering very hot or cold weather, you need to choose your footwear accordingly. In hot weather, the emphasis should still be on durability and protection. It is hard to overheat a wet foot, so repeated dunkings can keep your feet cool and comfortable. More important, perhaps, is allowing your feet to dry thoroughly each day and keeping your feet and footwear clean, potentially to the point of cleaning or sanitizing with powders or soap. This is especially true in tropical environments with high risk of bacterial and fungal infections.

In very cold, wet, or windy paddling conditions, even if your body is well-insulated, it is difficult to keep your feet warm when wet. During the planning stages, you should seriously consider the risks inherent in running whitewater in very cold or freezing conditions. It is vital to plan for some mitigating factor, such as easy rescue, a fully set up riverside camp with hot soup on the stove, or high confidence in a dry descent. Insulated, flexible, neoprene boots are important here, and should be worn over dry suits with integrated booties. For information on protecting against and treating a nonfreezing cold injury known as immersion foot, see chapter 11.

LOWER BODY

Do not forget your legs. Wearing a pair of long underwear under nylon pants is often enough for cool weather; adding waterproof paddle pants protects against wind, rain, and waves, as well as the small amount of water sloshing about in the bottom of a canoe on blustery days. In very cold weather, adding fleece pants or heavyweight long underwear is a great idea, but not at the expense of not having a dry pair in camp. Simply upgrading your two sets of base layers—one for paddling and one for camp—to a heavier weight is a good solution.

Splash, or paddle, pants are a great option for river and cold-weather or warm open-water travel. These are uninsulated and somewhat baggy waterproof pants with a semiwaterproof waist and ankle cuffs. Some models claim to be fully waterproof, but in the event of a swim, you will be soaked unless you are in a full dry suit.

Some styles of paddle pants have integrated feet, meaning that you will have dry feet no matter where you go. However, these are in effect lightweight waders and will trap water inside during a long swim. How much water they trap is a point of debate; some call them "death pants," but others argue that the pressure of the water outside the pants keeps them from ballooning up. They can be a great option for cold-weather travel; do your own experiment beforehand in controlled conditions to see how they function when submerged.

Lightweight neoprene pants, often marketed as HydroSkins, are another great option, especially if you expect to be in the water often for wading or swimming and the weather or water is cool but not very cold. At first they can feel constrictive, but if they are well fitted, they will become more comfortable over a short time. Neoprene clothing should fit the body snugly without restricting range of motion.

UPPER BODY

Your own personal comfort and body characteristics play a huge role in what kind of apparel makes the most sense for you in various conditions. Regardless of the weather conditions, all upper-body layers should be worn under your personal flotation device (PFD) at all times.

A long-sleeved cotton shirt can be a godsend in very hot or tropical conditions, where the weather is hot and the water is warm. This option provides ventilation as well as sufficient coverage to help prevent heat illnesses and skin infections.

In warm or hot weather with variable water, you might wear a synthetic or wool T-shirt as a base with a thin wind jacket as an outer layer, or a long-sleeved base layer with no outer layer. When the weather and water are both cold, a long-sleeved base layer, fleece vest, jacket, and paddle jacket all worn together can up the insulation level. For wet, windy, or cold conditions the addition of a more substantial outer layer takes the system to the next level.

A simple rain jacket is an inexpensive and effective outer layer for someone just starting out or anyone in mild, damp conditions. Some rain jackets bridge the gap between an ordinary rain jacket and a splash top with full front zippers, neoprene neck closures, and latex wrist gaskets; these are great expedition tops but are less commonly available than other options.

Loose sun shirts, hats, and frequent water breaks in the shade are key on hot desert rivers like the Rio Grande in Texas.

The next step up is a dedicated paddle jacket; these are usually made of a breathable waterproof fabric like Gore-Tex and are pullovers with neoprene or latex neck and wrist gaskets. The top level of outer-wear protection is the dry-top, a pullover jacket with latex cuffs and neck, plus a tight neoprene and fabric tunnel closure around the waist. The idea here is that in a swim, you will stay nearly dry in the jacket, though some leakage is common. Latex neck gaskets can be rather uncomfortable over time and are not strictly vital for canoeists; neoprene closures work well. Latex is more comfortable and functional for the wrist gaskets, however. Gaskets on paddle jackets are designed for kayakers whose spray skirts and kayaks provide a full-coverage waterproof system. Canoeists will be soaked in a swim no matter what kind of jackets they are wearing.

For dedicated whitewater paddlers and playboaters, a dry-top is a great option, but for expedition canoeists it might be overkill. A great middle-of-the-road option is to borrow from the sea kayaker's wardrobe; a dry or semidry jacket designed for sea kayaking often has all the best of the above features—latex wrist gaskets, neoprene or rubber cinch neck closure, and a tight, water-resistant waist—with the addition of a large, deep hood that can fit over a helmet, a wonderful feature for a canoe outer layer.

For many paddlers, the rain jacket is where the decision begins and ends. You probably already have a rain jacket with a hood, and it means

Basic splash pants and jackets make a big difference for a modest cost. Here they are worn on the Clarence River in New Zealand.

you need to carry only one item for several jobs. The sea kayak style anorak—basically a semi-dry-top with a hood—can be a somewhat more substantial option.

DRY SUITS AND WET SUITS

Dry suits function by keeping all water outside of the suit through the use of tight latex gaskets and waterproof fabric. The latest-generation dry suits are durable and highly functional garments that are well suited to expedition use in the early season, cold weather or water, or continuous rivers and open-water situations where a swim would be long and your continued functioning is vital to survival. Overheating is much less of a worry than you might expect, as the suit breathes and exchanges heat well, and you can always simply take a swim to cool down. Good dry suits are costly, but they can be tailored to fit you and repaired over time by some manufacturers.

Neoprene wet suits serve a similar purpose at much lower cost, but less effectively. They function by trapping a thin layer of water between the rubber fabric and your skin, and then holding the resulting warmth in place and insulating it. Most full wrist-to-ankle surfing wet suits are overkill for expedition use and would quickly become uncomfortable; better are Farmer John style sleeveless wet suits, which allow the arms full range of motion with minimal constriction of movement.

GLOVES

Hands get cold fast, and on an expedition they are usually wet, often in harsh conditions. Even in mild conditions, protecting your hands is vital; once injured, they likely will not heal during the expedition. In environments where your hands are often cold and wet, while repeatedly being warmed, chilled, and exposed to sun and wind, a variety of superficial skin injuries can result. These can be prevented by covering your hands and keeping them as warm and dry as possible.

For mild weather and day-to-day use, thin, fingerless rowing or cycling gloves are great options. In colder weather and on the river, neoprene gloves of varying thicknesses are the norm. Look for a good grip on the palm of the glove, as plain neoprene can slip at times. The thicker the gloves, the harder getting a firm grip on your paddle will be, with a corresponding lack of control and increase in hand fatigue, which can potentially result in tendinitis. For cold, wet conditions, another option is neoprene mittens, like the Toaster or Hand Jacket, which keep your fingers together and thus much warmer, at the cost of rope handling and some control and dexterity.

For cold-weather flatwater paddling, mountaineering-style mitten shells work very well for wind and rain protection, thought they are cumbersome for rope handling and not recommended for river work. The advantage with these is that your hands can stay warm and dry, and you can easily add fleece gloves or mittens if necessary. Another option is pogies, nylon or neoprene shells that cover and protect your bare hands where they grasp the paddle; these are much beloved by some cold-weather boaters.

HATS
In cold or windy weather, keeping your head warm is also important. A low-profile fleece or neoprene skull cap worn under the helmet is an easy and lightweight way to increase the body's insulation. An ordinary beanie or toque is great for use without a helmet. Always have a separate warm hat for camp if this is part of your paddling costume.

Safety and Rescue Gear

The last "layers" you put on are some of the most important ones: helmet, personal flotation device (PFD), and personal rescue gear. These items protect you when incidents take place on and along the river and help you manage the risks of the river environment, both for yourself and for other members of the expedition. Both your helmet and PFD should be purchased new, as the history of a used item is usually unknown.

HELMET
A whitewater helmet is protective headgear consisting of a hard plastic, carbon fiber, Kevlar, or polymer shell over a padding and strap system. Many modern helmets are half helmets, reaching only to the tops of the ears and around the back of the head. A full helmet covers the entire head and sometimes the face and chin and is still a functional style. Most modern helmets are multiple-impact designs, but it's best to buy a new helmet to ensure your protection.

A helmet that fits and won't slide off the head is vital for whitewater. Matching colors, like this Clarence River, New Zealand, paddler's, is a plus.

More important than style or model is the fit of a helmet and how well it stays on your head; when trying on helmets, play with the straps and padding options to ensure a fit that is snug but will be comfortable over several hours. A big concern is that during a swim, the helmet might slide forward to reveal the back of your head or backward to reveal your forehead. An impact driven by the force of the river on one of these areas can be damaging or fatal. Helmets like those made by WRSI, Sweet, Shred Ready, and Predator seek to prevent this sliding with coverage of the back of the head and a strap system that keeps the helmet in place when fitted correctly. Wearing a baseball cap and sunglasses under the helmet is acceptable only if they do not impair the fit and seating.

PFD

Your personal flotation device, or PFD, is a key piece of your gear. Every team member needs to have one, and it should be worn snug and fully clipped and zipped from the time the group pushes off in the morning until the last boat is onshore. When you're not wearing it, your PFD should be attached to a boat, tree, or pack or otherwise stormproofed. Consistently following these principles means less chance that someone on your expedition will lose a PFD and everyone will be ready to swim or perform a rescue if necessary while under way.

PFDs come in five styles, which are regulated in the United States by the Coast Guard, but the only options for canoeists are Types III and V. A Type III PFD is the standard vest most people wear and has 16 to 18 pounds (7.2 to 8.1 kilograms) of flotation. A Type V PFD is termed "special use" and for our purposes is usually referred to as a rescue vest because it has various features that support the skills of professional swift-water rescue practitioners; these can have 22 to 26 pounds (9.9 to 11.7

kilograms) of flotation. Both come in high- and low-profile versions, with the lower-profile vests allowing a slightly wider range of motion for canoeists and kayakers. Buy a new PFD and replace it when it starts to fade and abrade.

In Canada, a distinction is made between life jackets and PFDs: life jackets are emergency flotation devices required on large boats and ships, and PFDs are designed for constant use on smaller watercraft. Look for the government approval label on the PFD.

PERSONAL RESCUE GEAR

Canoeists also carry several items of personal rescue gear, equipment that can be vital and is worn on the person, often strapped or clipped to the PFD or body for easy access. (Usage is discussed in chapter 11.)

Knife. If the expedition is using lines on the boats for any purpose, including painters, throw bags, or rigging, team members should carry knives. When a line and a person are in the current together, the chance of getting dangerously tangled is high, and the one way out is immediate rescue or self-rescue with a knife. Serrated knives will cut through rope faster, but if used frequently, they will dull and are difficult to sharpen. Certain models have clips and attachment systems that allow the knife to be kept secure and accessible on the outside of the PFD but quickly be released for use, even while in the water. These are tools with a specific purpose and should not be in normal use outside of an emergency.

Whistle. Every expedition member should have a loud, durable whistle like a Fox 40 attached to his PFD. The whistle allows for communication when team members are out of sight and yelling distance of one another and aids in finding lost or swept-away paddlers in an emergency. Adopt an agreed-upon system among all the members so everyone knows what each pattern of whistle blasts means; this way, the signals can mean more than just "Help!"

Towbelt, or pigtail. This handy tool is basically a carabiner linked to a metal ring with webbing-sheathed elastic. It is attached to the releasable belt of a rescue PFD and gives a trained swift-water rescue professional more options in extricating a person or boat. It is more useful in kayaking than canoeing, however. The pigtail is sometimes attached to a longer length of webbing or a small throw bag to increase the user's options.

Throw bag. A throw bag is a synthetic bag, usually with a cinch top, that contains a length of floating line 50 to 100 feet (15.24 to 30.5 meters) long and is used in river rescue.

Flip line. A 4- to 10-foot (1.2- to 3-meter) length of 1-inch (2.5-centimeter) tubular webbing with a carabiner at one end is attached around the waist to be used as a quick anchor, attachment piece, or to right a raft.

Medical kit. In addition to the larger expedition medical kit, it is helpful for each boat to have a small dry bag available all day with tape, ibuprofen, bandages, gauze, triangular bandages, and Band-Aids. If the main kit is readily accessible, this might be less useful.

Packing for the Water

One of the keys to your comfort, health, and happiness during a long day on the water is having your food, water, and other necessities close at hand when you need them. Following is a list of items you may want to have at hand while on the water:

Sun protection: sunscreen, lip balm, sunglasses with retaining strap, shirt, hat, bandanna

Water: water bottle with 1- to 3-liter capacity depending on the weather and environment, H_2O treatment

Food: leftovers, snacks, bars, treats

Layers: long-sleeved base layer, fleece pullover, splash or dry-top, wind jacket

Gear: map, map case, compass, GPS unit, camera

Rescue gear: saw, knife, throw bag, whistle, carabiners, small pin kit (as outlined in the Rescue section of this book.)

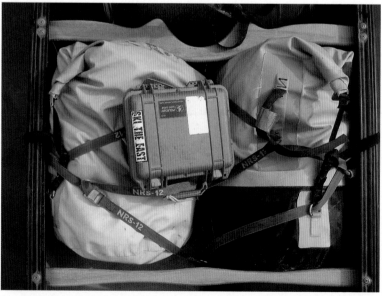

A small dry box, like this Pelican Case, is useful for storing small, crushable items you might need during the day.

There are many creative ways to organize and secure all the small and sometimes awkward items and keep them right at hand, and your system need not be complicated or expensive. One easy method is to use 1221- to 1830-cubic-inch (20- or 30-liter) dry bags for extra layers and outerwear, as well as a carefully packaged lunch and snacks. Unfortunately, even the best PVC and coated nylon dry bags can get punctured and abraded easily; to protect the dry bag, put it in a slightly larger synthetic canvas daypack. This makes it easy to carry and secure in the boat, and it also creates a small storage space between the daypack and the dry bag for things like fuel bottles, grills, and wet socks.

Finding small but important items like lip balm in a dry bag can be frustrating, and they can be easily lost. To protect these items as well as breakable ones like sunglasses, a hard-sided waterproof container like a Pelican Case, OtterBox, or ammo can is a wonderful, if unwieldy, option. This can be put in the top of your daypack or clipped to the D-ring at your feet.

CHAPTER 4 | IN CAMP

Camp life on a canoe expedition, including choosing an appropriate campsite, setting up shelters and a kitchen, hygiene, water treatment and storage, clothing for camp, and other aspects

This book is about going beyond the basics and using the canoe to travel through the landscape, and to do it with style. Style means different things to different people. The capacity and ease of transport a canoe can provide is used by some to support traditional styles—packing canvas tents, axes, woodstoves, and wannigans. To others, style means dedicated teams pursue lightweight descents on rivers around the world, while some prefer guided groups that leave them resting comfortably at the end of the day in folding chairs on the banks of remote northern rivers with fresh bread baking in Dutch ovens. The elements of style extend through technical travel and life on the water but come home while in camp. Style need not be heavy, expensive, high impact, or even skill intensive.

Choosing a Camp

It is always amazing how, at the end of a wet, cold, and exhausting day, the simplest patch of waterlogged and boggy ground can seem like joyful deliverance; there are only good camps and great camps, depending on the time of day and how badly you want to devour vast quantities of macaroni and cheese and lie down. The diversity of environments you can journey into by canoe negates a thorough discussion of specific camp preferences here, but a few general comments can be made.

If there are impacted or designated campsites, use them. Creating new campsites or new tent spots where functional ones already exist increases the impact on an area drastically. One patch of flattened grass will quickly be camped to death in heavily trafficked areas. Most cared-for backcountry areas that see significant traffic have volunteers or employees that build, maintain, and retire campsites throughout the seasons. Use designated

Elements of Style

No matter how you handle the details, the elements or principles of good style are the same:

Be organized and take proper care of all gear. Routines, systems, and clear expectations support organization. Every member of the expedition should know where everything is and take responsibility for its care. Personal gear should be kept on the body, in the tent, or in the pack. Do not leave personal or group gear alone without making it fully stormproof.

Keep it light and simple. The right gear, skills, and systems are used to focus on keeping things light and simple. Canoe expeditions need not carry mountains of gear to be functional or comfortable.

Be self-sufficient. The team is dedicated to being self-supported and self-contained as much as possible, seeking outside help or resupply only when required by emergency situations or route length. The team is prepared with the right gear, planning, and skills to achieve this.

Leave no trace. Follow the principles of Leave No Trace ethics and adapt them to the specific environment you are traveling through. Travel and camp with these principles in mind.

Manage risk. Take appropriate risks, demonstrate self-awareness in decision-making, and make appropriate decisions based on reason.

Exhibit good expedition behavior and teamwork. Support the goals and needs of others while being kind, helpful, and working hard.

Remember the priorities. The number-one priority on an expedition is the care and safety of the team members, followed by the care of the gear that supports that safety, and finally care of the environment.

campsites where they exist; where they do not, choose durable spaces that don't need to be altered.

If your team is large enough, a few members can act as a scouting party to look for an appropriate place to set up camp. There are several things to scout for when choosing a campsite. It should have a flat, protected area where you can set up your tents, with enough room for everybody; a protected spot for a kitchen that has access to water, a nice view if possible, and trees and rocks for tarp anchors; a dry place to use as a bathroom that is at least 200 feet (61 meters) from water sources and has good soil and vegetation (alternatively, you might use a portable toilet option like a groover). It can be nice to set up the site so that the kitchen, tents, and bathroom form a large triangle if possible. This way the bathroom is always accessible, while the 100 to 200 feet (30.5 to 61 meters) between the kitchen and tents means folks with different sleeping schedules will not be inconvenienced. Thinking of a canoe camp as a house is a helpful one: the bathroom is never in the living room, and you don't stay up late chatting in someone's bedroom—you do it in the kitchen.

You also want a protected storage area for canoes and gear that is close to the water, yet high and dry, and has very solid anchors such as tree trunks or large rocks. A landing beach is nice, if one is available. If you are in bear country, you also need to gauge a site's suitability for bear precautions. Avoid ideal bear habitat; make sure there are no nearby carcasses or recent bear sign. It should have a good line of sight from camp to kitchen, and room to keep the kitchen area well away from the tents.

Depending on the environment, you may also need to make sure your campsite will have an escape route in case of flooding. If you are on a river, know the flow profile and flood potential. Rain 100 miles (161 kilometers) away can easily result in a 2 a.m. scramble to higher ground; even worse, in a river canyon, you could be trapped. When scouting for a potential camp, look for clues that indicate how high the water level *regularly* gets and *can* get. On most rivers, little vegetation grows in regularly flooded beds, while large debris piles and some patches of stunted or sandy, low vegetation usually mark beds that are seasonally flooded in spring. Flotsam lines, like those at the beach, are also a great indicator. Local knowledge can also tell you if camping 1 vertical foot (.3 meter) above the high-water indicators is smart or if 10 feet (3 meters) would make more sense. The U.S. Geological Survey Water Resources website (http://water.usgs.gov/) gives seasonal flow profiles. In extreme cases, rivers can rise 20 to 40 feet (6 to 12 meters) in several hours. Rivers in monsoon areas, in desert canyons with impermeable surfaces, or in mountains during severe weather events are most likely to see drastic rises outside of seasonal variation.

Generally, rivers that are fed primarily by aquifers are fairly stable throughout the year; rivers that are fed primarily by spring or seasonal rains peak quickly and can be low later in the season; rivers that are fed primarily by snowmelt will peak in late spring or after long warm spells and rain and can be quite low later in the season; and rivers that are fed by lakes maintain normal flows longer through the season. Unfortunately, predicting potential flows relies on many factors and is challenging to do with any certainty, and few rivers have one primary source.

Because of the flow constriction, rivers in canyons can rise quickly and flood with little warning. What is a 1-inch (2.5-centimeters) rise in a wide, calm section of river could be a 2-foot (61-centimeter) rise in a constricted, steep section. In a desert canyon, dry arroyos and wash, along with poor soil absorption, often result in flash floods that can impact an area quite far from where the rain is actually falling. Flash floods build quickly, happening over minutes or tens of minutes, though not seconds. Tropical rivers in monsoon trajectories can get shockingly big. Research ahead of time, look for indicators of potential flooding, and make sure you have an escape route.

On large lakes, wind usually blows onshore, meaning from the water toward camp. Finding protection starts with scouting; rock formations are good and thick trees are best, though watch for dead limbs or trunks that might fall in a windstorm. Wind can actually push water to one end of a lake and hold it there, increasing the water level temporarily and potentially causing flooding of camps and low-lying land.

Depending on the region, wind tends to blow upstream. Rivers that flow through rough terrain into the ocean or large lakes can sometimes be on a diurnal "inhale-exhale" cycle powered by temperature. Water stays at about the same temperature both day and night, but mountain surfaces and air can change drastically, causing convection air currents. Glaciers also can cause evening winds.

Making Camp

Having a ritual when making camp is a special part of an expedition. On every trip, regardless of length, this ritual will develop, but it can be helpful to structure it on the first day so that all expectations are on the table and no resentment can build over time. Laissez-faire group work on an expedition can lead to poor functioning or unhappiness, especially in a group that is large or has specific high-reaching goals.

Once the scouting party has decided on a campsite, they should relay the camp plan to the rest of the group.

This is probably the last time the group will be together and focused for a few hours. If a plan for the night or any important information needs to be passed on, this is the time to do so.

Your first task when you arrive at the chosen campsite is to unload, clean, check, and stack your boat. As a habit, every evening you should empty your boat, scrutinize it for damage, check all knots and lines, and give it a cleaning. Minor repairs, such as loose bolts, broken seats, or frayed lines, are easily taken care of in that moment, while larger repairs will need as much time as possible before the next morning's launch as adhesives may need to set or cure.

Wash the boat with the bailer to remove all the sand and debris that can accumulate over a long day. The easiest way to do this is to sit on one of the decks in about 10 inches (25.4 centimeters) of water, with your feet on

Unloading the boats at the end of the day can be a group effort. These paddlers are on a Clarence River trip in New Zealand.

the river- or lakebed, and scoop water first into the bow to wash everything toward you, and then scoop it out. The more water you use, the easier it is. If there is clay or thick mud, this may need to be brushed off and then rinsed. This simple daily cleaning decreases the wear on both the boat and your packs, and getting into a clean, shipshape canoe every morning is a great way to start the day.

Once you've finished cleaning your boat and making any necessary repairs, look around and see if any of your team members need help with theirs. A general rule on a group expedition is to complete your own work before helping others, and then help others before moving into camp.

When moving the gear from the boats to the kitchen and tent areas, doing it together in one trip saves time and energy. Racing ahead to claim the best spot is bad style.

Before settling into camp each evening, any expedition gear that will not be needed until the next morning—canoes, paddles, food for later in the trip, and so on—should be secured and attached to solid anchors. Strap all the paddles together. Put food packs or barrels in the shade (take proper precautions if you are camping in bear country; see *NOLS Bear Essentials* or a similar book for details). Store map cases, bailers, and throw bags off the ground in a closed duffel or spare pack, or take them into the tents.

Things that might be needed, like the repair kit, extra fuel, and the group library, are tied in but accessible. Many people also clip their PFDs and helmets onto a canoe seat.

One effective method of securing the gear is to line up all the packs that will not be used at this camp, along with the duffels and gear, and turn the canoes over on top or in front of the line. Then take one painter from the canoe on the end, run it through each canoe's grab loop, and secure it on the far boat. Repeat this procedure with the painter on the other end of the outermost canoe, so all the boats are secured together on both ends. Then run lines out to at least one or, ideally, two to three nearby trees or very large boulders and tie them in. Also tie the lineup of gear to the boats or anchors, creating a tight overall package with very little slack. The bottom line is that everything should be secured from potential wind, animals, and flooding. An efficient, high-functioning team can be off the beach and at camp in twenty to thirty minutes, with the unloading zone left totally clear.

Once you've secured all the unneeded gear, the next step is to set up the tents and the kitchen. The cook for the night will appreciate a hand moving the food barrels or packs containing the rations to the kitchen spot. If it's getting late and you're cooking individually instead of as a group, you might want to eat dinner as soon as you have your tent set up. You also need to make time for self-care. Changing into warm or dry camp clothes, changing socks and footwear, washing your face and perhaps your body, rehydrating, snacking, and taking personal time are all key elements of living sustainably on a longer trip.

Securing the boats and gear every night is a worthwhile habit for all paddlers. Desolation Canyon, on Utah's Green River.

Shelters

TARPS

Using tarps as your primary shelter is as old as canoe expeditioning and can be done comfortably and with style. A good tarp has six to twelve reinforced grommets and about 30 square feet (2.8 square meters) per person of durable synthetic fabric. Nonwaterproof tarps work well if you seal the seams and set them up so that they shed water, or you can use a tarp made from a material such as siliconized nylon, though this is often less durable. Blue polypro tarps from the hardware store are a good low-cost option. If you reinforce the grommets with good tape prior to use, they are very durable, though they might not last as many trips as a higher-quality—but much more expensive—nylon tarp.

A tarp is incredibly easy to use. Tarps are lighter weight and cheaper than most tents, they can last longer, and with no zippers to wear out, they are a great choice for desert environments. They do take a little more ingenuity to set up, but this can be fun and demonstrates creativity. In areas with lots of insect life, having mosquito netting that hangs down from the edges of the kitchen tarp, attached either permanently or with Velcro, can mean the difference between cooking in heaven or in hell.

In environments with frequent rainfall, like the Bonnet Plume River in Yukon Territory, a kitchen tarp can make in camp life much more pleasant.

The conditions that make tarp use uncomfortable are bugs, wet, wind, and cold; while these things can make tarp use dangerous at their extremes, small amounts of them do not hurt. Generally, if it makes sense to use a tarp as your sleeping shelter, conditions might not require a kitchen tarp. In certain environments that have larger or poisonous animals, such as grizzly country or tropical rainforest, sleeping under tarps is probably not a good idea.

In most environments, rain or snow falls often enough to warrant bringing a large tarp to serve as a shelter for a kitchen, with the same criteria as above. Cooking tarps are best set up high, with lots of head room, when protecting against sun, vertical rain, or light snow, and set up lower to the ground in higher winds or horizontal rain and snow. Cooking with a fire under a synthetic tarp, even a very high one, is not recommended. Instead, carefully use a liquid fuel stove, which can be done in much tighter quarters.

To set up a kitchen tarp where there are no good trees, wrap or clove-hitch the ridge line of the tarp to the grip end of a paddle shaft, then use pegs or other anchors to secure the working ends of the ridge line to the ground. A trucker's hitch tightens the tarp and gives you a solid start on your tarp; secure the corners next and the middle last.

TENTS

The best tent is a quality tent, and one suited to your needs, intended uses, and the environment where you will be camping, as well as your personal preferences. Tents are expensive, but over the life of the tent, well-made ones actually cost less than poorly made ones. In other words, buying one well-made tent is cheaper than buying multiple poorly made ones that you would need to replace as they wear out. In some places, a mountaineering tent with doubled-up poles is the only viable option; in others, a simple tarp is more than enough. On various canoe expeditions, I have stayed in campsites with little cover and 85 mph (140 kph) winds, and I have been snowed on, weathered typhoons, and had rather pleasant stretches too.

On a canoe expedition, weight and size of the tent are still an issue, but less so than with backpacking, as on most expeditions you will not need to carry the tent very far. Still, the ounces add up, and you may regret the extra weight on the portage trail. The weight and space saved by judicious tent choice often grows more noticeable as the journey lengthens from days to weeks.

Even more important qualities in a tent are durability and water resistance. Test the tent in tough conditions before relying on it for comfort and survival. If most of your route is in protected forest campsites, a highly wind-proof tent is less vital, though waterproof full fly coverage remains key.

In spring or during a major flood, the beach this lightweight tent has been pitched on in Hess River, Yukon Territory, would be under water. The woody debris, lack of vegetation, and smoothed river sediments are all clues.

Generally, how you set up and peg out a tent is as important as the tent's inherent sturdiness; this is even more the case for tents that are not freestanding, like tube and pyramid tents. Start by using sturdy pegs, trees, and large rocks as anchors; you should have six to twelve of these solid anchors. Attach the p-cords from the base of the tent, out 3 to 4 feet (.9 to 1.2 meters) to the anchor, then back into a trucker's hitch to allow a strong and adjustable finish.

Even the best waterproof tent floors will eventually leak, so it's a good idea to take along a sheet of nylon or 6-mil plastic that is about 6 inches (15.2 centimeters) wider and longer than the tent's interior. Place this plastic sheet under the tent if setting up on a dry, abrasive surface, or center it inside the set-up tent on wet days. If the sheet is under the tent and extends farther out than the tent's sides, water will pool under the tent when it rains

With frequent high winds and no shelter, this camp in Þjórsá River, Iceland, is only feasible with good stormproofing and a well-anchored mountain tent.

In areas of high wind, multiple anchoring points and significant anchors are required. These tents in Ahuriri, New Zealand, have twelve anchoring points with about thirty pounds on each one.

so remember to fold it under. Folded up, the sheet can also provide a platform for sleeping out in the open or standing on while changing.

Ultraviolet radiation will destroy tents, especially in the Arctic and far southern latitudes and in places like Australia and New Zealand. Limit UV exposure by pitching your tent in the shade when available or taking it down during the day if laying over.

The Kitchen

Planning the kitchen starts during the goal discussion before the expedition. Some people need fancy, elaborate, hot meals three times a day for the trip to be a success, while others would happily subsist on much faster, simpler fare. What you pack for the kitchen also depends on the important decision of whether your main activity is going to be camping or paddling. Going into a trip with people having different expectations often does not end well. The kitchen gear needs to support all tastes and goals, and it should be simple, durable, and multiuse. Talk these things over, make compromises, and build in flexibility. The camp chef's motto is "do more with less."

GROUP KITCHEN GEAR

Cooking as a group of more than four presents big challenges, with the only benefit being community building through group work. A division of labor, perhaps rotating day to day, will give everyone more free time and keep the kitchen from having too many cooks. Cooking in small groups does not mean you have to cook separately; it only means that you need not take along a large and unwieldy collection of kitchen gear, and the cook or cooks will not be stressed and overworked.

To eat well and stay happy and functional on your trip, all you really need is a stove and fuel bottle, fuel, a spatula, pot grips, and a small pot. A frying pan and lid can make a nice addition to your kitchen, though the classic cast-iron pan of years past may be overkill. NOLS uses a pan made by the Banks Fry-Bake Company that is lightweight and durable and can be used to easily bake breads, cakes, pies, pizzas, and casseroles. One of the great joys of a long canoe trip is being able to bake these items. A simple frying pan with a lid is all you need, but if you are cooking for more than three or four people, you might consider including more versatile baking and cooking gear such as a Dutch oven, reflector oven, or Outback Oven. Few people will decry the added weight when you hand them fresh cinnamon buns.

When choosing a pot, plan on roughly 1 quart (1 liter) of volume per person. A second pot of a slightly smaller size is a great help for making elaborate or two-part meals, like pizza and soup or pasta and brownies, or if anyone in your group has specific food preferences, such as vegetarian or gluten-free. Pots can be hot and heavy, so a pot grip can come in handy and help avoid burns in the kitchen. Multitool pliers or lightweight pot grips made for backcountry use often do not work as well with full pots and pans, as they can't handle the weight or may slip. A better bet is a sturdy pair of Chanellock pliers.

No matter how close the water source is, having a water container of around 2 to 5 gallons (7.6 to 19 liters) greatly increases your efficiency in the kitchen. Not having to get up to fill pots and pans means less movement around the stove and a safer kitchen, and not using personal water bottles avoids spreading germs.

PERSONAL KITCHEN GEAR

Your most basic personal kitchen gear consists of a bowl and a spoon. A good bowl has about 1 quart (1 liter) of volume at most, and depending on your appetite, it could be a bit smaller. A screw-on or clamp-on lid is helpful for storing leftovers and packing lunch. Plastic is fairly durable, though cheap plastic bowls don't usually survive more than a few months' use; a 1-quart (1-liter) wide-mouthed Nalgene container may be the strongest and longest-lasting plastic bowl. A metal bowl is a great option, as it is durable and can be used as an extra small pot when sanitized. A lightweight ceramic bowl also works well if you are careful. Use what you have. For a utensil, a spoon is more versatile than a fork or spork. Plastic works well but has the potential to snap or wear out before the trip is over. Stainless steel flatware is fairly light, durable, and easy to clean and sanitize.

KNIVES

There are arguments both for and against knives in the camp kitchen. Knives make cutting a few select items in the kitchen easier, but they also risk cutting hands or fingers, which you want to avoid at all costs on a canoe expedition. You can use a thin metal spatula or turner in place of a knife to cut vegetables, cheese, and meat. have one or two people in the group carry along a small knife for special culinary circumstances, and leave the Bowie knife at home.

You can find a full discussion of backcountry cooking and equipment in *NOLS Cookery* and nutritional information in *NOLS Backcountry Nutrition*.

Fires

In many environments, having fires can be a wonderful and efficient part of an expedition if done responsibly and following Leave No Trace principles. Even if cooking on fires is a goal, a functional stove and adequate fuel should still be part of the kitchen gear as a backup when needed to warm a paddler who unexpectedly becomes a swimmer, ease a rushed morning, deal with a medical emergency, or provide food in an unexpected ten-day downpour.

Wildlife

In some environments, wildlife can make your camping life much more difficult. Animals are usually more afraid of humans and our smells than we are of them. However, in commonly traveled areas where animals have access to human food or have otherwise interacted with humans with no ill effects, they become habituated to us over time. In such cases, the likelihood of interacting with them is much higher. Truly wild animals are rarely a cause for concern, with some notable exceptions like jaguars in the Amazon, polar bears in the High Arctic, crocodiles and snakes in Australia, or hippos in Africa. If you are planning a trip to one of these places, it's imperative that you thoroughly research the specific strategies for dealing with such animals when camping and traveling in the area. This book will focus on some of the more commonly encountered animals. For more information on wildlife interactions, check out *NOLS Bear Essentials* and *NOLS Soft Paths*.

INSECTS

Insects can be omnipresent companions on a canoe trip, but they need not be a major nuisance. The main tools in your arsenal are chemical and physical barriers. Chemical barriers include bug spray, lotions, and chemical-soaked clothing, but these can be hit-and-miss when it comes to keeping blackflies and mosquitoes at bay. DEET, a toxic pesticide, is a common ingredient in insect repellents and is the only consistently effective agent; however, it is illegal in Canada at concentrations over 30 percent and is not recommended for children in large concentrations or frequent applications. Check the label and local warnings before using. If you do use DEET-based chemical barriers, apply it to your clothing, not your skin. Even DEET may not fully deter the biblical swarms of blackflies and mosquitoes you find in parts of Canada at certain times of year, but it is the only really effective chemical across regions.

Physical barriers include head nets, bug shirts, and tarps with mesh netting, along with things you might already be taking, like a tent, a hooded wind jacket, long pants, shoes, and a bandanna or scarf. Physical barriers offer the best protection if used correctly. Some species of blackflies may still manage to work their way in through seams and gaps, and mosquitoes can bite through thin fleece and other fabrics, making a wind jacket a key item. Head nets are common, cheap, and lightweight, and they provide excellent protection; in northern latitudes, bug shirts are something to consider.

SNAKES

Rattlesnakes are the most common dangerous snake in the United States, but you can largely avoid them by knowing their habits and daily and seasonal times of activity, staying out of tall grass with low ground visibility, and giving snakes a wide berth and not antagonizing them. Water moccasins—also known as cottonmouths—are a venomous snake found in the Southeastern United States. Their bites are very painful and can even be fatal. If you are traveling in a place that has multiple species of aggressive poisonous snakes that sometimes hunt near water, such as India or Australia, consider wearing knee-high, bite-proof boots or full hiking boots and gaiters when you're in camp.

SMALL MAMMALS

Small mammals are more a nuisance than anything else, with the main risk being that mice, raccoons, squirrels, or other animals may eat or ruin your food. The best ways to avoid unwanted attention from these creatures are to camp and cook very cleanly, and do not leave anything out when you are not right there. A closed barrel is protected against small wildlife, but an animal can chew through a dry bag in seconds, so it's a good idea to hang it up off the ground. Small mammals are mostly an issue in frequently used campsites due to habituation.

An additional risk if camping in lean-tos, log shelters, or overhangs is hantavirus, a virus sometimes present in the urine and droppings of rats and mice, especially deer mice. The disease is contracted when people breathe in dust containing this airborne pathogen while sleeping close to rodent droppings, so if you suspect the presence of mice or rats, consider pitching a tent instead.

BEARS

For the majority of canoeists, the large wildlife we are most worried about is bears. In areas with large wildlife, especially bears, the basic precautions are to travel, camp, and sleep in groups; make a lot of noise when entering a new spot while traveling or making camp; and keep an immaculately clean kitchen, leave smelly items in it, and sleep away from it.

Black bear habitat ranges all the way from Alaska to Mexico to Nova Scotia, and they are often present in traditional canoe country. They are not aggressive animals, but black bears are curious and can easily become habituated to humans and our food. When cornered or if females feel their cubs are threatened, they can become dangerous. In addition to the above basic precautions, consider carrying a canister of pepper-based bear spray in black bear country, especially in well-traveled corridors where black bears are known to be present.

Grizzly, or brown, bears are usually larger, more curious, and more likely to stand and fight a threat than to run away like a black bear. The same three precautions are key in grizzly country, but you should take them to the next level. Your kitchen, sleeping area, and toilet area should be 200 feet (61 meters) apart from each other, depending on the terrain, and in addition to food, all smelly items—toothpaste, sunscreen, shampoo, soap—should be left in the kitchen. Team members should travel in groups at all times, even when going to the bathroom, and make loud bear calls to announce their presence. Areas of low visibility are more likely places for an encounter, as neither you nor the bear can see each other. Bear spray is effective against grizzly bears, and you should consider carrying enough bear spray for each small group to have at least one canister.

Carrying a gun as a bear deterrent is questionable, as shown by various studies, including a 2012 study by Tom S. Smith, a wildlife biologist, that showed that having a gun in a bear encounter has no effect on the outcome of the encounter. Being able to load, aim, and accurately fire a gun at a bounding target is the province of trained, expert marksmen (and perhaps lucky ones)—not your average canoeist. Bear spray is easier, safer, and will teach the bear that humans are to be avoided, all without destroying the animal. Polar bears, the only bear species known to actively hunt humans, are an exception. If you are planning on traveling in coastal areas in the High Arctic, where you might encounter polar bears, you may want to carry a shotgun that you have extensive practice with. Having secondary options like bear bangers and bear spray is also a good idea, especially if you are only ending your trip on the coast.

Hygiene

A backcountry expedition should be viewed as an opportunity to live and travel in the wilderness, rather than to survive in spite of it. This extends to self-care and hygiene in significant ways. Some seem to have the idea that basic cleanliness and routine do not apply when in the wilderness or on an expedition. This is an absurd notion. In fact, these things become even *more* important on a group trip, as the proximity of people's bodies and the lack of abundant hot water and dishwashers mean that a person's germs rarely stay personal for very long.

The nature of canoeing is that water is abundant, so washing should be abundantly easy. Establish rituals like washing your face every morning and night, brushing and flossing every day, and leaving the kitchen spotless after each use. Make time, particularly on warm and sunny days, to swim or disappear behind a bush to wash with a dromedary bag hung from a tree.

Bathroom use needs special attention, as it is fecal-oral contamination that is by far the most common and easily transmitted of all expedition ailments. Countless canoe expeditions have been laid low by a foul lack of simple hygiene. This can be avoided by making hand washing an expected ritual after pooping and before cooking. A group or individual going on a dump run leaves camp with someone assigned as a hand washer waiting with good, foaming, concentrated soap and a full dromedary of water. After dumping, the group or individual touches nothing before the hand washer gives each person a dose of soap and turns on the water. Scrub your hands, fingers, fingernails, wrists, palms, and forearms for a full twenty to thirty seconds before rinsing.

The notion of thriving, or living, rather than surviving is an important one, but in terms of self-care, you probably do not need an electric razor, deodorant, shampoo, or makeup to take good care of yourself, so some sacrifices might be necessary.

Water Treatment and Storage

Along with poor personal hygiene, drinking unsterilized water is the other chief cause of gastrointestinal illness on canoe trips. Having the ability to disinfect water on your expedition is a fundamental necessity, especially in more popular canoe areas where heavier use often means more microorganisms in the water. For our purposes, treating or purifying water refers to disinfection, i.e., killing microorganisms such as parasitic worms, viruses, protozoa like *Giardia* and *Cryptosporidium*, and various bacteria.

Even in remote wilderness, it is still important to treat your water; better to be safe than sorry. See *NOLS Wilderness Medicine* for more information on water treatment and gastrointestinal illness.

Another worry in more populated areas is that water may be polluted or contaminated by farm runoff, paper mills, and industry. Heavy metals, hydrocarbons, and pesticides are just a few of the contaminants you can come across. If the expedition will be going through areas with polluted or silty water, the group gear should include enough water storage capacity to avoid using water from the contaminated waterway. In hot, dry weather, plan on about 1.8 gallons (7 liters) of water per person per day for drinking and cooking. If temperatures are moderate or cool, 1 gallon (4 liters) per person per day might be sufficient.

The sturdy 5-gallon (19-liter) high-density plastic water cubes, like the Reliance AquaTainer, that are often used on rafting trips work well, though many other options exist. Side-country waterways (rural areas in between backcountry and frontcountry) polluted by agriculture or industry often have potable water available in nearby parks, campgrounds, or river or lakeside villages or farmsteads, so when traveling in these areas, you rarely need to carry more than a couple days' worth.

SETTLING WATER

If a river is silty but clean and unpolluted, you can make clear drinking water with just a few simple steps. Using several bailers, fill a large, open container like a 15.8-gallon (60-liter) barrel or a canoe with river water, and let it sit for several hours or overnight. Most of the particles will settle to the bottom, thanks to gravity, and you can carefully scoop the water off the top and put it into other containers. If using a canoe, place it on a very soft, even surface—like a sandy beach—first, as a few hundred pounds of water can result in punctures or deformation to the boat on sharp or uneven surfaces. Tie the canoe up before filling. The hull will be under significant stress and should not be totally filled. Place it on a slight slope, if possible, and fill just a third of the hull.

Another option to aid in the settling process is to use aluminum sulfate, or alum, a type of salt that when mixed into silty water will bond to particles and clump them together, causing them to settle out. About 1 to 1.5 ounces (29.6 to 44.4 milliliters) of alum powder mixed into 1 quart (1 liter) of water creates a concentrate that can be used throughout a trip; about 3.4 ounces (100 milliliters) of the alum concentrate can settle 10 to 15 gallons (38 to 57 liters) of silty water in less than an hour. Do not drink the alum-silt mixture at the bottom, which is an aluminum derivative and toxic when ingested. As with any settling method, the water must still be disinfected.

TREATING WATER

Whether you are drawing the water right out of a lake or river or it has been settled, it needs to be disinfected before use. The options are to use heat, filtration, or chemical means. Heat simply involves bringing the water to a rolling boil. While highly effective in disinfecting water, this requires significant time and fuel.

Filtration involves the use of a hand pump or gravity filter with a pore size of 0.2 micron. Filters physically remove bacteria and protozoa, but they will not remove viruses. The disadvantages to filters are that they can be expensive, may require time and energy to use, need to be cleaned regularly, and can develop microcracks. The advantages are that they produce potable water without the use of chemicals and remove the most common microorganisms in North America, *Giardia* and *Cryptosporidium*. Filters using ultraviolet light are becoming more common and claim to be 99.9 percent effective at inactivating microorganisms. Follow the manufacturer's instructions on use with any filtration system.

The most commonly used water treatment method is chemical disinfection, using iodine- or chlorine-based tablets, drops, or strips. This method is fast, easy, and effective, and it adds little in the way of weight or cost. Iodine is less useful because of the taste and chemical content; chlorine tends to have less aftertaste than iodine.

The easiest and cheapest way to treat water in large quantities on an expedition is to carry along a small hard plastic bottle filled with chlorine bleach (6 percent sodium hypochlorite) and topped with an eye dropper. The warmer and clearer the water, the less solution is required, and if a quicker turnaround is needed, much higher quantities of solution can be added. A conservative general rule is five drops of chlorine bleach in 5 gallons (19 liters) of water for twelve hours.

Away from contaminated or silty water, or for small amounts of water such as the liter in your water bottle, it is more effective to treat as you go. Boil water used for cooking, and treat drinking water in the bottle with small chlorine tablets or a two-part chlorine solution like AquaMira.

Dressing for Camp

In camp versus on the water, the same concepts apply: wear layers, stay dry, and maintain homeostasis, keeping your body temperature as stable as possible. The key is to have separate clothing options for camp apart from those for the water. You need a reliable system for getting warm and dry on arriving at your campsite, especially because you're likely to experience a splash or swim at some point during your trip. Conversely, in hot weather, you need clothing that will help keep you from overheating while in camp. If your expedition will involve both extremes, it's a good idea to have a flexible system that tends toward preparing for colder weather. See appendix A for sample gear lists, including clothing options for various climates.

COOL OR WET CONDITIONS

Unless you are portaging, the cardiovascular workout of a day on the water does not really turn up your body's thermostat, and no matter how warm the air is, a long swim or wet travel can slowly deplete your body heat and leave you in need of warmth upon arriving in camp. Taking two sets (top and bottom) of long underwear means that even if one set stays wet for the entire trip, you will have a dry set for camp, but this requires committing to keeping the dry set dry even if it means putting on a wet set before launching each morning.

Warm layers like long-sleeved wool base shirts, plain fleece pullovers, warm hats, and synthetic puffy jackets together make a great and flexible system. Wind pants and jacket create a durable outer layer that you can add or subtract as the weather and your metabolism change. In very cold weather, puffy or fleece pants, gloves, and an extra puffy jacket or parka complete the picture.

Having dry feet for about half of the day—eight to ten hours—is vital in cool or wet environments, as feet are highly susceptible to cold injury (see the discussion of immersion foot in the section on nonfreezing cold injuries in chapter 11). Warm, dry camp shoes and socks are necessary. The best choices include good-condition, water-resistant sneakers or light, soft boots like L.L.Bean hunting shoes or Blundstone work boots. Galoshes can go over a pair of sneakers, providing a more flexible, if slightly less durable, system. Options abound for keeping feet warm and dry in camp in cool and wet conditions. If it's very cold, you may need insulated boots.

HOT WEATHER

On the other end of the spectrum, in hot and sunny weather, having full skin coverage and loose, breathable layers is a matter of health as well as comfort. Humans do not deal well with heat, and everything from skin health to decision-making can be affected when you are in the beating sun. Although cotton is not a good choice when you are cold or wet, a loose, long-sleeved cotton shirt can be perfect for camp on a hot summer day. You can still wear full-coverage footwear, such as durable boots or sneakers with socks, but you'll want thinner socks in this environment so that they won't overheat your feet and are easier to clean. Sandals can be a good option for camp in warm weather, but watch out for insects, sunburn, and poking sticks.

RAINGEAR

Proven, durable raingear is a must in nondesert environments. Waterproof, breathable fabrics like Gore-Tex are lightweight and effective, though they are expensive and ultralight varieties can be fragile and must be well cared for. Gore-Tex also can succumb to leakage when the fabric is under pressure or has been used hard for a few months. Vinyl or PVC foul-weather gear does not breathe, but high-quality sets, like those from Helly Hansen, will last much longer and resist abrasion better than the more advanced fabrics like Gore-Tex. When canoeing, as opposed to backpacking or many other physical activities, you are not usually generating a lot of body heat, especially in conditions when you would need raingear, so breathability may not be a factor. Use what you have and experiment with what you like.

One way to make raingear, particularly Gore-Tex, last longer is to put it on only when it is raining or snowing. Wearing it around camp as a warm layer, wind layer, or style item increases wear, and better and much cheaper options for wind and warmth exist. Not storing it wet, sitting on it, or wearing it while moving through dense brush also help with longevity. Weight-conscious paddlers may, however, use their raingear for multiple purposes at the cost of increased wear.

The Good Life

There are certain small accoutrements that are not strictly vital to your existence on a canoe trip but can help lend that important feeling of living with wildness rather than surviving in spite of it. Practiced skill and intentional living enhance this feeling, but it can be aided by thoughtful gear choices made ahead of time.

Finding time to relax can be difficult on a long expedition, but it is vital. A few small items can provide a lot of stress relief. Here, a paddler relaxes on Richardson Lake in Maine.

BOOKS

Surviving without a book on an expedition is strictly possible, but many, including me, couldn't endure it. A good book is one that can be shared or read aloud in some moments, and a great book is all that as well as one that speaks to the land or people you are traveling through and with. Reading Sigurd Olson in the Boundary Waters, Robert Service in the Yukon, or Thoreau in the Maine woods can help engender powerful connections with your environment, while having journals or logs from past explorers, like John Wesley Powell on the Green or Colorado River or Alexander Mackenzie in interior Canada, can evoke an element of history that is nothing short of magic. Group texts, like science books, poetry anthologies, or canoe-specific technical works, together with route guides and not-in-use maps can make up a community library that all can use and learn from—and share the burden of carrying.

CAMP CHAIR

A square of closed-cell foam will suffice as a butt pad and changing platform, but for those with long or injury-prone backs, as well those seeking more comfort, a small camp chair is an important luxury. Folding chairs like those from Crazy Creek work well, though a better choice may be a foam-free nylon chair with metal stays. Hammocks can make excellent chairs as well, and the backpacking versions are tiny and lightweight.

SPECIAL FOOD

Apart from the protein and calories, treats like gourmet jerky or preserved meat, chocolate, candy, and power bars are nice to have for personal use, as is chili paste or hot sauce, and items like multivitamins, vitamin C powder, and fruit bars can be an investment in your health. Label everything well, and limit the quantities to avoid adding a lot of weight and make them feel like treats.

This may come as a shock to you, but coffee, tea, and hot chocolate are not vital group amenities. It might be best to have individuals pack their own preferred hot beverages and brewing arrangements.

MUSICAL INSTRUMENTS

Musical instruments are hard to justify from a packing perspective, but in camp they are beyond price. A fiddle, guitar, or harmonica is a potent tool for entertainment and group bonding, and being away from recorded music makes everyone's voice sound better.

CAMERA

Building a video and photograph record of your trip is a worthy endeavor, but it takes time, expensive equipment, and some skill to do well, and significant skill to produce anything someone outside of your family would want to see. As for equipment, great options run from high-end digital SLRs with high-definition video and sound capture ability all the way to simple point-and-shoot cameras.

For shooting while on the water without interrupting the flow of the day, some of the low-cost, high-quality, waterproof and shockproof digital point-and-shoot cameras will fit well in the front pocket of a PFD or paddle jacket. This is a great option for most people, but the lack of significant or interchangeable lenses and the ability to shoot in RAW format, as well as the lower quality of the image processor, will deter most higher-end photographers.

Caring for higher-end equipment need not be a massive or expensive ordeal. Pelican Cases are rugged and waterproof and fit all camera and lens sizes, and though they are expensive, they tend to last longer than most cameras. Ammo boxes and dry bags are much lower-cost options but are not as long-lasting or waterproof. If the whole kit is worth over $1,000, it's not a bad idea to buy a short-term insurance policy against accidental damage for the length of the trip; being afraid to take out your camera because it's expensive negates having the camera along in the first place.

Talented photographers are often the first ones invited when building a team, and having this skill in the group is definitely something to think about. That said, many professionals relish the idea of being able to leave their equipment at home and just relax on the river.

BINOCULARS OR MONOCULARS
Binoculars and monoculars are wonderful tools for birding and spotting wildlife, as well as picking out distant river features and portage trails.

PERSONAL ELECTRONICS
Many people cannot live without some kind of personal electronics. In the front or side country, I may take a simple MP3 player, but on a true back-country trip, I usually leave mine at home and ask others to do the same. This is a judgment call and is best decided as a group before the trip.

An iPod Touch, iPad, Nook, or Kindle can last weeks in certain conditions, and when paired with a good solar panel or biofuel charger, the battery can last indefinitely, giving you access to all the bird guides, recipe books, and other material you could ever want, at a savings of several pounds.

BASIC SKILLS

Loading and rigging, paddling concepts, basic strokes, and basic maneuvers and drills

As an expedition paddler, you need to master a repertoire of skills, including how to properly load and rig the boats and execute a variety of strokes and maneuvers. You also must have a knowledge of basic paddling concepts.

Loading

The process of moving gear from shore into the canoe will depend on the loading zone, the amount of gear, and the team's experience level. The fol-

Learning how to effectively maneuver a canoe is a lifelong progression. Hess River, Yukon Territory.

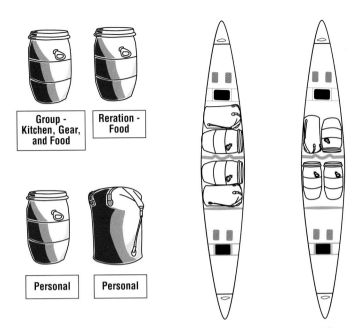

Group -
Kitchen, Gear,
and Food

Reration -
Food

Personal

Personal

There are a hundred ways to load a canoe, and most of them work. Consider keeping the heaviest items lower in the boat and closer to the pivot point.

lowing recommendations are part of a flexible system that should be adapted as necessary based on the situation at hand and team members' judgment and experience.

Most expedition canoes can safely carry hundreds of pounds of people and gear, but they need to be supported by water to do so. You should avoid loading boats on land, as the weight of the gear can damage and deform the hull. Also avoid having the canoe "bridged," meaning partly in the water and partly on land, with open air between the two points of support, because a sudden addition of weight can deform the hull. That said, in certain situations loading on land may be the only option, particularly on steep and vegetated riverbanks. If so, load the boat on level ground and then the whole group should move the boat to the water together. When attempting to move a loaded canoe from land to water remember that canoes are just pieces of gear, and while they should be treated with diligent care, they are not as important as any person's safety.

It's a good idea to tie up your boat while loading or have one partner stand and hold the boat while the other loads. A gust of wind or the pull of current can cause an unattended boat to move surprisingly fast. Having all of the gear intended for your boat within arm's reach before starting to load will make the process smoother. Packs and barrels, particularly those with a full ration of food, can weigh about 80 pounds (27 kg), so lift with your legs and keep your chin up and back straight. No pack needs to be carried solo; a very heavy pack can be moved short distances with two people carrying it. This can also work toward creating a culture of teamwork instead of one of brute strength, risk, and competition.

When you are loading a boat, you need to be aware of its trim, which refers to how a canoe sits in the water as a result of its load. The trim has a significant effect on the boat's efficiency and how it handles. Generally, the trim of the boat should be neutral at all times; this means that when paddlers and gear are in the boat, it should sit level both from bow to stern and from side to side. Always trim the boat so that it is balanced, and learn to handle it in that state.

The closer the majority of the weight is to the pivot point, the easier the boat will turn under steering forces. If you have two heavy packs and two light packs, which is often the case on an expedition, with each canoe carrying two food and two personal packs, put the heavy pieces close to the yoke and the lighter pieces close to the bow and stern thwarts.

When each paddler is about the same weight, load the boat so that it is balanced and hop in. If there is a significant weight discrepancy between paddlers, say 20 pounds (9 kilograms) or more, it may be necessary to switch the load around so that the boat is not plowing into the water or popping a wheelie. Trim is also important from side to side, and most canoeists can tell when the boat is overloaded on the left or right. Fix this immediately, as it increases the risk of capsize and can result in a backache at the end of the day from sitting at a slight angle.

The load should be as close to flush with the gunwales as possible; any gear that sticks above the rails is unsightly and might catch on branches, lines, or rocks. It also significantly decreases the stability of the boat: as weight rises above the waterline and then the gunwales, the craft becomes increasingly top heavy and less stable.

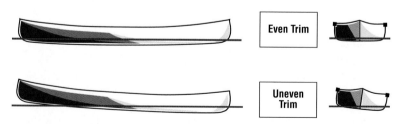

Even or neutral trim makes the canoe much easier to maneuver. Uneven trim has specialized uses, however.

Loading the canoes close to high-consequence water requires communication and planning. Nisutlin River, Yukon Territory.

For travel on remote or continuous rivers, it can be a good idea to pack boats so that each is as self-sufficient as possible, with tents, stoves, food, and clothing in every boat. That way, if a boat is lost or the group is separated in an emergency, members on a single boat will still be able to function if they need to make camp or survive alone. On very remote or exploratory expeditions, consider having some form of emergency communication technology in each boat, in case the boat with the satellite phone, personal locator beacon (PLB), emergency position indicating radio beacon (EPIRB), or other beacon is lost.

At the campsite, it is usually best to agree the night before on a time when the boats will be untied rather than at wake-up time. That way, all team members can plan out their morning routines and be ready to start carrying boats and loading together. It works well to have each pair load and rig their own boat and then help others until the whole group is ready to move. The process will become quicker and more efficient as time goes on.

Rigging

The need for a rigging system and what type you should use depend on where you intend to use your canoe; a focused river canoe used on a route with continuous whitewater needs a reliable and secure rigging system, but a focused flatwater canoe used on a calm lake route might not. Generally speaking, in moving water all gear should be secured so that in the event of a capsize, the safety boat or swimming paddlers need only rescue one thing rather than several. If the packs are waterproof, the tied-in gear will also serve as flotation as it displaces water in the swamped canoe.

GRAVITY RIG

On a lake route, a gravity rig—simply placing gear in the boat without tying it down—might be enough, depending on conditions. Rescuing a swamped, loaded boat with tied-in gear in the middle of a windy lake is very difficult. You might need to secure the swimmers and either tow the boat to shore or wait for it to be blown there at the risk of losing it. Ideally, you would not be out in those conditions, but storms often come up abruptly and unexpectedly. With a gravity rig, you may be able to T-rescue the boat (see chapter 11), pluck the swimmers out of the water, and capture a few key packs, though it is all a dicey proposition in rough conditions.

Many rivers are "pool and drop" in nature: each set of rapids or section of moving water begins and ends in a calm pool where rescue is easy and a capsized canoe whose load was gravity rigged can be put back together without the worry of losing much gear. Still, a securely tied-in load on a continuous or pool-and-drop river is probably the best option, as it is on an open lake, although this requires situational judgment.

DIAMOND RIG

One highly effective method for securely rigging a canoe for downriver travel is the diamond rig. Three metal and vinyl D-rings and four rope D-rings form the basis for this system. The three D-rings are installed on the bottom of the canoe on the centerline under the bow thwart, yoke, and stern thwart, and the rope rings are placed just under the gunwales halfway between the thwarts, as described in chapter 2.

You then lace the load together with a cam strap, a 15- to 20-foot (4.6- to 6-meter) piece of 1-inch (2.5-centimeter) flat webbing with a cam buckle sewn to one end. Other options are tubular webbing without a cam buckle or quality rope, but for ease of use, the cam strap is worth the extra cost.

Starting at the bow, you place the buckle on the seat, then thread the strap through the floor D-ring under the bow thwart, over the load, through the gunwale rope ring, over the load, down to the floor D-ring under the yoke, over the load, through the other gunwale rope ring, and through the buckle, and then cinch it tight. For added security, and to avoid having a loose piece of webbing, the tail can be finished with a half hitch or a slippery half hitch just behind the buckle, and any spare strap can be laced across the load. The straps should not go around or over the thwarts,

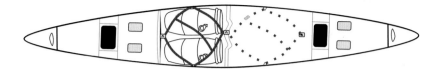

The diamond shape of the cam strap rig secures all the gear in the canoe, making it rigged to flip, but this rig requires a bit of practice and close attention to detail to be fully effective.

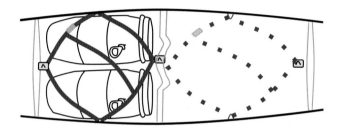

A close-up of the diamond rig. Note that the cam strap is threaded through four D-rings—two on the bottom of the hull and two at the gunwales.

should not be twisted, and should be neither loose nor too tight; they need only be tight enough to prevent any movement of the load.

Repeat the process on the stern compartment. The straps share the D-ring under the yoke. These two diamond-shaped (when viewed from above) straps will hold the gear in place if the boat capsizes and will keep the load from shifting during aggressive maneuvers. Odd-shaped or small pieces like 1,831-cubic-inch (30-liter) barrels, fuel jugs, water jugs, rocket boxes, or portable toilets might require a little creativity, but as with the larger pieces, it is a good idea to thread the strap through a handle or hard point on each item so that even if it slips out from the load, it remains attached.

SECURING THE LITTLE STUFF

After the big pieces have been loaded and secured, the smaller but rather important pieces of gear still on the beach need a secure home as well. The key here is to attach every single item to the boat, while keeping the area around your seat, knees, and thighs free of anything that might entangle. A daypack might be clipped into the bow or stern or on top of a low-lying load, while the spare paddle can be strapped on top as well or jammed down the side of the canoe between the load and the hull. Map cases benefit from a 2- to 3-foot (61- to 91-centimeter) length of p-cord, which you can use to attach them to a pack or thwart with a releasable hitch, like a

Dry bags secured to the hull of the canoe with cam straps in a diamond rig.

thief's hitch. Water bottles need straps or clips to hold them in; taping a spare length of webbing to each bottle and then clipping it to a pack or ring is an easy solution.

Basic Paddling Concepts

If you are a novice paddler, before building a team and planning an expedition, you need to learn some basic paddling concepts and skills. You may have observed seasoned professionals appear to execute these maneuvers without thinking, but this comes only with practice and experience. It is vital that you tackle them in detail in order to achieve ease of execution, muscle memory, and good style.

You cannot learn how to paddle simply by reading the next few pages and looking at the photos. Growth in paddling skill comes with significant practice, qualified instruction, exposure to new ideas, and an open mind. And a good paddler never stops learning and growing. There are several good paddling schools in North America that focus on canoeing, including Zoar Outdoor in Massachusetts, Nantahala Outdoor Center in North Carolina, Rocky Mountain Paddling Center in Alberta, and Madawaska Kanu Centre in Ontario, as well as national bodies that organize instruction, such as Paddle Canada and the American Canoe Association. For short-term paddling instruction, the above schools are great choices, but for high-quality paddling instruction along with expedition skills and wilderness leadership, NOLS is the leading option.

POSTURE AND TORSO ROTATION

The largest and strongest muscle groups in the body are located in the back, chest, and stomach, and it is these core muscles that provide the power in most correctly performed strokes. Using your arm muscles is a sure way to get buff, but proper technique uses the large and efficient core muscles, as the arms tire quickly and cannot provide the needed power over time.

While paddling, practicing proper torso rotation is necessary both to provide the required power and to lessen your chance of injury. Efficient torso rotation is best achieved when you are kneeling comfortably in the canoe, with most of your weight on your knees and some on your butt resting on the seat. It is helpful to think of your arms only as a conduit to transfer power from the engine of your core muscles to the force applicator of the paddle and blade.

Initially, the novice paddler must actively and deliberately engage these muscles by rotating first to the off side, the non-main paddling side, and then to the on side, the main paddling side, in effect unwinding the coiled spring tension of the torso into the paddle and from there to the water. How this concept does or does not apply to specific strokes will be addressed shortly.

Over time, you will create muscle memory for this set of motions and it will feel natural, as with many kinesthetic endeavors. It is important for the beginner to develop good habits through proper instruction and skilled role models, as bad habits can be hard to break.

Paddler's Box

To ensure that you are rotating your torso properly, it can be helpful to imagine that a small flatscreen television is attached to your chest, with the screen pointing to the sky. The rectangle's longer sides are perpendicular to your chest when your outstretched arms are right in front of you. Whatever stroke you are doing, rotate your body from the hips up and turn this "paddler's box" toward the work of your stroke; this keeps your shoulders forward and in line, preventing injury, and engages the large core muscles.

Separation of Upper and Lower Body

Another tip in setting yourself up for proper torso rotation is to visualize a strict separation of your upper and lower body. From feet to hips, your lower body should move very little in relation to the boat; it remains connected to the boat through your feet, knees, thighs, and butt and is the platform or turntable on which the rest of the body moves. From hips to head, your upper body serves as the power unit that interacts with the water through the force applicator of the paddle. Maintaining this separation is a great help in achieving proper torso rotation, as well as in setting up the paddle for tilting the boat as part of maneuvering the boat.

PIVOT POINT

The pivot point is the fulcrum, or balance point, of the boat. On a well-loaded canoe, the pivot point is located on the bottom of the hull on the centerline and under the yoke. Generally, the farther away from this point you apply force and steering strokes, the more they will affect the boat.

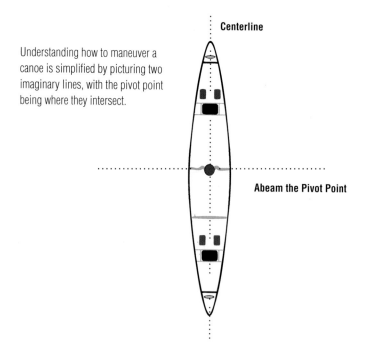

Understanding how to maneuver a canoe is simplified by picturing two imaginary lines, with the pivot point being where they intersect.

Centerline

Abeam the Pivot Point

FOCUS ON THE DIRECTION OF TRAVEL

As in almost any sport, you need to focus on your direction of travel rather than any obstacles. A downhill skier in the forest is more likely to hit a tree if she looks at one; to her, maintaining rhythm means looking between the trees. The same principle is true if you are behind the wheel—if you look at a cow on the side of the road, you might start to turn toward it.

On the water, you should have a peripheral awareness of your surroundings but spend most of your time looking in the direction you want to go and working aggressively to get there. This focus on points not immediately in or around the boat increases stability as well. The novice often tends to focus on the boat or paddle, the intermediate paddler on the currents or obstacles around the boat, and the expert on the eddy he intends to hit or even the bottom of the entire set of rapids.

STEERING FORCES

A variety of forces can turn a boat, including wind, currents, and strokes; these are called *steering forces*. Understanding how to increase and decrease the power of these steering forces is vital to controlling the boat effectively in constantly changing conditions and environments. The farther a stroke or other input is from both the pivot point and the centerline, the larger a steering force it will exert. This chapter focuses on paddler-initiated steering forces; using external steering forces, like waves, currents, and wind, is covered in the following section.

ON-SIDE AND OFF-SIDE STROKES

While paddling, you can apply power through on-side and off-side strokes. These two sides exist in relation to your orientation and which hand is where. If your right hand is on the grip, then the right is your off side and

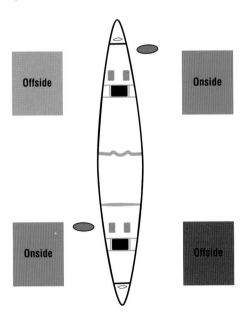

Tandem paddlers have opposite on sides. The stern paddler never uses his or her off side, while the bow paddler does occasionally.

the left is your on side; if you switch hand positions, the off side and on side also switch. Both off-side and on-side strokes are done with your hands in the same position; they do not switch, and the majority of tandem strokes are placed on the on side. This terminology is helpful in discussing stroke stages and biomechanics, as well as in differentiating types of strokes.

In a tandem boat, you and your partner paddle on opposite sides and switch only during a break if tired or sore. A racing stroke that involves constant forward strokes and frequent switching of sides has no place in whitewater paddling and is unnecessary in expedition paddling as a whole. Using core muscle groups to avoid arm fatigue and proper steering strokes to maintain direction is more efficient over time and more effective in rough water.

CATCH, POWER, AND RECOVERY PHASES

A stroke can be broken down into three simple phases: catch, power, and recovery. This helps beginners slow down and learn, and it can aid specific coaching and deliberate personal growth.

Before beginning a stroke, you sit facing forward at neutral, with an intact paddler's box and the paddle held loosely in front of you in both hands and parallel to the water. The *catch phase* begins the stroke as you move the blade toward and into the water. In the *power phase*, you apply force to the water through the blade until it has moved through the proper length of the stroke. In the *recovery phase*, the paddle is removed from the water and returns to the start position of the catch phase.

Strokes

This section describes the four basic canoe strokes, variations of these strokes, and compound strokes consisting of two basic strokes performed one after the other. The descriptions given here are meant as a reference or starting point; to gain proficiency, you must practice on the water and spend time with more experienced paddlers or instructors. If you are just starting out, focus on the basic paddling concepts, as described above, rather than on specific strokes. Concentrate on gaining an understanding of boat control and how water works, and master the basic strokes before delving into the more complex strokes.

BASIC STROKES

Basic canoe strokes are the building blocks that you put together to perform maneuvers. The four basic paddling strokes are the forward, back, draw, and pry strokes. Once you have learned these four strokes, you can start practicing the whitewater and flatwater maneuvers detailed later in this chapter and in part II. The descriptions of how to perform each stroke are divided into the catch, power, and recovery phases.

Forward Stroke

The forward stroke occurs in front of the body and is accomplished with a deceptively simple movement. Many paddlers spend their entire lives working on tweaking and improving this stroke in order to achieve more power and greater efficiency. Over the course of a long paddling day on expedition, you might do more than fifteen thousand forward strokes, which means that the slightest inefficiency in your technique can result in a massive waste of energy, and the tiniest anatomical fault might lead to fatigue and injury.

Catch. The forward stroke begins with your arms held in front of your body, with your elbows slightly bent and an intact paddler's box. You then swing the box slightly to the off side to wind up your torso: the blade comes forward as your shoulders turn to the off side. Next, you drop the blade toward the water and raise the grip hand to eye level, placing the entire paddle outside of the boat. The paddle shaft as viewed from the bow will be vertical, but as viewed from the side it will be sloped at about a 45-degree angle. The blade enters the water cleanly and silently as far in front of your knee as possible without leaning or sitting forward.

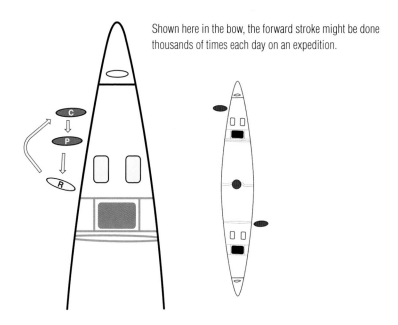

Shown here in the bow, the forward stroke might be done thousands of times each day on an expedition.

The vertical paddle shaft placed outside the boat sets the paddler up for a strong stroke. Here, the power phase began before the catch phase finished, leaving the blade partially out of the water.

The catch phase finds the paddler's arms nearly straight out in front of him and the torso prepared to rotate.

Power. The power phase starts with the paddle shaft vertical as viewed from the bow. Your shaft hand is just above the gunwale, and your grip hand is at eye level and just outside the gunwale. Your shoulders and torso are turned slightly to the off side, with the blade engaged on the on side. The power phase starts as your torso unwinds and force is applied to the water. Keep the shaft vertical and close to the gunwale as your torso unwinds. The power phase of the stroke is stopped just before the paddle reaches your knee. The blade travels only about 18 inches through the water, depending on your body. In moving water, the length of each stroke is kept short and the stroke rate is kept high to maintain control; on flat water, the stroke rate will be lower and the length may be slightly longer and more relaxed.

Any power applied to the blade at the extreme end of the stroke, particularly behind your hip, is largely wasted because of the blade angle—it is pushing water up rather than moving the canoe.

Recovery. The blade decelerates at your knee; take it out of the water by slightly dropping your grip hand and knifing the blade out. The recovery moves the paddle and your body back into the start of the catch. When the blade comes out of the water, rotate the grip so that the blade is parallel to the water and is "feathered," turned to cut through the wind. Imagine being a pizza chef taking pies out of the oven with a giant spatula—do not let the pizza slide off into the water. Your grip hand can stay roughly at the level of your eye and chin, moving in a small orbit in front of your torso. In whitewater, where maintaining momentum is often necessary for some moves, keeping a vertical paddle shaft through the recovery, rather than feathering, can increase stroke cadence and therefore power.

Back Stroke

The back stroke is approached similarly to the forward stroke, but in reverse.

Catch. The blade enters the water at your hips, with your torso turned slightly to the on side and the paddler's box intact, but with your shaft arm slightly bent.

The back, or reverse, stroke is almost the same as the forward stroke, but done in reverse.

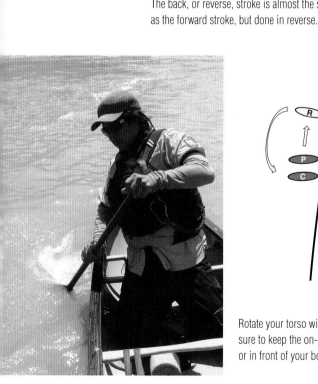
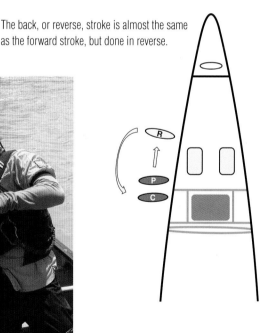

Rotate your torso with the shaft, being sure to keep the on-side elbow beside or in front of your body.

Power. The power phase begins when the blade is fully submerged and you begin to rotate your torso to the off side. The shaft is kept vertical as viewed from the bow, with similar hand positioning in relation to the boat as the forward stroke.

Recovery. The blade decelerates when it reaches the limit of your reach. Remove it from the water by dropping your grip hand, just as in the forward stroke.

Draw Stroke

The draw stroke moves the boat toward your on side. The draw is one of the simplest ways to apply a steering force and has a number of important variations. The draw stroke involves placing the blade outside the canoe and pulling water toward the hull—in effect, moving that end of the boat toward the paddle. When a draw is combined with an understanding of the canoe's pivot point, basic maneuvers and steering forces begin to make a

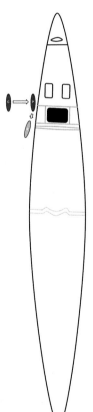

The power in the draw comes less from rotation than from your arm and torso muscles contracting together.

This draw is a standard draw into the hip.

lot more sense. The draw stroke is made to your side, and it is helpful to remember that the power face of the blade is used in every draw, stern draw, and cross draw.

Catch. In placing the blade for the initiation of a draw stroke, it is important to "face your work"—that is, to rotate your torso and shoulders to your on side, where the draw stroke is going to occur. Beginning at neutral, rotate your torso so that your shoulders are close to parallel with the gunwale. This may be uncomfortable at first, so try not to overextend to the point of injury. Once you are facing the on side, hold the shaft vertically as viewed from the side, and submerge the blade in the water at arm's length.

Power. Applying power to the water is a matter of moving the boat toward the shaft as a fixed point. It

The paddler is bending at the waist to add power to the draw.

is helpful to deliberately tighten your stomach and torso muscles as if you were doing a sit-up or crunch to help fully engage those power centers. Nevertheless, you cannot avoid using your arms for some of the power in a draw stroke. Keep your arms fairly straight with elbows slightly bent; your arms do not fully collapse into your body when bringing the paddle toward the boat.

Recovery. Do not bring the blade all the way to the boat, which could cause the paddle to get sucked under the boat and perhaps even pulled out of your hands. To avoid this, decelerate the blade several inches to a foot from the gunwales, depending on your body size; in this zone close to the hull, the power of the draw diminishes anyway. Drop your grip hand forward while keeping your shaft hand stationary, which will cause the blade to pop out of the water. You can then move the blade in the direction of the next stroke. Alternatively, you can feather the blade in the water and set it up for the catch phase without taking it out of the water.

Pry Stroke

The pry stroke moves the boat away from your on side. The pry can be one of the most powerful strokes in your toolbox when your body is engaged and you use the boat to amplify it. It is in some ways the opposite of the draw stroke in the effect is has on the boat, but it is in the same family in that it causes the boat to move around the pivot point in relation to where you plant the paddle and apply force. This stroke is most useful in the stern. In the bow, it is sometimes used only until the paddler learns how to do the cross-bow draw, but the bow pry is still an effective stroke that should not be wholly forgotten. It is helpful to remember that the back face—not the power face—is used in all pry strokes.

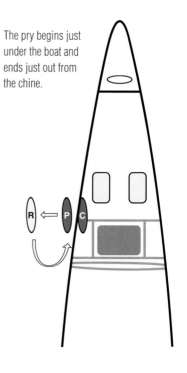

The pry begins just under the boat and ends just out from the chine.

Catch. The pry begins with the same body and paddle position as in the recovery phase of the draw stroke: your torso is rotated toward the on side, and the shaft is parallel to the gunwale. Holding the shaft in place against the gunwale with your shaft hand, move your grip hand to eye level, rotating the paddle to vertical and sinking the blade into the water.

Power. Ideally, the power phase starts with the shaft against the gunwale and the blade in the water under the hull, with your grip hand out over the water. Your shaft hand then uses the boat as a fulcrum and the paddle as a lever to amplify the force applied to the water; this is why it is such a powerful stroke. As with the forward stroke, at a certain angle the blade ceases to move the boat and starts to just lift up water and waste energy. The power phase is over before this happens. Beware that this stroke exerts a great amount of force on the hull and might damage non-Royalex hulls over time.

Recovery. To recover, drop your grip hand forward toward the gunwale, knifing the blade out of the water behind your hips. Feather the blade back into the neutral position.

VARIATIONS

The four basic strokes move the blade on two axes and can basically move the boat in any direction. Certain variations on the above strokes give you more power and efficiency, and these two bonuses become vital assets in moving water, rough conditions, and over long distances. The variations mostly name a change in the angle or position of the blade or shaft. Paddlers also classify these variations by where they occur, such as bow draw or stern pry.

Steering forces are energy inputs that turn a boat, and strokes are paddler-induced steering forces. The closer a stroke is to the pivot point and centerline of the canoe, the smaller the steering force it will exert—that is, the less the stroke will turn the boat. Conversely, the farther you place the blade from the pivot point, the larger the steering force you can exert. A normal forward stroke should exert a small steering force, because it is close to and parallel to the centerline and fairly close to the pivot point. One of the main variations in strokes thus deals with the placement of the blade in relation to the pivot point of the canoe—in other words, changing the angle of the shaft during the power phase.

The big caveat here is that your body position must stay comfortable and loose; if you overextend your body to increase your steering force, you will lose strength and the overall effect is lessened. There is, then, a sweet spot when moving away from the pivot point without overextending. Clinics and drills are a great way to find out where that sweet spot is for your body size and type.

Stern Strokes

A stern stroke is a variation on the draw and pry strokes. The catch, power, and recovery are all roughly the same, save that you change the angle of the shaft from vertical, moving the blade closer to the stern and farther from the pivot point. The draw and pry cease to be done at the hip and become something new, the *stern draw* and *stern pry*.

The best way to experiment with this new idea is to practice flatwater drills and slowly move the blade back every half dozen draws or pries. You will feel the increase in power as the blade moves closer to the stern, with the limit being the shaft at about 40 to 45 degrees to the gunwale. Torso rotation remains

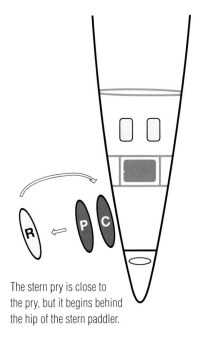

The stern pry is close to the pry, but it begins behind the hip of the stern paddler.

The paddler has finished the catch phase of the stern pry and is prepared to lever the paddle for the power phase.

important; do not put either stroke under power with your arms out of the paddler's box.

Bow Strokes

Strokes moved closer to the bow are mostly variations on the draw but do not move as far from a hip draw as in the stern stroke. As the bow paddler, when you attempt to move the blade closer to the bow, you will notice an increase in power, but you are limited by the fact that this extension will, at a certain point, crush the paddler's box, and your arms will cross and lose power.

Cross-bow Draw

This draw is used in the bow to move the bow toward your off side. The cross-bow draw, also called the cross draw, is the first of the off-side strokes, meaning that it is done on your off side, but with the same hand positions—grip and shaft—as a stroke on the on side. This is done for speed, efficiency, and stability.

Catch. Begin with the paddle held in a neutral position and with an intact paddler's box. Then rotate to the off side while maintaining the same hand positions on the paddle; the result is a significant rotation of the torso. Now put the blade in the water, with your shaft arm fairly straight and your grip arm bent close to, but still in front of, your body.

Power. The power phase begins with the shaft at an angle to the water and your torso wound up as a result of the extension of the off-side reach. Be cautious about grabbing too much water, particularly during an eddy turn; you can get pulled off balance or even risk injury. Having the blade just in front of the knees and about 18 inches (46 centimeters) from the hull is the sweet spot for most people. Force is applied by unwinding your torso slightly while pushing out with your grip arm. The power phase ends a few inches from the hull for the same reason as in other draw strokes: the blade can be pulled under the boat and out of your hands in some situations.

Recovery. Drop your grip hand to knife the blade out of the water,

The bow paddler is using a cross draw to turn the boat in an eddy on the Hyland River in Yukon Territory.

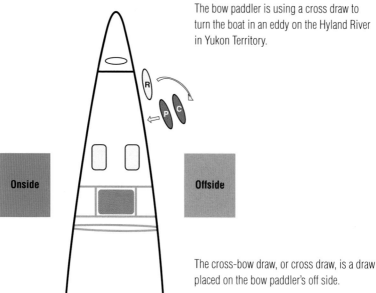

The cross-bow draw, or cross draw, is a draw placed on the bow paddler's off side.

Bow Pry versus Cross-Bow Draw

Both the bow pry and the cross-bow draw serve a similar purpose: moving the bow toward the off side. One achieves it with an on-side stroke and the other with an off-side stroke. Which is better? There isn't a simple answer. The cross-bow draw is often more stable than the bow pry in whitewater, particularly in eddy turns where the cross-bow draw ensures that the paddle is on the inside of the turn, making it easier to initiate and maintain tilt. The bow pry can be applied faster and puts less stress on the paddler, but it is harder to get the same strength of steering force. For quick side slips and other fast maneuvers, however, the bow pry is worth exploring.

and then either return to neutral for an on-side stroke or perform another cross-bow draw. In moving water, only one cross-bow draw is usually needed to perform a maneuver; if the first or second does not move the boat, then the third or fourth will not either. In flat water, multiple cross draws are more common. The cross draw can also be feathered back to the catch phase.

Cross-Forward Stroke

The cross-forward stroke is just an off-side forward stroke and is most useful in a solo canoe for maintaining momentum in moving water without losing angle or direction. The cross forward and its variations allow you to adjust or maintain course and boat angle without a momentum-robbing steering stroke. In a tandem boat, it is only used in the bow, and even then it is employed infrequently, depending on the skill of the paddler and the needs of the river.

Catch. This stroke follows a similar progression to the cross draw: beginning in a neutral position, rotate to your off side while keeping your paddler's box intact and your hands locked in position. Your grip hand comes up to face level, and the shaft becomes vertical, with your shaft hand over the gunwale. The blade enters the water 12 to 18 inches (30 to 46 centimeters) in front of your knee and is sunk to the throat.

Power. The paddle then traces a similar position and trajectory to an on-side forward stroke, but because your hands are reversed in position, your arms will cross and lose power if you take the stroke all the way to your hip. Instead, depower the blade early—at your knee—and turn the grip so that the blade is parallel to the boat but still in the water. While the cross forward requires significant rotation, it does not gain as much of its power from that rotation as a normal forward stroke does, again depending on your body type. Instead, it comes from bending at the waist and using a crunch motion to engage your core muscles as in the draw. Taller people, however, may find rotation to be a source of power as well.

Recovery. Finally, slice the blade up and toward the bow. If that is the end of the off-side effect, slice the blade all the way out of the water and reset. If another cross forward is required, you can set up the blade for the next stroke without taking it out of the water; this is called an in-water recovery. Cross forwards are often done in series, as they are forward, momentum-building strokes and can also be correction strokes.

COMPOUND STROKES

The above strokes can be performed in series to create highly effective steering forces. A compound stroke is two basic strokes done one after the next, occasionally with a deceleration or loss of power between them.

Forward into Stern Pry, or River Pry

The forward into stern pry is also known as the river pry because it is so effective on the river for building and maintaining momentum while also turning the boat. Only done in the stern, this compound stroke begins with a forward stroke that is depowered between your knee and hip, and the recovery phase is replaced with the catch phase of a stern pry. The blade does not leave the water between the strokes. It is important to focus on rotating your torso the extra 15 degrees or so at the start of the stern pry so that

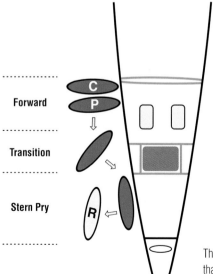

The J-Stroke is a compound stroke that begins with a forward stroke and ends with a stern pry.

throughout the stroke you are facing your work with proper form. The thumb on your grip hand faces the sky as the stroke transitions from forward (shaft vertical) to stern pry (shaft angled), so that your hand, wrist, and arm can stay in line, preventing fatigue and injuries, particularly tendinitis.

J-Stroke

The traditional and widely used variation (or origin, depending on your perspective) of this stroke involves the same progression as the forward into stern pry, except that your thumb is turned *down* during the transition between the forward stroke and stern pry. This keeps the power face of the blade engaged throughout the stroke, rather than switching faces as in the river pry. Called the J-stroke and any number of other regional and institution-specific names, this compound stroke is extremely efficient and rhythmic and is ideally suited for extended flatwater travel. The downsides of the J-stroke are that it is a less powerful stroke than the river pry and can cause tendinitis in paddlers with tighter grips. Its best use, then, is not in making aggressive turns or movements, but in holding the boat on course in moderate flatwater conditions. Very stiff paddle shafts can sometimes increase the possibility of tendinitis with this stroke.

STATIC VERSUS DYNAMIC STROKES

Most of the strokes mentioned so far rely on the paddler applying power to the water by actively moving the blade, termed *dynamic* strokes. In certain situations, however, it is more effective to use *static* strokes, taking advantage of the power of moving currents and apparent currents by placing the blade in the water and keeping it stationary, letting the water apply force to the blade. Examples of moving currents are the swiftly flowing water on the other side of an eddy line or a large wave passing under the boat, while apparent currents include the stationary water moving past a boat with momentum.

Static strokes still rely on good form and torso rotation, as the currents used can be quite strong, and the more stationary the blade is, the more effectively the force of the water can be transferred from the blade to the paddle, through the paddler, and to the boat. Some strokes, like the crossbow draw, are often static, and in some maneuvers, such as when entering and exiting eddies, many of the strokes used are static in order to work with the water rather than against it. You can modify the basic strokes that you have learned by making them static; a draw can be performed as a static bow draw, for example.

SWEEPS

Sweeps are not vital strokes in a tandem boat, but they might be an avenue for growth if you are an intermediate paddler trying to push yourself. In a solo boat, sweeps are much more effective and performed slightly differently. Sweeps are simple strokes that combine the building of forward momentum with a slightly more pronounced steering force than in a forward stroke, but less than in a draw or pry. In a tandem canoe, the paddle traces an arc from the end of the boat to your hip (tip to hip or hip to tip), whereas in a solo canoe, the paddle makes an arc from one end of the boat to the other (tip to tip).

Forward Sweep
The forward sweep is an onside stroke done in the bow or stern to move that end of the craft toward your off side.

Catch. From a neutral stance, drop the shaft down to the level of your navel, and extend the paddle out over and roughly parallel to the water. The thumb on your grip hand is pointing up, and your grip arm is bent while your shaft arm is straight. The blade enters the water along its side edge and is mostly submerged, leaving the shaft at a slight angle to the water. The stern paddler plants the blade in line with the hip, while the bow paddler plants the blade forward and close to the bow.

Power. Rotate your torso, keeping your arms and the paddle in roughly the same orientation, except to straighten your grip arm to lever the blade against and apply more force to the water.

Recovery. Drop your grip hand to bring the blade out of the water, and turn and feather the blade back into position for the next stroke.

Back Sweep
The back sweep, or reverse sweep, is an on-side stroke done in the bow or stern to move the bow toward your off side, with the blade tracing a path from your hip to the bow. This is an antiquated and ineffective stroke in the bow. In both the bow and stern, it most often results in a back stroke rather than a sweep because this is what feels strong. The bow draw is much more effective and harder to get wrong. A series of stern pries is much more effective in the stern. It's not a good idea to attempt back sweeps as a beginner, as it usually enforces bad habits.

BRACES
A brace is a static stabilizing stroke that is placed far from the canoe to effectively double or triple the boat's width and stability. The brace only provides a point of contact with the water; the righting force of the stroke comes from levering off of that point and requires your knees and hips to snap the boat back into position. Any stroke can be a force that increases stability, but only braces have no other function and no other stroke is as effective in righting the boat or keeping it stable.

High Brace

A high brace is basically a static draw placed in line with your hip. It is used to stabilize both intentional and unintentional tilts to your off side. In a high brace, the draw is held to provide a point of contact against which you can apply force and use your hips and body to snap the boat back to where it needs to be. Your grip arm elbow should not be above or behind your head, as this risks significant injury to your shoulder, just as when the draw is used for other purposes. The blade and shaft should be perpendicular as with the draw, although the primary need is not in moving the blade to the boat, but in holding the blade stationary as a platform. A strong snap of the hips combined with pressuring the on-side knee into the hull and lifting the off-side knee against the thigh straps provides the full righting force of the high brace.

After the initial moment of pressure, the tension on the water will usually disappear unless there is a significant current. You can move the blade slightly from side to side to increase the pressure; this is called sculling, or a sculling brace.

Righting Pry

An alternative to the high brace is the righting pry. To execute this maneuver, you perform a pry at your hip and follow through with a hip snap and

a shift of weight and force on the knees, righting the boat. The righting pry is more challenging to apply correctly than the high brace, but because it is transferring power directly from the water to the boat, it can be more powerful.

Low Brace

When the tilt is toward your on side, a high brace can be hard to do without moving your weight out of the boat; a better alternative is a low brace. Place the blade close to parallel with the water level, ideally on the surface. Slap the blade down and lever off of this point of contact

The blade is slapped down on the surface of the water and complimented with a snap of the hips.

As the partners practice tilting, the stern paddler is ready to do a low brace to guard against capsizing.

to right the boat or protect it from tilting any farther. To be effective, you should break at your waist and rotate forward and low into the canoe once you have executed the slap, while transferring your weight from the on-side knee to the off-side knee. This lowers your center of gravity and makes the brace more effective.

In some more advanced maneuvers, the low brace can be used as a stable point around which a heavily tilted boat will pivot in conflicting currents. Using the low brace as a pivot, often described as "spreading the peanut butter," can result in a back stroke, killing momentum. It also puts the emphasis on the paddle for stability and can lead to poor body position. In a tandem pair, both paddlers can do high braces at the same time, but it is often more effective if the paddler whose on-side gunwale is closest to the water level places a low brace, and the other paddler performs a high brace.

Basic Tandem Drills and Maneuvers

As a pair of paddlers achieve basic competence in strokes and begin to understand steering forces, they are ready to start building their first maneuvers as a team. Much of the challenge of canoeing ceases then to be a purely singular challenge and becomes one of collaboration, communication, and shared effort. Solo boating can grow out of this tandem understanding of water, boat, and paddler—and vice versa—but much of your learning will occur as part of a high-functioning pair.

The various combinations of similar or different strokes performed by the two members of the team will move the boat in different ways. The ideal way to learn and gain understanding of these maneuvers is by performing drills together on calm flat water, so that no steering forces, such as wind or current, can confuse you and your partner and obscure the effects of the force you are applying. With time and practice, these drills will grow into effective tandem maneuvers.

TURNING

Turning the boat as a team using basic strokes simply requires applying different steering forces on bow and stern. For example, the bow paddler can apply a draw while the stern paddler executes a pry, or vice versa.

SIDE SLIPS

A side slip is a lateral movement of the length of the canoe to the left or right, with no change in the angle of the boat in relation to shore. A running side slip is similarly a lateral movement but is done under power. In moving water, the side slip is a great way to avoid obstacles without opening up the angle of the boat and risking a potential broach or pin. It can kill forward momentum but is a good way of moving slowly across the grain of the river when entering a chosen line. This is best done by a team; solo paddlers will have trouble effectively side-slipping more than a boat width or two and are better off driving forward or backward away from obstacles.

Depending on which way you want to side slip, either the stern paddler uses a draw or stern draw while the bow paddler uses a cross-bow draw or pry, or the stern paddler uses a stern pry while the bow paddler uses a draw. The key is to match each other's power so that the angle of the boat does not change; this is mainly the stern paddler's job, as he can see the angle of the boat better and either communicate a need for more or less power or supply the correct amount himself.

After practicing this maneuver to the left and right, switch sides and repeat. The goal here is that eventually you and your partner will stop thinking about what strokes you need to execute the side slip and just move the boat intuitively. This takes practice, but slowly your reaction time will decrease. To that end, a simple game of chicken between two boats works well in practicing side slips, as well as stroke combinations in general, and helps decrease reaction time. Ideally done on flat water, one boat stays stationary while the in-play boat moves to a spot five to ten boat lengths away. The in-play boat charges the stationary boat head-on, as fast as possible, with the stationary boat staying in place and pointed directly at the

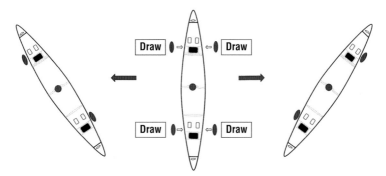

If the tandem pair both executes draw strokes, the boat will spin left or right, depending on where their on sides are.

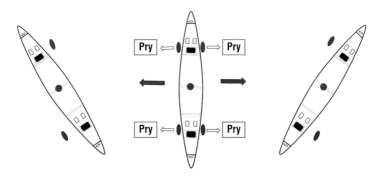

If the tandem pair both executes pry strokes, the boat will spin left or right, depending on where their on sides are.

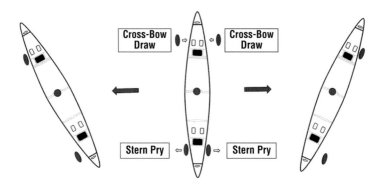

If the bow paddler executes a cross draw and the stern paddler a stern pry, the boat will spin left or right, depending on where their on sides are.

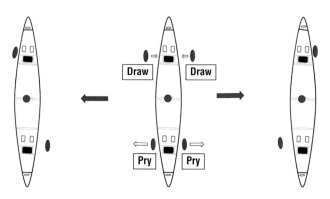

If the bow paddler executes a draw and the stern paddler a pry, the boat will move laterally left or right.

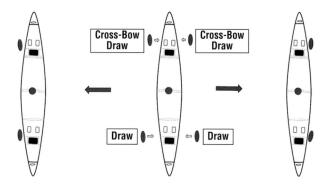

If the bow paddler executes a cross draw and the stern paddler a draw, the boat will move laterally left or right.

bow of the moving boat. At the last second, or at a gradually decreasing distance, a paddler on the stationary boat calls out a direction, left or right, and the partners on the moving boat have to smoothly side-slip one way or the other.

SPINS

Spins are very simple moves in which the boat spins in place to the left or right. Spinning the boat in a 360-degree circle is useful as a drill in that it helps the tandem pair practice changing the boat angle through stroke combinations.

With both paddlers drawing, the boat spins in a circle.

Spinning the boat requires the two paddlers to apply force with the power faces of their blades facing in opposite directions while the blades are still parallel to the sides of the canoe. For example, if the stern paddler applies a stern draw and the bow paddler applies a draw, the boat will spin one way; if the stern paddler applies a stern pry and the bow paddler applies a cross-bow draw or pry, the boat will spin the other way.

As a drill, this reinforces stroke combinations that help the tandem pair change the angle of the boat. Doing a number of simple spins to the left and right and then switching sides is a helpful progression, as it encourages both paddlers to experiment with stroke combinations to achieve results, rather than getting locked in to one set way of moving.

TILTING

Tilting refers to setting the width of the canoe at an angle to the surface of the water; this engages the chines of the boat and changes the shape and depth of the canoe in the water, making more aggressive maneuvers possible. This is sometimes also called *leaning*, but this term can create dangerous confusion, as it conjures an incorrect image of the paddlers being at an angle, rather than the boat, with their weight out of the boat.

Proper tilting begins with pressuring one side of your body through the contact points of your butt against the seat and knee against the knee pad. Separating your lower and upper body at the hips is vital in effectively tilting. Tilting can occur in conjunction with the paddle, but with a fully loaded expedition canoe, both paddlers must work together using their body weight to tilt the boat. With the increasing feeling of instability as the canoe tilts to one side, you may be tempted to either grab the gunwales or lean forward over your knees, but it is important to avoid doing either. Maintain hold of the paddle and keep it engaged in whatever stroke pattern is needed, while you sit up straight or even lean back a little.

The danger with tilting is that your head can cross through the imaginary wall that rises up from the gunwales of the canoe. With this shift in weight out of the canoe, the boat will be much less stable. The objective is

to remain fully in the canoe, with your center of gravity close to the centerline; in other words, keep your head in the boat. It is helpful to try to form a C-shape with your spine as viewed from the front or back, with the open part of the C facing away from the lowered gunwale. Practice tilting together with your partner until you both are comfortable with it. The next steps are to hold the tilt over time and to slowly increase the degree of tilt, until you can comfortably dip the lowered gunwale all the way to the water and hold it there.

Practicing initiating and maintaining tilt begins on flatwater as shown here on the Green River in Utah.

The paddler is tilting downstream in preparation for crossing an eddy line and carving a turn.

CARVING

The next step in initiating and maintaining tilt is to do it under power and execute carving turns. Carving is the act of turning the canoe on an arc while moving forward; to accomplish this, the boat must be on a tilt. With an alpine ski or an ice skate, when the flat surface of the ski or blade is lifted off the snow or ice and only one sharp edge is engaged, the whole object tends to turn, or carve, to that side; if the left edge is engaged, the ski or blade carves left, and vice versa. The mechanics of carving with a canoe are similar. And just as skis or ice skates can be designed in certain shapes so that they carve more effectively, some boat hulls are designed to carve and will react to tilting under power better than others.

Carving significantly increases your canoe's stability in moving water and makes momentum easier to build and maintain. In addition to its effect on turns, carving can be used to move in a straight line with the need for fewer correction strokes, sometimes called paddling against the carve or against the arc. This is particularly effective in solo boats, where you initiate and maintain tilt to your on side while continuing to paddle forward. The boat carves to the on side, while the forward stroke turns the boat to the off side. These two forces can cancel each other out, resulting in a straight path. The bow wave resulting from the carve also arrests much movement. Although often described as a straight path, it is more the shape of a wave, especially in a solo boat.

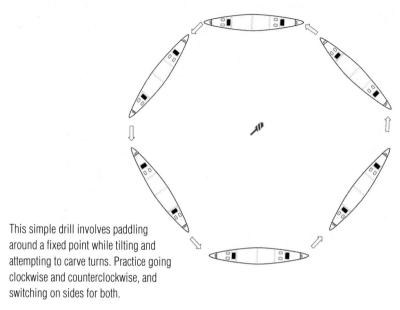

This simple drill involves paddling around a fixed point while tilting and attempting to carve turns. Practice going clockwise and counterclockwise, and switching on sides for both.

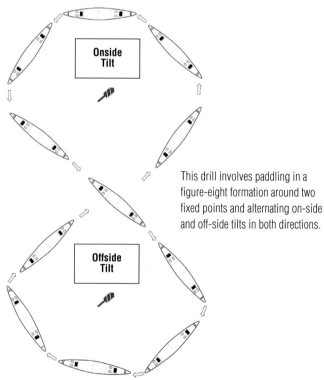

This drill involves paddling in a figure-eight formation around two fixed points and alternating on-side and off-side tilts in both directions.

To practice carving turns as a tandem pair, accelerate normally while on flat water, then together initiate and maintain tilt and see how aggressively the boat will carve a turn at different speeds before adding a few steering strokes to initiate a more aggressive arc. All boats will carve a turn much more effectively with a few stroke combinations, such as the ones practiced while spinning and turning. In addition, you can now add sweeps to great effect.

A more advanced drill to practice carving turns involves carving a circle around a central point such as a buoy, pole, or even an imaginary rock. Maintaining the tilt toward the center, paddle the canoe around in a circle with different stroke combinations, such as only sweeps, only forward strokes, or forward strokes plus a limited number of stern pries. Repeat with on-side and off-side tilts, and advance into seamlessly connecting two circles in a figure eight, with one circle on-side and the other off-side.

WARP AND WEFT

A final drill that is helpful for getting a team of paddlers of any level on the same page before starting down a river, or for novices in developing communication, reaction time, and tilting comfort, is a technique called warp and weft. The boats line up bow to stern, one to two boat lengths apart, to form a slalom course. At a signal, the last boat in line charges forward as fast as possible and weaves through the slalom course at speed, while carving turns and using a variety of strokes. The other boat pairs watch, cheer, distract, and look for points of feedback. When the in-play boat is halfway through or is finished, depending on the number of canoes, the next boat goes. This rolling progression can continue until everyone is feeling good or is too tired for more. It is good practice on many levels.

Routes don't always work out as planned, but it is often these experiences we value and remember the most. North Branch Big Salmon River, Yukon Territory.

TRAVEL SKILLS AND SCIENCE

Canoe routes by their nature follow the land, seeking low points in the landscape and low-resistance areas that ease travel. Sometimes the routes you planned out beforehand don't seem to make sense when you are traveling them. They may revert back on themselves and even disappear. Sometimes they don't look like canoeing habitat at all, and it is such routes that require your imagination the most.

There are purely practical travel-related reasons for delving into scientific study of the landscape. Canoe routes are selected based on land characteristics, and to travel safely and efficiently on an expedition, you must understand the landscape and how it came to be. Any understanding of travel techniques must be informed by an understanding of the set of overlapping sciences that describe how water behaves, in all its myriad forms and phases, and how rivers and lakes form and change over time. This knowledge will smooth your way and help you travel into and through the land.

This section gives an introduction to the science underlying canoe routes and travel skills, focusing on building a basic scientific understanding of the main factors that influence our canoeing environment, and then deals in depth with river forms and whitewater travel, open-water travel, and the various skills associated with wilderness canoe travel in addition to paddling.

WATER SCIENCE

*An introduction to the sciences underlying canoe routes
and travel skills on water*

To build a connection with the natural world and develop good back-country travel habits as a paddler, you need a basic understanding of the underlying sciences. These include hydrology, the study of water, often moving; limnology, the study of fresh water, often still, as in lakes and ponds; geology, the study of Earth; and geomorphology, the study of landforms.

This chapter looks at the processes and elements that make up our water systems, examines river anatomy and formation from geologic and hydrologic perspectives, and describes the forms and features that you may encounter on moving and open water. Although a survey of the biology and ecology of canoe-route water systems is beyond the scope of this book, it is often the biotic river environment that holds the most wonder for the paddler. Delving into fish or caribou migration, plant succession on point bars, or bird identification will enrich any canoe voyage and engender a deeper appreciation for and understanding of the natural world.

Water

Water forms the environment for expedition canoe travel. Understanding the science and issues behind the simple union of hydrogen and oxygen, including the various phases of water, the hydrologic cycle, and weather, is the necessary starting point for this discussion of how the science of water influences travel in this environment.

PHASES OF WATER

Water is the only element that becomes less dense when it undergoes a phase change from liquid to solid; ice floats, and if it did not, many bodies of water in the world would freeze solid, with drastic effects on climate

Water interacts with the landscape in sometimes startling ways. This waterfall is on the Skógafoss in Iceland.

and the basic habitability of our planet. In fact, water is most dense at 39 degrees Fahrenheit (4 degrees Celsius), meaning that in the Arctic, as well as in the colder seasons at midlatitudes, waves do not break and aerate as easily because the water has achieved or is close to achieving its greatest liquid density. Very warm water behaves differently.

HYDROLOGIC CYCLE

Also known as the water cycle, the hydrologic cycle describes the flow of water through different phases and environments on a macro scale. It is often explained by following a drop of water down a river from the mountains to the sea, where it evaporates, joins a cloud, and is blown inland to condense and fall on the mountains again. In reality, the movement of water in the cycle goes in all directions, often skipping

The hydrologic cycle is more of a tangled web than a straightforward circle. Boundary Waters, Minnesota.

major parts and staying in some places or forms, such as underground or in an ice cap, for millenia. Still, the general flow is accurate and is the first step in understanding the waters you canoe on.

WEATHER

Weather is one of the primary driving forces of the hydrologic cycle, in a certain sense its engine, the system of water and heat transfer that manifests in various forms. The "fuel" that drives weather is energy in the form of solar radiation. The sun emits a huge amount of radiation in a usually even pattern, but in reaching Earth, it heats different areas more than others. This differential heating of the atmosphere causes heat and moisture to concentrate or dissipate all around the world, and these differences in density are behind every aspect of weather: clouds, local winds and jet streams, snow- and rainfall, monsoons and hurricanes. Generally, heat and moisture tend to move from areas of higher to lower concentration on a molecular level, and this drives the whole process. Climate is simply weather averaged through the seasons and over long periods of time.

In terms of the hydrologic cycle, heat can cause water to evaporate or sublime into a vapor that is highly mobile; this vapor is then moved over time to an area where it can condense and either fall or settle on the surface as a liquid or solid, where it awaits evaporation or sublimation once again.

Wind tends to blow "down" the pressure gradients created by heat and moisture density, and it is the borders between high- and low-pressure systems that we call fronts. Imagine a big pile of air, which is dense and under high pressure. Nearby is a depression, or air under very low pressure. The air will flow toward the low pressure to fill in the gaps, creating wind and, when the fronts collide, storms.

Moisture-laden air can drop its moisture as precipitation only if it reaches its current dew point, the temperature at which vapor will turn to liquid. When wind blows moisture-laden air to a higher elevation, such as when a front hits a mountain range, the localized pressure the air is under will drop, causing it to cool. This lowers the dew point, causing precipitation to occur; this is called *orographic lift* and is a prime cause of why more precipitation falls at higher elevations in arid environments. Similarly, if the moisture-laden air is blown to an area of low pressure, it can cool and precipitate.

Understanding and Differentiating Rivers

Rivers are bodies of water that flow downhill on a bed surface from a *source* to a *mouth*; they are bounded by riparian *banks* that form a *channel*. There are many other names for these hydrologic systems, including creeks,

The forms that rivers can take vary enormously, but follow common patterns. Yellowstone River, Wyoming.

burns, streams, and rivulets, but for the purposes of this discussion, the word *river* is used as a generic term for all sizes of beds and flows. Rivers function much as the circulatory system does in a human being, transporting nutrients, carrying away waste, and protecting and rejuvenating the landscape. Much of human history and prehistory involves rivers: migrating by river, settling and farming by rivers, and harnessing their energy and life-giving forces for purely human needs. Many peoples throughout history have conceptualized rivers based on their characteristic environments, giving names to short sections of a river rather than thinking of it as one unit.

The three primary factors that differentiate rivers are gradient, flow, and geologic structure. These three elements are deeply interrelated, but for simplicity's sake we will consider them one at a time.

GRADIENT

The average slope of a riverbed or section of riverbed is called the *gradient* and is often measured as a percentage of a 45-degree angle, similarly to how road grades are measured and marked. A 10 percent gradient, or grade, is equal to about a 5½-degree slope, which is quite a steep river. More commonly, the gradient may be measured as the elevation lost over a set distance, such as 10 feet per mile (3 meters per 1.6 kilometers). Gradient measured as elevation over distance is more helpful, as few rivers maintain an even gradient for long. For example, a river may have 500 yards (roughly ½ kilometer) of a high gradient followed by 1.2 miles (2 kilometers) of a low gradient, resulting in an overall percentage grade that tells us very little about what the river looks like.

Gradient can be pulled off a topographic map with some precision and is often noted in guidebooks for more commonly run rivers, but no amount of research can give you a complete picture of what a river actually looks like. A loss of 160 feet per mile (30 meters per kilometer) might indicate a continuous slope of gravel and cobbles or a stretch of flat water between two 50-foot (15-meter) waterfalls. While this is an extreme example, it shows that gradient is only one factor in figuring out the lay of a river.

LAMINAR FLOW VERSUS TURBULENT FLOW

The flow of a river can be divided into laminates, several thin layers of water uniformly coursing downstream. This concept can be helpful in understanding how currents work and how a canoe needs to be handled to achieve certain maneuvers and goals. A log floating in one laminate will stay in that laminate unless it is acted on by an outside force. Similarly, a laminate will maintain the same direction and place in the channel unless it runs into an island, rock, or any other obstruction.

Unfortunately, this is not the whole story. Rivers usually function in a combination of *laminar* and *turbulent flow*. The distinction comes from the fact that laminar flow is perfect—there is no friction or contact between the laminates, which does not happen in a river. On a straight, uniform section of calm moving water, the flow can be near-laminar, meaning it is close to flowing as a series of parallel laminates, though it would be impossible to identify a single "laminate" from the flow. In a rapid or in the presence of an obstruction, these theoretical laminates dissolve into chaotic turbulent flow that follows different rules. Still, it is helpful to remember that a piece, laminate, or moving water will continue downstream until acted on by an outside force, usually an obstruction.

FLOW

The *flow* of a river is the volume of water moving past a certain point per unit of time and is calculated by determining the size of the occupied channel and the velocity of the current. It is usually measured as cubic feet per second (CFS, or ft³/s) in the United States and as cubic meters per second (CMS, or m³/s) in the rest of the world. CMS is often described as a separate unit of flow called a *cumec*, which is equal to 1 m³/s or 35.5 ft³/s. A cubic foot is about the size of basketball, whereas a cubic meter weighs more than 2,000 pounds. When the flow of a river reaches an open body of water such as a lake or ocean, it is often called *discharge*, which is

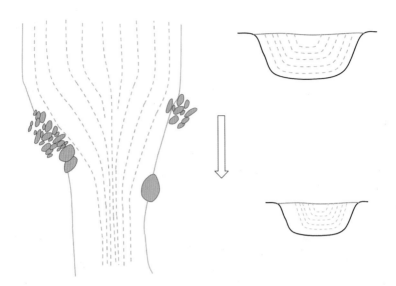

A river flows in laminates, and obstructions and constrictions often affect how the laminates move. Here, the laminates are spread out and uniform above the rapid but are forced together below.

measured over days, months, or years and in units of cubic feet, meters, or acre-feet, a volume equal to an area of 1 acre (4,046 square meters) covering 1 foot depth (30.5 centimeters) of water, or 43,560 cubic feet (1,233 cubic meters).

GEOLOGIC STRUCTURE AND BED MAKEUP
The surrounding geology has a big impact on the structure of a river. The river is always changing the surrounding rocks and soils, and vice versa. The route a river takes is not necessarily the shortest path between two points, but it does seek the path of least resistance. This means that tectonic fault lines, glacial valleys, and plains tend to have rivers in them, as gravity works on water. Rivers also seek out the most erosion-prone bed surfaces over time, changing constantly through flood and erosion.

Geomorphology

Any canoe trip longer than a few days will inevitably see a finger pointing toward a canyon wall or cut bank and sparking the question, spoken or not, "How did that get there?" Geology, the study of Earth, is one way to answer that question, and more specifically, fluvial and limnal geomorphology provide a more focused picture and additional tools to answer that

In canyon country—the Split Mountain Canyon on the Green River in Utah—the way the earth changes is often on display.

question. *Geomorphology* refers to the study of landforms and how they change over time; *fluvial* and *limnal* are just fancy ways of saying "pertaining to rivers" and "pertaining to lakes," respectively.

Geomorphology is sometimes divided into several different categories related to the forces of change: fluvial, referring to change by water; igneous, change by volcanism; eolian, change by wind; hillslope, change by gravity or mass wasting; tectonic, change by tectonic shift; and glacial, change by glaciation. Every canoe route is littered with examples from these different categories, some more obvious than others.

Mount Aoraki, or Cook, is New Zealand's highest peak and is the largest and tallest massif in the Southern Alps. This beautiful, jagged, glacier-encrusted mountain is over 13,000 feet (3,900 meters) high; however, without the geomorphologic forces of change described above, it would be over 62,000 feet (19,000 meters) high, and much of the land to its east and west would not exist. Over time, glacial, tectonic, and hillslope forces have, in part, shrunk the mountain to its present size, and high precipitation rates have washed the enormous amount of resulting debris as bed and suspended load downstream and deposited them in the ocean, an example of fluvial change. This created huge alluvial fans that rose above sea level and formed what is now the Canterbury Plain, a 15,000-square-mile (38,850 square kilometer) area that is one of the only flat areas in the South Island. All the rivers and lakes that drain the mountains there and trace lines across the plain and nearby regions are colored by this geologic history of change.

SEDIMENT TRANSPORT

One of the primary "jobs" of a river is to move material downstream, creating new land, carrying nutrients to lakes and oceans, and changing the landscape to create new forms and habits. This material can range from massive, car-sized boulders to the finest clay and sand particles and is divided into two categories based on particle size: bed load and suspended load.

Bed load. Generally, larger particles up to massive boulders that roll, slide, and bounce along the bed surface of the river.

Suspended load. Generally, smaller particles like clay, silt, and sand that float in the water; the permanently suspended very small particles are sometimes said to constitute the *wash load*.

On large, higher-gradient rivers, especially in the mountains, a paddler onshore can occasionally hear the deep rumbling sounds of boulders being rolled along the bed surface and knocked into each other by the force of the current. During floods, enormous quantities of material can be moved, sometimes totally changing the river environment, and it is then that you are most likely to hear and see evidence of heavy bed load movements. The power of these events is unbelievable and cannot be understood until

Sediment Transport

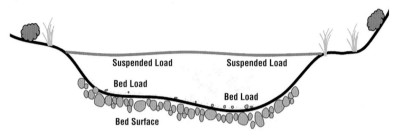

One of the goals of a river is to transport sediment, both smaller particles suspended in the current and large ones rolling and skipping along the riverbed.

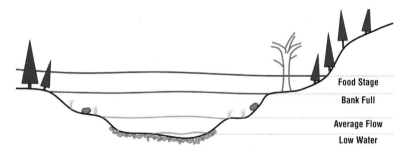

Using small clues from the vegetation, sediment, and bank structure, you can tell how high the water is—and how dangerous.

you have witnessed them. The force a river exerts increases exponentially with the speed of the current; when the speed is doubled, the force increases to the sixth power, meaning that if the volume of a river is held constant and the speed of its flow doubles, the laws of hydrodynamics state that objects sixty-four times larger can be moved.

On more mellow rivers, maybe far downriver from the above example and out in the plains on the way to the take-out, you might hear a gentle, slightly abrasive ticking sound that grows louder when you put your head in the boat or near the water. This is the sound of the billions of tiny particles in the water hitting and rubbing against the hull of the canoe and each other; it is the sound of mountains being washed to the sea.

UPLIFT AND SUBSIDENCE

Some of the most dramatic rivers of the world owe their attractive character to a tectonic process known as *uplift*. The Grand Canyon of the Colorado River is a perfect example of the power of uplift, though it can also

The surrounding land is fairly even, but the Rio Grande in Texas has cut a deep canyon.

be seen in many of the sand- and mudstone canyons in the American Southwest. Millions of years ago, the Colorado flowed across an enormous flat plain in what is now northern Arizona. Over millions of years, as tectonic forces slowly pushed the plain up in elevation, the Colorado River basically stayed in place because it eroded through the plain at a roughly similar speed in a process known as *downcutting*. The river became entrenched in a canyon because the path of least resistance was down through the bed surface rather than into the increasingly steep walls; the uplift of the surrounding plain increased the gradient so much that the erosion rate speeded up as well. Thus the Grand Canyon was formed.

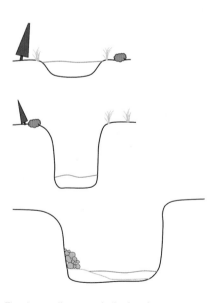

The sheer wall canyons in the American Southwest are often caused by uplifted land.

Uplift is not completely uniform, however. Occasionally, it can upend a river valley and cause the river to reverse the direction of its flow or spill a lake out into inflowing streams.

Subsidence is the opposite of uplift, referring to a process by which the surface is depressed by a weight or pulled down by tectonic forces. This too can change, affect, and create river systems.

Tributaries tend to flow into the main channel pointed downstream rather than up, meaning that the angle between the two channels is smaller upstream of the confluence than downstream. This is especially true in mountainous or hilly terrain, where tributary creeks can look like the fletchings on an arrow fired downriver. An interesting exception to this general rule is the occurrence of barbed tributaries, which flow into the main channel pointed upstream. These occur most frequently in mountainous terrain that has, at some point in geologic time, experienced an uplift event.

Surprisingly, lake systems in Yellowstone National Park in Wyoming are being uplifted on a local scale. Imagine putting a finger under one edge of the bottom of a bowl of soup; lifting that edge tilts the plane and spills the soup. Similarly, volcanic activity under the park is lifting the lakes and flooding one shore, allowing paddlers to canoe through a dying forest. Some volcanologists believe that a massive high-pressure blister of molten rock and gas is causing the localized uplift.

GLACIATION

The last ice age ended about 11,000 years ago, but its effects can still be seen throughout the Northern Hemisphere and, to an extent, the Southern Hemisphere. The Canadian Shield, a massive igneous province that covers half of Canada, was scraped clean of organic soils during the advance and retreat of the Laurentide Ice Sheet. It was also divoted with depressions that were eventually filled with meltwater at the beginning of our present warm period. This created the incredibly complex and rocky lake systems of east and central North America. The glaciation also built and deposited

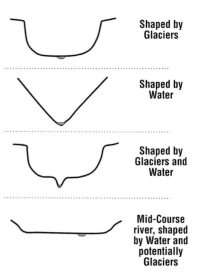

Shaped by
Glaciers

Shaped by
Water

Shaped by
Glaciers and
Water

Mid-Course
river, shaped
by Water and
potentially
Glaciers

A few dramatic examples of how water and ice and carve river valleys.

The Devilshole Creek valley in the Yukon was once filled with ice, and the characteristic U-shape it has today is evidence of the huge power of the glacier.

the countless eskers, moraine fields, erratics, and till fields that we see near waterways across the continent.

Glaciation still actively affects our landscape and has done so drastically in recent times. Many northern and midlatitude mountain river valleys, especially if they are not following a depression between faults, known as a *graben*, conform to formerly glaciated valleys. In recently glaciated regions, especially formerly glaciated regions with few forces of change acting on them, the river valleys created by ice excavation are clearly U-shaped, whereas river valleys formed by downcutting by liquid water are V-shaped.

Anatomy of a River System

WATERSHEDS

Traditionally, a watershed was defined as the dividing line between two *drainage basins*, and it still carries this meaning in British English. In North America, however, the term refers to the catchment basin itself and is always modified by the name of the body of water that carries or collects the waters in that basin.

For example, all the rivers and lakes that drain into Hudson's Bay can be said to constitute the Hudson's Bay watershed, a 1,560,400-square-mile (4,041,400-square-kilometer) region of dizzying size and diversity. Incidentally, the watershed formed the basis for the original land grant to the Hudson's Bay Company, which said that they would control all the land that drains to the bay. This watershed is a massive and complex mosaic of thousands of major and minor watersheds, all contributing water to the bay. Take, for example, the Rupert River, a massive river that drains a 17,000-square-mile (44,000-square-kilometer) slice of northern Quebec. The Rupert is part of the James Bay watershed which is part of the Hudson's Bay watershed. It is one of many such contributing watersheds and is also broken up into several tributary watersheds, such as the Natastan, Lemare, Marten, and Nemiscau, all between a few hundred and a few thousand square miles in size

Watersheds also include all the drainages, tiny creeks, and springs that complete the farthest uphill reaches of the liquid system.

The final piece of the watershed puzzle is human interaction. People have been engineering the hydrologic environment for ten thousand years, since the first canals were dug near farming settles in the Middle East, Egypt, and the Indian subcontinent. Today billions of gallons of water are pumped and moved by canals and viaducts for shipping, drinking, industrial use, and farming. Interestingly, in the above example, the mighty Rupert has been dammed and diverted as of 2009. Roughly 70 percent of the Rupert River watershed now has its outflow in an enormous underground

The watershed, or drainage basin, of a small mountain tributary (Stewart River headwaters in Yukon Territory) is shown in red, with the outflow at the bottom of the valley. The even smaller contributing watersheds are show in orange.

This power station in Iceland shows a completely reengineered river system with a dam and channelized riverbed.

pipe 1.9 miles (3 kilometers) long; it discharges into a reservoir system with already built hydroelectric facilities.

Several concepts help illustrate watersheds in practice, and understanding these will aid you on your expeditions.

Heights of Land

The divide between two watersheds is often called the height of land, meaning the high line between the two drainages. The portage that carries a team over the height of land is often a special milestone, as it can mean that upstream or lake travel has now come to an end and you will soon be traveling downstream. Long expeditions often have routes that hop from one watershed to another, stringing them together with creative ascents and portages. The Northern Forest Canoe Trail traces a route across New England that is 740 miles (1,191 kilometers) long and contains eight heights of land or significant watershed crossings. Many of the world's largest rivers are developed for some or most of their length, meaning that if you want to paddle through wild or semiwild country for 400 or 500 miles (644 or 805 kilometers), you may have to cross a height of land or otherwise access a watershed creatively.

Endorheic and Exorheic Basins

A watershed that does not flow into the world's interconnected ocean system is called an *endorheic basin*, or an internal drainage system. These are more common than you might think. Much of the Intermountain West in the United States is endorheic, with all of the water from places like Lake Tahoe and the Great Salt Lake evaporating or seeping into desert soils and aquifers. Most of Central Asia is endorheic, as are parts of central Africa and various locations in North Dakota (Devil's Lake) and Minnesota. In rocky landscapes, localized bogs can have no outflow for part or all of the year. These types of closed watershed systems are still very much a part of the global hydrologic cycle.

An *exorheic basin* is a watershed that eventually flows into the world's oceans. Amazingly, the Colorado River, one of the largest rivers in the world, has ceased to be part of an exorheic basin; as a result of human use and transport of its water, it no longer flows to the sea every year.

Anatomy of a River

SOURCE
Determining the source of a river has been a recurring goal for explorers and surveyors interested in records, law, and boundary making. For your purposes as a paddler, the source is less important than the *sources*—that is, the multiple headwaters of the river or river system that together form the paddlable stream. The river might be navigable almost within sight of the headwaters, or it might travel 62 miles (100 kilometers) before you can put blade to water. River sources can be glaciers, lakes, or springs or aquifers.

Glaciers
Rivers fed wholly or in part by glaciers often are very cold and have high suspended loads of glacial sediment, making the water milky white or

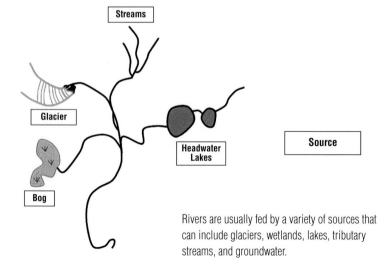

Rivers are usually fed by a variety of sources that can include glaciers, wetlands, lakes, tributary streams, and groundwater.

The Hofsjökull (Hofs Glacier) dominates the mountains in the background, feeding various streams that eventually make up the Þjórsá River, Iceland's longest.

turquoise; this can also result if the river flows through recently glaciated geologic regions. The flow profile of a glacier-fed river is often *diurnal*, meaning that solar radiation during the day, particularly the warmer second half of the day, causes an increase in melting and therefore flow. At night, during cold snaps, or on lower-radiation days, the flow can slow or stop. Over the course of the year, rivers fed by glacier runoff will peak in flow later in the spring or summer than other rivers, because their sources are at higher elevations and need a more advanced season to begin melting. This is true not just of glacier-fed streams, but of all those with sources in mountainous areas that receive significant snowfall.

Lakes

Lakes receive multiple inflows from glaciers, rain, rivers, and other lakes, and they store this water and release it more slowly throughout the season. Because of this, rivers with lakes in their headwaters can be relied on to

An interesting example of the complexity of watersheds and groundwater transport can be found on the borders of the Black Forest in southwestern Germany. The Danube River rises here and is the second-largest river in Europe in terms of length and discharge, but after several miles (a few dozen kilometers) of existence, just as it is starting to feel like a real river, the water disappears into the ground. Over the course of less than 100 feet (30 meters), the river disappears into the Donauversickerung, or Danube sink, a vast cavern system of porous limestone. More than 500 CFS (14 cumecs) of water can disappear at peak flows, and it travels 9 to 25 miles (15 to 40 kilometers) underground to join the Rhine River on the other side of the Swabian Mountains.

have more regular flows later in the season. Also, these rivers are often more likely to be navigable from the headwaters down.

Springs or Aquifers

Groundwater makes up a large percentage of the total liquid water on Earth and takes the form of subterranean rivers, lakes, and massive aquifers of saturated porous rock and sediment. With an elevation change, these sources often come to the surface as springs. Navigable rivers can start at a single spring; however, more often springs are just one source of many that together create a navigable flow.

COURSE

The course, or path, of a river can be described in many ways, and because of the breadth of different rivers and river types in the world, classifying the parts of a river is difficult. One way of generally describing course is the Bradshaw Model, in which the river between the source and mouth is imagined as a continuum, with river depth, width, and suspended sediment load *increasing* and gradient, bed rockiness, and suspended sediment size *decreasing* as one moves downstream. This influences how we classify and understand different types of river courses, their channels, and how we might travel up or down them.

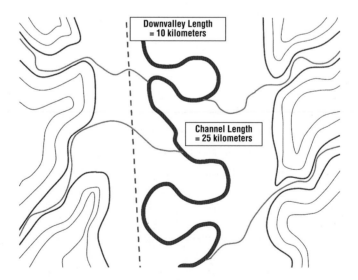

Sinuosity is the measure of how much distance a river travels to connect two points. In this example, the river takes 25 kilometers to move 10 kilometers down the valley, giving it a sinuosity index of 2.5.

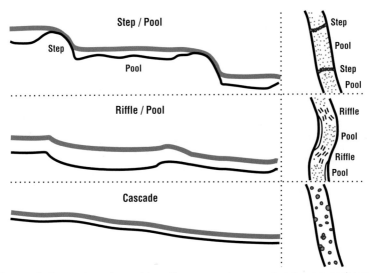

River gradient ranges from step-pool to continuous cascade, as seen here in cross-section and from above.

The course of a river can be described in terms of its channel and bank environments, and how these change over time. Rivers are delineated on the criteria of gradient, flow, and geologic structure, as well as sediment and vegetative cover.

Rivers can be low-gradient, such as meandering or wandering rivers, or high-gradient, such as rapid, step-pool, or cascade-focused rivers. Braided rivers can fall into either category, though they rarely exceed a slope of a few degrees. Native Americans usually did not refer to a river by one name, but instead provided appellations based on food resources and physical characteristics. Although the following classifications provide a good insight into river type, no river holds to any one type throughout its entire length, but is in fact an amalgamation of types throughout its course.

High-Gradient Rivers or River Sections

A high-gradient river or river section usually has an average slope between 1 and 15 percent and can extend up to overhanging waterfalls. Generally, a high-gradient river falls into one of the following categories:

Cascade. A cascade has a gradient between 8 and 15 percent, has no pools, is continuous, and has a bed made up of boulders.

Step-pool. A step-pool has a gradient between 5 and 20 percent, well-developed pools, and sections of rocky, high-gradient topography.

Rapid. Also called a *plane*, a rapid has a gradient between 1 and 4 percent, infrequent pools and point or braid bars, and often whitewater.

The headwaters and upper reaches of a river system often have a magical quality to them, and it is a special treat to be able to paddle a river from near its source. Here are the upper reaches of Marvelous Creek in Yukon Territory.

Riffle-pool. A riffle-pool is similar to a step-pool but has less gradient, at 1 to 2 percent, a network of potentially shifting channels, and point and braid bars.

Low-Gradient Rivers

A low-gradient river is *usually* described as one of the following, but because of the variety of land types, perfect classification is impossible:

Braided river. A braided, or *anabranching*, river has multiple interconnected channels between the banks; these channels continuously change and move across the bed surface. There is a big difference between the *occupied* channel and the *actual* channel during normal flows, though during floods there may be one massive, shallow channel. The constant formation and destruction of cobble, gravel, or sand bars and islands is a common feature. The gradient is relatively high, and flow is characterized by rapid changes, either seasonally or day to day.

This river type is relatively rare and is usually found only in watersheds whose upper reaches include recently uplifted and fast-eroding mountain ranges, such as in the Canadian and American Rockies, Alaska, the Himalayas, and New Zealand. The mountainous terrain and soft, erosion-prone landforms provide abundant sediment and can lead to accumulations of woody debris, including strainers and logjams, below the treeline or brushline. Water levels can fluctuate widely, carrying more wood into the river. Braided rivers are popular canoeing rivers because of the speed and

In erosion-prone mountainous areas, braided rivers are common. Large floods rearrange and flush out huge quantities of particles from silt to boulders as in the Taipo River in New Zealand.

challenge of the water, as well as the beauty and remote quality of the landscapes they flow through.

Anastomosing river. An anastomosing river is a specific type of braided river. It is characterized by braided channels that experience slower rates of change and are more permanent. The sediment load is lower than in a traditional braided river, as is the gradient, but the most defining factor is the presence of significant organic life in the water and riparian zone. The banks might be of compressed clay or other sediment with similarly small particle size, but they are anchored with significant vegetative cover. Examples of anastomosing rivers include sections of the Columbia and Yangtze Rivers and the Amazon.

Meandering river. Sometimes technically referred to as a *single-thread sinuous* river, a meandering river is characterized by a relatively low gradient. Flow can be high or low and is more stable than in other types, and the channel is potentially deeper and wider. The river has a medium to low sediment load and size per unit, but it can have a high overall load and erosive force if the volume is high.

This creek in Iceland, the Álftavatn, is an example of a fast-changing braided stream.

Shield river. A shield river is one that flows over a geologic shield at some point in its course. Geologically, a *shield* refers to a massive continuous region of stable Precambrian bedrock, often with very little topsoil on it as a result of glaciation or slow organic development. Shields make incredible paddling country, as these rivers drain poorly and usually have amazing formations of granite close to the surface. The channels of shield rivers tend to resist erosion and therefore change extremely slowly; fur trade journals from two hundred years ago describe rapids identical to those you may encounter today.

A river that flows through shield country looks and behaves very differently than its mountain and plains

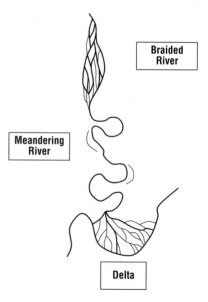

Braided and meandering channels and deltas are three common river forms, but they might not all be found on the same river.

Shield River Country

With its shallow, rocky soils, poor drainage, and northerly latitude, the Canadian Shield is classic canoe country. The Canadian Shield dominates the eastern and central portions of northern North America, covering nearly half of Canada and parts of the northern tier of the United States, as well as significant parts of Greenland and Baffin Island. Canada contains one-fifth of the world's available fresh water and has more lakes than any other country, in part because of the shield. Across the Atlantic at similar latitudes, paddlers find surprisingly familiar canoe country in much of inland Scandinavia as a result of a granitic shield formation known as the Baltic, or Fennoscandian, Shield. On the other side of the world in North and Western Australia, however, the Australian Shield creates environments that differ in quantity of water, flora, and fauna.

counterparts. Poor drainage in shield country, along with depressions left in the rock by glaciers and ice sheets, results in a thick cover of lakes of every size, from potholes to some of the Great Lakes. These lakes often drain into one another, creating short, often steep connections between them.

The Boundary Waters Canoe Area Wilderness, which straddles the U.S.-Canada border, is another example of a classic shield environment. Here huge lakes outflow into waterfalls that plunge directly into another lake. The water flows in the traditional manner for only a tiny percentage of the course, however, so it is unclear whether these outflows can be considered rivers.

Some shield rivers may have the characteristics of high-gradient and step-pool rivers, but only for short stretches; over the length of a shield river, the gradient is often medium to low. The French River, for example, a key part of the old Voyageur Route from Montreal to Lake Superior and beyond, flows with no perceptible current between parallel cliff walls before tumbling over a steep cascade or rapids into another lake or long, riverlike pool. This dramatic step-pool character makes shield rivers like this great learning rivers, as well as being almost as easy to ascend as they are to descend.

Shield rivers with short sections of higher flow or gradient can explode into stunning cascades and gorges, particularly where they tumble off the shield into basins on their way to the ocean. The northern edge of the Canadian Shield is one such place, and power companies want to harness the energy being expended by dozens of huge rivers flowing off the shield for hydroelectricity. Many dams and diversions have already been built here.

In shield country, exposed bedrock can impede and reroute the movement of water, creating unusual forms. The Boundary Waters in Minnesota is a prime example of this type of water movement.

MOUTH

The outflow, or mouth, of a river is a dynamic place and can take multiple forms that are often in flux. A river can discharge into another river, a lake, or the ocean, and it is these destinations that best describe mouth characteristics.

Confluence

The junction of two rivers is called a confluence. One river ceases to exist after the union for classification and naming purposes, but in reality the two waters meld together and become something new. As an example of this arbitrary naming structure, the Green River supplies more water and is longer than the Colorado at their confluence, but because of frontier politics in the nineteenth century, the blended river was named after the state of Colorado.

Deltas

The huge volume of sediment that a large river discharges at its mouth occasionally is held in place by shallow, calm water or a lack of ocean or lake currents to wash it away. These delta-shaped alluvial deposits often form constantly changing fans with significant wetlands, various slow-moving channels, and dense concentrations of life because of the fertile soil

This false-color satellite image of the Lena River in the Russian Arctic shows the incredible complexity of a large delta. In some places, it is 100 miles or more across.

and robust nutrient influx. Deltas are key habits and are often beautiful places to paddle, if hard to navigate in. A delta that forms where a river empties into a lake is known as an *inland delta*, and the often characteristic channels that diverge from the main river and do not rejoin it are called *distributaries*.

Some river deltas have grown to enormous sizes over thousands of years and have come to be ecologically vital features on a continental or global scale. The mouth of the Mississippi River forms a huge and populated delta, while the Danube ends in a delta that plays a key role in shipping, pollution filtration, and bird migration. The northern Russian deltas of the Ob, the Yenesi, and especially the Lena discharge a vast percentage of the world's fresh water and are the subject of intense study related to climate change.

Estuaries

Where a river mouth discharges into the ocean, the zone of interplay between the freshwater river and highly saline ocean is called an estuary. These zones are often characterized by shallow, slow-moving water and thick sediment deposits from river discharge; as a result, estuaries are often teeming with life supported by the nutrient-rich environment and the unique habitat provided by the protected and brackish water. Tidal forces have a big influence on estuary function as well as navigation; some rivers show evidence of tidal forces 62 miles (100 kilometers) or more from the ocean.

Life Stages of a River

The essential element of river environments is *change*, and over the thousands and even millions of years of their life span, this constant process equates to a progression through general life stages, from young to old, with the potential for renewal or rebirth. Generally, the older a river is, the more tributaries it will have, the slower it will move, the wider and deeper it will be, and the larger floodplains it will have.

Young rivers. A young river often has a steep gradient and high-velocity flow, with few tributaries, significant sediment transport per volume, and high erosive force. The channel or surrounding relief is often V-shaped, as the river is cutting vertically rather than horizontally. The Black Canyon of the Gunnison in Colorado, and the Grand Canyon of the Colorado River are young rivers.

Middle-aged rivers. A middle-aged river has a medium to low gradient, as well as medium velocity and high-volume flow as a result of having multiple tributaries and a larger watershed. The channel or surrounding relief is more U-shaped. The Mississippi and Danube Rivers can be classified as middle-aged.

Old rivers. An old river has a low gradient, little velocity, and a small sediment load per volume, but because it has an enormous volume, it does move significant quantities of material. The Nile, Tigris, and Euphrates Rivers can be classified as old.

Rejuvenated rivers. A rejuvenated river is a middle-aged or old river that has been uplifted or tilted by tectonic forces, and thereby had its gradient increased while keeping some of the advanced forms and features. The Colorado River can be classified as rejuvenated, particularly the middle canyons.

Open Water

Rivers are only one part of the liquid freshwater aspect of the hydrologic cycle. Open water in the form of lakes, ponds, swamps, and bogs painted across the landscape can make for fantastic paddling, particularly in northern North America, where they are accessible and in some places undeveloped. These structures fill because of a number of factors that may include poor drainage; large inflows; a high water table; or being located in an endorheic basin, bedrock, or permafrost substrate. They are often formed through glaciation, river change, fault-block tectonics, volcanism, or as a consequence of mountain building or glacial rebound.

Interestingly, rivers are usually longer lived than lakes over geologic timescales. Rivers will continue to drain a watershed and change drastically in the process, whereas lakes cannot adapt to changed forces very well and often will fill with sediment or have their outflow cut down enough to drain them.

There is an enormous amount of detail associated with limnology, the study of open fresh water, but as an expedition paddler, you do not need to know as much detail about lakes as you do about rivers. Lakes are usually stable, and when you see one on a map, you have a pretty good idea of what it is going to look like, with some variation in bank structure. Canoe travel on lakes and other open water relies more on an understanding of navigation, weather, and physical structure than on detailed classification. A basic understanding is helpful, however. Following are a few select definitions of various open-water structures.

LAKES

Lakes in exorheic basins are usually filled by one to many rivers and creeks. In an endorheic basin, a lake is often the terminus of the watershed and has no outflow; such lakes often have high mineral and salt content.

This small gravel-bottomed pool in Mt. Mueller, New Zealand, is a good example of tarn.

A bog is a type of wetland that accumulates slowly decaying plant matter. This bog is at the Nulhegan River headwaters in Vermont.

Although some conjoined lakes can have two different names, if they are at the same surface level, they are the same lake.

Lakes are usually classified based on their source, the geology of their formation, and their level profile, which refers to whether they are growing or shrinking over time or seasonally. Formation can occur through river change, glacial retreat and melt, volcano or meteor crater, or depression through tectonic and glacial forces, for example. A *pothole*, or kettle lake, is usually a round, shallow body formed by the retreat of a glacier and filled with rain- or meltwater. Lakes that dry up or disappear with some regularity are called *ephemeral* lakes. The lakelike bodies of water behind dams are called *reservoirs*. Among the many other kinds of lakes are crater lakes, salt lakes, oxbow lakes, and glacial lakes.

PONDS
Generally, a pond is a body of water in which enough sunlight reaches the entire bottom of the lake to allow vegetation to grow there. Ponds are often smaller and shallower than lakes.

Tarns are shallow, gravel-bottomed mountain ponds formed by glacial action.

BOGS AND SWAMPS
Bogs are shallow wetlands usually found at mid to high latitudes. Usually fed by rain and meltwater, bogs are filled with decomposing plant material

that produces an acidic, tannin-rich flow. In contrast, swamps are wetlands that are usually found in warmer regions than bogs and have a more active vegetative cover. Swamps can be very big and are usually fed by rivers and streams or are tidal.

River Features and Hazards

BENDS

Among the most important and universal features of rivers are bends, turns in the path of the river. If you have ever canoed on a very sinuous stream— paddling, for example, 25 miles (40 kilometers) to travel 6.2 miles (10 kilometers) as the crow flies—you understand the scope of how rivers can bend. When viewed from above, many large rivers show evidence of incredible wandering over time. Bends, meanders, oxbows, and oxbow lakes abound, as do clear meander scars, dried-out or boggy channels that, because of different soil composition and water content, have sharply different vegetative cover and physical structure. Viewed from above, they can be quite beautiful. Following are some of the features and terminology associated with river bends.

Meander. Named after the Meander River in Turkey, this refers to an accentuated bend that defines a meandering river, usually a mature or mid-course river type, which traces a snakelike pattern across the landscape. Over time, erosion and deposition cause the channel to move, make the bends more extreme and the river more sinuous. Interestingly, if a meandering river is uplifted, it can resume the downcutting it discontinued earlier in

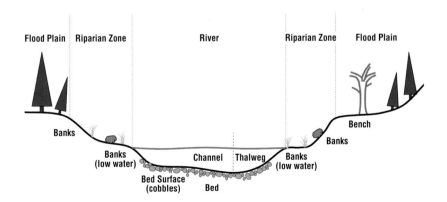

A few common terms for river structures.

The Stewart River in Yukon Territory has shifted across the landscape over time, leaving lakes and scars on the land.

its life cycle and create *entrenched* meanders, a common feature of canyon rivers in the desert Southwest. The straight course of a river between bends is sometimes called a *reach*.

Oxbow. A meander that has become so sharp or extreme that it almost traces a teardrop shape is called an oxbow. Over time, the process that creates oxbows can straighten the channel or move it laterally, side to side. This essentially cuts off current from the oxbow, and the river eventually will build a bank and isolate it, creating an oxbow lake, or *rincon*.

Point bar. Point bars are shallow, sloping beaches of sand, gravel, cobbles, and/or boulders that form on the inside or just downstream of river bends. They can be the size of a doormat or a football field, depending on the bank structure, flow, gradient, and sediment load of the river.

The confluence of two waterways is a special place: Bonnet Plume River and unnamed creek in Yukon Territory.

Braid bar. Braid bars are formations of sand, gravel, cobbles, and/or boulders that occur mid-channel on a braided, wandering, or meandering river. They can be formed in midchannel or can be point bars and banks that have been cut off from shore and re-formed. A braid bar can turn into an island if enough vegetative cover develops and has an opportunity to grow and secure it.

Cut bank. A steep-sided cut bank may form on the outside of a river bend as a result of the erosive

Cut banks usually appear on the outside bends of rivers with soft banks and significant erosive force. In many cases, they are made of material that was deposited long ago by the same river.

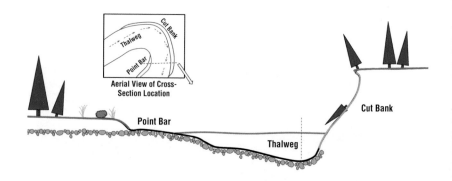

The mechanics of point bars, cut banks, and thalwegs are closely interwoven.

forces of the river cutting into the land. These are often disturbed, sheer faces of sand and gravel with trees and vegetation hanging or suspended from the top, making them primary sources of sediment and woody debris in the middle course of a river.

If a river tries to find the path of least resistance in flowing downhill, why does it end up with an improbable number of bends? This is a complicated question whose answer requires delving slightly into hydrodynamics, but is easy to understand if you have ever stood on the sandy beach on the inside bend of a wild river.

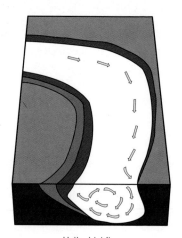

Helicoidal flow.

River bends form and change over time through the process of erosion and deposition on point bars. The fascinating and counterintuitive part of this process is that almost none of the *suspended*, or floating, sediment load is deposited on the inside of a bend to form point bars; instead, these features are formed out of the bed load by something called *helicoidal flow*. The primary flow is on the river surface and moving downstream, and when this flow reaches a bend, it flows above and across the bed surface toward the outside, or concave side, of the bend rather than parallel to the bed surface.

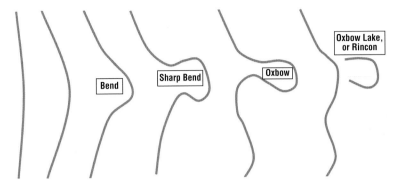

As the river shifts, the bends tend to get sharper until the river breaks through, leaving a dead channel.

When a river rounds a bend, centrifugal force causes a slight elevation difference between the inside and outside of the bend. This results in more pressure on the higher elevation outside of the bend and more erosive force in total. The difference in elevation and pressure between the two sides of the bending river creates a pressure gradient, and the force of this gradient causes a secondary flow, or current, to move in opposition to the primary flow along the bed surface. This type of secondary flow is called heliocoidal flow, and it moves at a slight downstream angle from the outside of the bend across the bed surface and to the inside of the bend or just downstream, following the pressure gradient.

Point bars, like this one on the Stewart River, Yukon Territory, usually form on the inside of bends from material eroded from the outside of the bend.

As it does so, it redirects part of the bed load to the area of shallower water on the inside of the bend, depositing it there and making the water even more shallow. The contributions that the eroding outside bank have made to the bed load are often included, and much of a point bar is made up of material from just on the other side of the river and a bit upstream. The helicoidal flow is often strong enough to push the material upslope to the surface of the river and deposit it at the water level. Thus, the genesis of a point bar. On rocky, steep-walled rivers, like Hells Canyon of the Snake River, sediment and erosion are minimized, but many of these processes still take place on some level.

RAPIDS

In order of increasing gradient, a river can take the form of a run, riffle, rapids, or cascade. The first indication of widespread *whitewater*, water that is temporarily aerated by extreme turbulence in the river to the point of being white and frothy in color, occurs at the level of rapids.

This turbulence can come from four different sources: gradient, obstruction, constriction, and flow. These four features, either alone or in conjunction, are what cause the formation of rapids and whitewater.

Gradient. When the slope of the river increases over a short distance, this causes an increase in velocity and usually a decrease in depth.

Obstruction. Any time an object is placed in a river current, it will create some level of turbulence. If the obstruction is large and heavy enough

Looking down on a rapid in the Rio Grande in Texas, you can see the side drainage that dumped the debris into the river, creating a constriction filled with obstructions.

Large ledges of bedrock obstruct the Hyland River here in the Yukon, forcing the water either over or around them.

to anchor itself on the bed surface and remain stationary, it will cause even more turbulence—often enough to create whitewater. Many such objects will create rapids, though interestingly, they will also increase pressure through either gradient or constriction, or both.

Constriction. A constriction works similarly to putting your thumb over the end of a garden hose: the channel becomes smaller and the pressure is increased. Most commonly, the banks of the river narrow, and because the volume of the river is constant, either the channel must get deeper immediately or the velocity must increase. An increase in velocity is the most common outcome, creating a set of rapids that often has water with a vertical profile—waves. Less commonly, the river maintains its width but gets significantly shallower, often because of bedrock intrusion, and this causes a similar increase in pressure.

Flow. A higher volume of water moving through a channel will cause an increase in velocity and therefore potential turbulence. An increase or decrease in flow can also engage previously unaffected features, such as deeply submerged rocks or canyon walls.

DOWNSTREAM AND UPSTREAM VS

In any set of rapids, obstacles in the current form certain current lines that tend to move at an angle downstream and away from the obstacle. Picture a

When viewed from river level, the V in the Gray Canyon on the Green River in Utah is harder to see, but it is still there.

This downstream V in the Rio Grande in Texas is obvious when viewed from above, though the observer might be too close to the edge.

large, dry rock alone in the middle of the river. It will have two lines of disturbed water trailing downstream of it, creating a large V-shape in the river, with the rock at the point of the letter. If the current has a high velocity, the lines will be much more obvious and appear to trail straight downstream rather than out at an angle. This is an *upstream V*.

Now picture two large, dry rocks side by side in the current, about 15 feet (4.6 meters) apart. There are now two upstream Vs. Where the two lines of disturbed water meet between and downstream of the rocks, a third

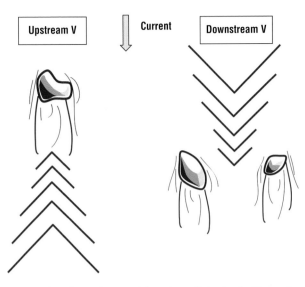

Training your eye to notice upstream and downstream Vs is a key tool for reading water.

V is formed, this time pointing downstream. This is a *downstream V*, with its tops as the two obstacles and its bottom as the clear channel. Particularly smooth or glassy downstream Vs are sometimes called *tongues.*

In practice, you can use these features in reading the water: upstream Vs point toward a potential hazard, and downstream Vs point toward a potential passage.

EDDIES

Downstream of a significant river obstruction, the area of less turbulent and occasionally stationary water with a reverse or upstream current is called an eddy. A complete obstruction of part of a river's flow, like that caused by a large, dry rock, creates a vacuum behind the obstruction. Because of Earth's gravitational pull, water seeks equilibrium, filling in all available spaces and having a flat, level surface. Because of this tendency, water will recirculate into the vacuum behind the obstruction, creating two opposing currents and an area of calmer, protected water. Obstructions that cause eddies to form can be rocks, islands, point bars, braid bars, or simply areas of riverbank that deflect the current.

The line of turbulent, confused water that extends from the obstruction downstream, marking the boundary between the two currents, is called the *eddy line*. The eddy line becomes wider and more turbulent as it moves farther from the obstruction. An eddy behind a rock or island will have

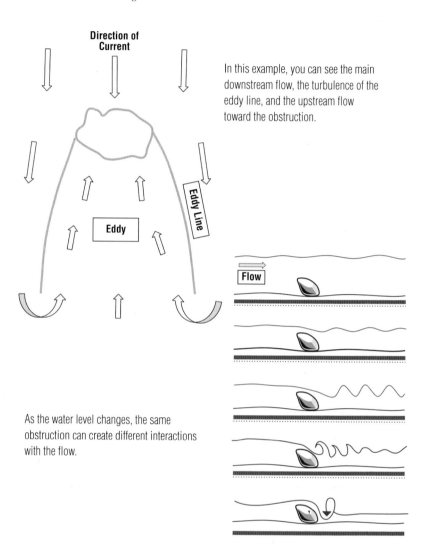

Direction of Current

In this example, you can see the main downstream flow, the turbulence of the eddy line, and the upstream flow toward the obstruction.

Eddy Line

Eddy

Flow

As the water level changes, the same obstruction can create different interactions with the flow.

two eddy lines creating an upstream V, while an onshore eddy will only have one.

The size of the area of protected water depends on the size of the obstruction. Very small obstructions cause very small eddies, sometimes called *microeddies*. These can be difficult for novices to notice and harder for them to use, but they are an important part of Class III maneuvering, especially on big-water rivers. Sometimes, an eddy is said to be flushing, meaning that while it is an area of calmer water that is moving upstream, the upstream water is not staying in the eddy for long, and your boat won't

This rock is obstructing the flow and creating a pillow upstream and a micro eddy downstream. An eddy is simply the river's way of filling in a vacuum caused by an obstruction. Reading and gauging the conflicting currents allows for multiple important maneuvers.

either. The downstream end of most eddies has water beginning to move downstream.

WET ROCKS
Rocks made wet by spray and errant waves are less prominent and sometimes difficult to see. There is still an eddy downstream of the rock, but the rock is harder to spot from upstream, and the eddy might be marginal or flushing.

PILLOW
If enough water is flowing into a rock but it remains above the surface, the water piles up vertically to form a pillow. A pillow may also be present with more exposed rocks but is not always.

POUR-OVER
When the water begins to consistently wash over a rock and cover it, this is known as a pour-over. An eddy may still be intact behind the rock if only a small amount of water is flowing over it. At the upper end, the eddy is eradicated and water is flowing over the rock and downstream. The rock is difficult to see from upstream, though it may be obvious from downstream looking up; there is often a small pillow or small wave upstream of the rock that may be the only indication of its existence.

Here, the water is fully covering the rock, but it is still obstructing the flow and creating a small recirculating hole.

HOLES

When the elevation difference downstream of a rock is great enough, or the volume of water going over it is large enough, you may encounter a hole. Holes, sometimes called *hydraulics*, are formed when the water is directed vertically down by the rock and it impacts the riverbed or other rocks; this impact causes it to turn back on itself in a circle, essentially creating something akin to a vertical eddy as the water and foam pile seek to fill in the vacuum created by the vertical fall.

Objects that get stuck in holes can sometimes stay there for long periods of time. Holes can range from the size of your fist to that of a tractor-trailer. In mild cases, they can look or be treated like traditional eddies, but they are different because water is flowing into the hole from both upstream and downstream, whereas in a true eddy the inflow is only from downstream.

All that may be visible from upstream of a hole is a single wave or pillow. When reading the water, you need to be aware that a hole will not be followed by more than one wave, whereas a true standing wave will exist in series. A helpful way to remember this is the saying, "Friendly waves have friends."

WAVES

A wave is a mass of water with a vertical profile and can come in a variety of complex shapes. River waves are stationary and are sometimes referred to as "standing." A breaking wave, or wave with a foam pile, can be similar in appearance to a hole, but most of the water flows downstream through the feature, rather than recirculating into the aerated water as is the case with a hole.

LOW-HEAD DAMS

A small dam that allows water to flow over its entire top is called a low-head dam, or weir. These man-made structures are used to regulate flow for a variety of purposes, but they often have dangerous hydraulics, almost always with a uniform hole along the base. Because of their uniformity and the fact that they usually stretch from shore to shore, these holes, even those below very small dams, are almost impossible to free yourself from if you get caught in one, and for this reason many paddlers call them "drowning machines." It is best to avoid low-head dams altogether and portage around them. While many are marked with signs and buoys, some are not and can be nearly invisible from upstream, so consult your map or guidebook to identify if there are any low-head dams on your route.

STRAINERS

Any feature on the river that allows water to pass through it but has passages too small for a boat or person to easily float through is called a *strainer* or *sweeper*. Most strainers are downed trees or bushes, but in some river environments, they can be rocks or rock formations known as *sieves*.

The high flow rate over this submerged ledge on the Rapid River in Maine helps create a large wave.

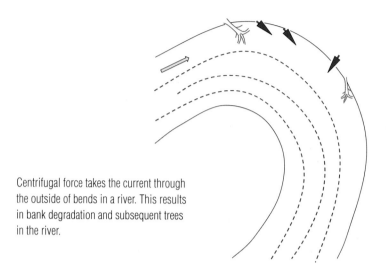

Centrifugal force takes the current through the outside of bends in a river. This results in bank degradation and subsequent trees in the river.

Frequently caused by landslides and mass wasting, rock sieves are surface strainers made of different-size rocks lodged together. Man-made items can also function as strainers, including dam intakes, culvert grills, filtration systems, pipes, irrigation equipment, diversion canals, low bridges, and even shopping carts.

Cut banks are prime woody debris locations, particularly of whole living trees. These trees can become hazards, if they are undercut and fall over into the river, which can occur along any bank or island. With the trunk horizontal or near horizontal, the limbs extend into the water, forming a fine, flexible net that can catch people, gear, boats, and debris. Alternatively, high water can flood forests and areas of stiff woody bushes or cane grasses, creating vertical strainers that are equally dangerous.

If we consider that 1 cubic meter of water weighs 2,204 pounds (1,000 kilograms), then a piece of gear or a person in the water upstream of a strainer can expect to be held in place or underwater with several thousand pounds of force by even a fairly mellow current. This is almost inescapable, and people onshore or in boats can do little to rescue that person or gear.

Underwater strainers, sometimes called *suck holes* or *tea strainers*, are particularly dangerous because they are difficult for paddlers to spot. Here, underwater suction is created. If this suction is strong enough, you or a partially submerged piece of your gear can get pulled under and be held there. These "caverns" in the river are the things of nightmares, as it can be extremely difficult to get free from an underwater strainer. The best clues

At higher flow, water would be forced into this nook of rock, sweeping anything in that laminate into it and holding it there.

At higher flow, this undercut rock in Desolation Canyon on the Green River in Utah would look like a normal canyon wall. The danger is that objects can be pushed into undercuts and held there, with no way out.

to look for are water flowing into an obstruction but not visibly flowing around or over it, the lack of a pillow or turbulence against the obstacle, and the lack of an eddy or the presence of boils downstream. This indicates that the water is going somewhere you cannot see, and there may be an underwater strainer.

UNDERCUTS

When soft sedimentary rocks are exposed to significant current, they can erode over time into overhanging structures. The water that caused the erosion is then pushing under the overhanging cliff, and at certain water levels the overhang can be submerged, at water level, or exposed. One way or another, an undercut represents an area where you or your boat can be pushed and held underwater indefinitely, with rescue challenging or impossible. These structures are less common in igneous and metamorphic rocks because of their tendency to resist erosion or crumble, but undercuts are still common enough here that you need to watch out for them.

The time of year may also make undercuts more of a hazard. Ice sheets often form on rivers early in the winter, and by late winter and early spring, the water level has dropped significantly and then begins to rise again from meltwater. During these periods, the ice can create massive undercuts along

Single strainers are often avoidable, but logjams, like this one on the Clyde River in Vermont, can stretch from one bank to the other.

the banks of a river, and in areas where open water flows into a fully frozen river, the bank should be treated as one massive, canoe-eating undercut.

LOGJAMS
When a high-gradient or seasonally fluctuating river flows through a forest, it will collect a certain amount of woody debris. When significant numbers of trees are eroded out and carried downstream by high-water events, they can pile up where obstructions in the flow occur, such as on the upstream end of an island, on large rocks, or at shallow or sharp bends in the stream. Water continues to flow through and under these rafts of intertwined wood, making them a hybrid of a strainer and an undercut, and very dangerous. A swimmer or boat swept under or into a logjam might not come out for a long time.

CLIFF SHOTS
In very young rivers and in confined, rocky gorges, current frequently flows directly into a wall, where it either forms a large pillow and circulates to the sides or undercuts the cliff to remove the obstruction. These features, known as cliff shots, have many of the characteristics of other obstructions, such as pillows and eddies. Avoiding them can be challenging when the entire flow of the river is charging into the wall.

Open-Water Features and Hazards

WAVES

River waves appear to stand still, but water is constantly cycling through them. Conversely, open-water waves appear to be moving, but little or no water is actually being moved; it is only energy that is being transferred from one piece of water to another. When that energy comes into contact with a solid object like a rock, reef, island, or shallow bottom, it changes form into a crashing wave.

Open-water waves are most often caused by wind blowing over the flat surface of the water.

Boat wakes can also create waves, but wind is the most important energy source. As wind blows across the surface, it puts pressure on the water and inputs energy into it, raising small pieces of water vertically and increasing the *sail area*—the area roughly perpendicular to the wind's direction, like a sail—of the water. Under constant wind, these small pieces of water will grow in a positive feedback loop, getting larger as more energy is input, creating a larger sail area and a bigger wave.

The highest point of a wave is the *crest*, and the lowest point is the *trough*; the vertical distance between the two is called the *wave height*. Perpendicular to the imaginary line measuring wave height is another line measuring the distance between two wave crests, termed the *wavelength*. The amount of time it takes for two wave crests to pass a stationary point is known as the *period*.

Understanding wave forces on the ocean can be a complicated effort, but those same forces acting on a small lake can be more easily understood because of the smaller scale. How wind builds waves is a product of four characteristics of the wind and the particular body of water: fetch, time, speed, and depth. All of these factors together affect how a canoe will handle and what tactics or strategies you need to use.

Fetch. Perhaps the most important factor is the open water surface area the wind has to work on, a distance called the fetch. Wind blowing down the length of a long, thin lake causes much larger waves than that same wind blowing across the narrow part of the lake, and very big lakes have larger potential waves

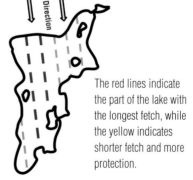

The red lines indicate the part of the lake with the longest fetch, while the yellow indicates shorter fetch and more protection.

Looking out from the lee shore of the Boundary Waters in Minnesota, you can see the waves rolling in.

than small lakes. One reason ocean waves can grow to be so large is the massive amount of fetch, or distance, the wind is effecting.

Time. A brief gust might cause ripples, but a sustained blow is required to build significant waves. Increased duration of a wind event causes more energy input into the water.

Speed. The wind speed strongly affects potential wave building. A higher wind speed means more energy that can potentially be applied to the water. A hurricane-force wind can create huge waves with only a short fetch, but a very soft wind needs a massive fetch to form significant waves.

Depth. The depth of the body of open water is an important part of how the energy input by the wind is manifested. The depth does not change the amount of energy in the water, but it does change how the energy is expressed. The same amount of energy that causes a relatively small, long wave in deep water will create larger waves in shallower parts of the lake near shore or over a reef or rock. Large, high-energy ocean waves turn from slow-moving swells to tall breaking waves as they move into much shallower areas. Consistently deep bodies like Lake Superior have more oceanic swell, while shallow lakes tend to have waves with a shorter period and more height, making them break more easily.

Wave Growth

Waves build based on the factors of fetch, time, speed, and depth, and they progress through certain stages, each with its own characteristics and management strategies.

Light winds produce small waves, like those here on Lake Mistassini in Quebec, but with increased energy input they can grow quickly.

The smallest are *capillary waves*, sometimes called cat's paws. These are only 1 to 3 inches (2.5 to 7.2 centimeters) in height, and if the energy of the wind is cut off, they will quickly disappear and return to normal as a result of surface tension. Once enough energy has been input into the water that the waves will continue to exist for a time after the wind calms, they are classified as seas or swells. *Seas* are waves that are influenced by land-forms, while *swells* are the more uniform, long-period waves unaffected by land and usually found offshore.

Two particular types of seas, or land-influenced waves, are rebound waves and refracting waves. *Rebound waves* usually form near cliffs, walls, or steep shorelines as waves hit these obstacles and rebound, or reflect, back into the oncoming waves. The result is a confused sea of chaotic water that is best avoided by paddlers. *Refracting waves* form near a change in the angle of the shore, such as near a cape, island, point, or bay. Here, an incoming wave hits the shore and is bent around the protruding shoreline, changing the direction of the wave. This is why a canoeist hoping to hide from waves behind an island is sometimes disappointed, because if the waves are big enough, they will refract around the sides of the island. If they are very large or the island is very small, the two sides of the refracted wave might even meet head on behind the island.

Once the energy driving wave formation is removed, it takes time for the waves to dissipate, or return to a normal, flat state. The amount of time

Even extreme winds, like these seen in a 75-mph typhoon on Inner Pelorus Sound in Marlborough, New Zealand, only produce small waves because the fetch is very short. The wind presents other problems, however.

it takes is relative to the amount of energy in the water and the ways it can be spent. With massive swells out in the sea, it may take a week or more for the energy to dissipate, whereas a 1-foot (30-centimeter) sea on a small, rocky lake might calm within less than an hour.

Breaking Waves and Surf

When a wave is forced to a wave height more than about one-seventh of its wavelength, it becomes unstable and begins to break, collapsing in a pile of aerated water down the leeward face of the wave. This increase in height and instability can be caused by either too much energy in the wave or a concentration of that energy due to a decrease in depth.

Whitecaps are caused by high-speed, long-fetch, and extended-duration wind events and are basically just small waves that break because too much energy has been input. These are the most common breaking waves on lakes and are an important clue in open-water decision-making on a canoe expedition. They are obvious even to the novice, and their appearance indicates building conditions that might not be suited for open canoes. They usually occur at around 10 knots of wind.

When waves impact a beach, they will break as a result of an increase in wave height caused by the decrease in water depth concentrating the energy in the water. How they break is in large part determined by the topography of the beach or obstruction. A reef or rock just under the surface of the water can cause a breaking wave called a *boomer* because of the noise it can

A beach break in the Pacific Northwest. Waves grow larger when they approach the shore because of the decreased depth in the body of water.

make slapping against the rock or other incoming waves. The wave gets steeper and collapses, breaking over the obstruction.

On a very steep beach, the waves might rebound as described above. On a moderate but consistently sloped beach, the waves might create a *dumping surf*. Here, the energy is concentrated abruptly and the wave height jumps and collapses quickly, sending the top of the wave down vertically onto the beach. On a shallow-sloped beach, the energy is less concentrated on the gradual slope, and the breaking wave is usually more of a rolling foam pile than a curling tube.

OPEN-WATER CURRENTS

A massive system of water movement occurs in the world's oceans, from huge "rivers" of current flowing in giant global circuits, transferring nutrients and heat, to localized wind- and tide-driven currents near shore. Ocean currents can be quite dangerous, but on lakes currents play a smaller role. Lake currents are most common near constrictions or narrowings of the shoreline, near inflows and outflows, or when influenced by tidal forces.

RIVER ENTRANCES

When scudding along the shore of a large lake, you may come across a place where a river interrupts the shoreline. Treat these areas with respect: the influx of water can cause confused waves, eddy lines, and dangerous currents. A wide, strong river creates the kind of conditions that can easily

Wave energy is dissipated on the beach in Rainy Lake, Minnesota.

capsize a canoe or push a group of paddlers far out into the lake when you have all been lulled into complacency by calm hours on flat water. Groups sometimes portage or track a little ways upriver and ferry across there instead. There are often banks or shoals of sediment deposit where the river meets the lake, and these can be some of the only flat places to camp on steep and rocky shores.

TIDES

The combination of the gravitational pull of Earth, the sun, and the moon, along with Earth's rotational force, causes a rise and fall in all surface land and water. This is obvious in large lakes and on the ocean shore as water is pulled around the world, raising and lowering water levels on a roughly twelve-hour cycle. Where constrained by shore formations and local bathymetry (underwater topography), this can create fierce currents and large water-level changes. On a tiny island in the middle of the Pacific, for example, tidal fluctuation might be minimal, while in the Bay of Fundy or on the north coast of Australia's Northern Territory, the tidal range might be up to 60 feet (18.2 meters).

REEFS, ISLANDS, AND POINTS

Reefs are hard submerged bars of rock or coral in open bodies of water. They often cause breaking waves, and at lower water levels or low tide, they can result in rebounding and refracting waves. Living and dead coral can form large reef systems only in the ocean, while rock reefs exist in both fresh and salt water. These formations can protect inshore travel even in rough conditions, but can occasionally make getting to or along shore quite difficult, depending on conditions and orientation.

On very large lakes, currents and waves can be confused or concentrated around islands and points. Waves commonly are refracted around them, creating confused and potentially dangerous waters. Islands and points can make good reference points for navigation and may provide protection on the side opposite of incoming waves.

RIVER MANEUVERS
AND STRATEGY

A bridge between the science and structure of a river and the basic strokes and concepts of paddling

You might have noticed by this point that the book uses a nested system. Learning the basic concepts of paddling helps you master the strokes, which you then put together into maneuvers and use to control the boat. When paired with an understanding of water science, you can use these tools to think critically about strategies and tactics for challenging situations like whitewater, rough flat water, and other special circumstances. In slow-moving water and small, low-consequence rapids, a lack of skill, experience, and focus probably will not hold you back, but it will prevent you from learning to control your boat in ways that will let you move into larger or more complicated water. Incidents can occur in water of any difficulty level, however, particularly when novices are not paying attention.

The next step in the system is to gain an understanding of more complicated river maneuvers, how to read water, and other strategies and tactics that build on the basic components and strokes introduced in part I.

River Maneuvers

CROSSING THE GRAIN

An understanding of how river currents move is helpful in picking and executing good lines—your intended path of travel—in whitewater. A canoe not under power is the equivalent of a floating log, and in the absence of turbulence or river obstructions, it will move downstream on the path it started on. Moving across the river requires momentum. This momentum can come from forward or back paddling or from current differentials or waves.

The application of this idea can be somewhat counterintuitive, as demonstrated by the following example. First, picture a steep, river-wide downstream V that compresses the current into the center of the channel;

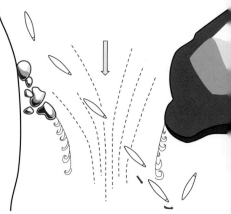

Above: The paddlers aim where they want to end up: river left. They paddle forward starting on the right and move smoothly across each laminate before eddying out on the left. If they lost their momentum at any point before the final eddy line, they would be pushed downstream and to the center.

Left: The paddler here on the Green River in Utah is pointed at the left shore and is paddling forward to get there. He is crossing the grain of the river from the center to the left so that he ends up on the left.

downstream, the water piles up in large waves that will swamp or capsize a canoe. Your group realizes this and makes a plan to eddy out on river right below the drop but beside the wave train.

The problem is, the current in the river leads into the wave train; that is to say, a floating log or canoe will end up in the wave train no matter where it starts above the drop. The counterintuitive part is that to reach the eddy on the bottom right, you have to start above the drop on river left and cross the grain of the

In the first two photos, the paddlers identify the large waves downstream, set an angle, and paddle across the grain to avoid them. In the third and fourth photos, they have lost their angle and momentum across the grain and are being pulled downstream and to the center. In the last photo, they cannot avoid the large waves on the Green River in Utah.

river while pointing the bow—and looking—at the eddy you want to end up in.

Starting on river right to end up on river right can leave the canoe unable to cross the grain and eddy line and will put it in the wave train because of the lack of momentum. The canoe can also cross the grain from left to right and end up on the extreme right of the downstream current and possibly sneak past on the margins of the wave train bypassing the eddy; this too would require crossing the grain. The reality might be different if the V is on a bend or more obstacles exist.

There are other ways of achieving the same goal, such as the use of a back ferry, but in pushy water, with a loaded boat and high consequences, crossing the grain is an important maneuver in your toolkit. During execution, both paddlers on a team must work together, anticipating and setting up for the move, looking where they want to go, and moving the canoe across the river.

SIDE SLIPS

The downriver side slip is identical to the drill discussed in chapter 5. It is a helpful move in complex and

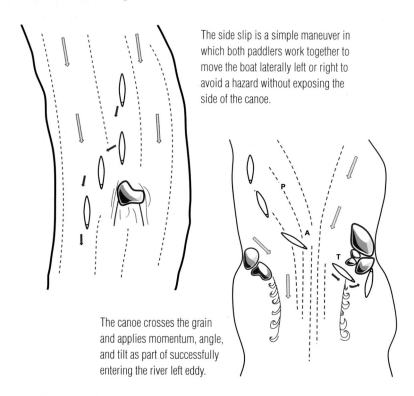

The side slip is a simple maneuver in which both paddlers work together to move the boat laterally left or right to avoid a hazard without exposing the side of the canoe.

The canoe crosses the grain and applies momentum, angle, and tilt as part of successfully entering the river left eddy.

continuous rock gardens with no truly clear passages, but not in pushy water. In this maneuver, you move the boat laterally left or right to avoid an obstacle without sacrificing all momentum and without opening the boat's angle to the current and exposing it to a potential broach or pin.

EDDY TURNS

You may want to use eddies as stopping and pausing points, as well as play features, but reliably doing so requires a rock-solid method of entering and exiting them. An eddy turn relies on using the water to do the bulk of the work and accenting it with a little boat handling and maybe a few strokes; the opposing currents on either side of the eddy line spin the boat, and the calm or recirculating water inside the eddy holds the boat.

A variety of models are used to conceptualize entering and exiting eddies, and the maneuver has various names as well. For the purposes of this text, the maneuver is called an *eddy turn* and is broken up into *eddying out* of the main river current and into an eddy and *peeling out* of the eddy and back into the main river current. The model employed in this text is based on momentum, angle, and tilt and is used to clarify the elements of how a boat behaves in an effective eddy turn and identify the common mistakes. The other models are based on similar ideas, differing only in emphasis. Following are details on eddying out of the main river current and exiting the eddy by either peeling out or using an alternative method, along with a few other considerations to make the maneuver easier, especially in a loaded expedition canoe, including the use of strokes to assist eddy turns, where to make the most effective eddy turn, and how to plan for the group.

Entering an Eddy: Eddying Out

Momentum. The setup for an eddy turn is vital, and it often begins with crossing the grain. The canoe is positioned upstream and moves forward toward the eddy, and its momentum allows the canoe to punch through the conflicting currents and confused water of the eddy line. Some eddies may require aggressive forward paddling, but most, with proper anticipation, require only momentum. This might take just a couple of strokes, or the river may provide the momentum, such as when you move from faster current to slower.

Angle. The orientation of the boat to the eddy line is a key element, as is, to a lesser extent, the angle to the downstream current. One analogy to consider here is that of a spacecraft reentering the atmosphere: if the angle of entry is too steep, the spacecraft will burn up; if the angle is too shallow, the spacecraft will bounce off. The angle between the trajectory and the atmosphere must be just right; in aerodynamics, this is called the angle of attack.

This concept of angle of attack applies to eddy turns in a similar way. If the angle of attack is too shallow or small, the canoe might bounce off the eddy line; if it is too steep, the canoe is in danger of capsizing or being flushed back into the river. The challenge in eddy turns is that the optimal angle is different for each eddy, and this ranges widely. Having an ideal angle in mind will keep you from being flexible based on different circumstances. The strength of the current, the momentum of the canoe, the width and turbulence of the eddy line, the differential between the two currents, and the desired arc of the eddy turn all help determine the optimal angle.

Tilt. When the bow crosses the eddy line, the canoe should be tilted. For a novice, it is helpful to initiate the tilt several feet before the bow crosses the eddy line, and as you gain confidence, initiate the tilt closer and closer to the line. The canoe should be tilted such that the lowered gunwale is facing the eddy and the exposed chine of the canoe is facing the main river current. Apply pressure with the knee on the destination eddy side while lifting with the other. A helpful aerodynamic analogy here is that of a plane banking, or turning, left or right. You might also picture a bicyclist tilting into a turn and tilt your canoe similarly.

A fully loaded tripping canoe has a ton of ballast and stability. Just showing your butt to the current will do little to tilt the boat, especially if you are a smaller paddler. It is often necessary to shift your hip right over to the gunwale in order to get a good tilt on the boat. The majority of tripping canoes have good secondary stability and will comfortably sit with the gunwale at the waterline. Stable tilt is created and maintained by having an upright upper body and a tilted lower body, as described in chapter 5.

Tilting changes the hull profile drastically; one chine is engaged and dropped deeper into the water than normal, creating a vastly more stable boat in conflicting currents. A lack of adequate tilt is the most surefire way to capsize on an eddy line, as the new current grabs the chine and side that should have been out of the water and pulls them down with surprising force. The upstream gunwale is always the one dropped in entering an eddy.

Exiting an Eddy: Peeling Out

All of the same principles apply to exiting an eddy as they do to entering one, though with a few small caveats.

Momentum. Momentum is just as important in peeling out as in eddying out, but you often will not have enough room to properly accelerate. A few helpful tricks are to use short, powerful strokes from the back of the eddy; start slightly downstream and change the angle at the last moment; or use static strokes placed in the main river current to pull the canoe out.

Angle. As with entering an eddy, the best angle of exit depends on what the eddy line looks like, how strong the current is, and where you want to end up in the river. Often in a peel-out, the current you are entering is stronger than the one you are exiting, so a steeper, more upstream angle is sometimes helpful. With more upstream angle, the turn will have a larger radius; with less angle, it will have a smaller radius. This is helpful in gauging where you want to end up in the river—far away from the eddy line or right next to it.

Tilt. The steepness of the exit angle means that the downstream current will be exerting significant force on the bow; this is when most

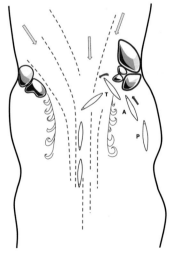

The steps of the eddy turn are reversed to successfully exit the eddy.

capsizes occur. The key to stability and an effective peel-out is setting and holding boat tilt throughout the maneuver. Dropping the downstream gunwale almost to the water level is not uncommon; this will stable the boat and help it carve into the turn.

Other Exit Strategies

The peel-out is not the only way to exit an eddy, and sometimes this maneuver might not make sense. If hazards exist near to the eddy line, it might be better to do a half peel-out, getting the boat turned downstream but leaving it on or very close to the eddy line and avoiding the hazard farther out. In some cases, simply turning around in the eddy and sneaking out the downstream end will allow you to avoid all hazards in the main flow parallel to where you started. This is sometimes the case in large wave trains where you cross the grain above the waves, end up in an eddy, and need to move downstream without reentering the waves.

Stroke-Assisted Eddy Turns

The smoothest eddy turns are accomplished with nothing more than momentum, angle, and tilt, and executing an eddy turn with no strokes at all is a helpful drill for developing paddlers—and we are all developing paddlers. In more challenging water, or for novice paddlers, you can add strokes to augment the existing steering forces. However, keep in mind that it's the currents that turn the boat; the strokes only help and aren't necessary in many instances.

In a stroke-assisted eddy turn, the bow paddler provides much of the forward power on the approach, while the stern paddler is providing some forward power, as well as judging and correcting the angle. Both paddlers initiate the tilt, and once the eddy currents have started to turn the boat, the bow paddler places a static draw or cross-draw stroke in the eddy to help the current turn the boat. This application of force can be conceptualized by picturing a bucket of peanut butter or concrete in the eddy; the bow paddler plants the blade in the bucket, anchoring the boat in the new current and allowing the rest of the boat to swing around the placement. The draw and cross draw are equally effective, and which one to use depends on where your on side is; the blade must be planted on the same side that the boat is tilted toward.

Eddy turns are sometimes described as on-side or off-side turns, referring to the side on which the turn is conducted. However, this can be confusing, as the bow paddler's on side is the stern paddler's off side. For our purposes, an on-side turn refers to its being on or toward the *stern* paddler's on side. A turn conducted on the paddler's off side might be slightly weaker than an on-side turn.

The stern paddler's job is to hold the angle until the bow paddler plants her blade in the eddy, at which point the stern paddler uses stern strokes to help the current turn the boat. For an on-side turn, the stern paddler uses a stern pry to augment the current's turning force; for an off-side turn, he uses a stern draw or sweep. The challenge with an off-side turn is that the stern paddler cannot do cross-boat strokes and therefore must apply force with his blade while tilted in the opposite direction; torso rotation and separation of upper and lower body are essential in an off-side eddy turn. Practicing this combination of maneuvers is important so that both team members are ready for must-make eddies without switching paddling sides ahead of time.

When exiting the eddy, again the ideal is to use a minimum of strokes and let the water do most of the work. The difference is that in an eddy, you will not be starting with momentum, so forward strokes are required to at least build momentum toward the eddy line. To make the turn sharper, the bow paddler can place a draw or cross-draw stroke on the downstream side of the boat once the bow has crossed the eddy line, while the stern paddler uses a low brace or a stern pry for an on-side turn or a stern draw for an off-side turn.

Where to Enter an Eddy
Nearly all eddy lines follow a similar pattern: some obstacle, change in depth, or undulation in the riverbank causes a vacuum in the river, and the water seeks to fill it. The closer you get to the feature that is creating the eddy, the narrower and sharper the eddy line is; as you go downstream from the object, the eddy line grows wider and more confused.

Performing an efficient eddy turn is based on letting the water do as much of the work as possible, so the most effective eddy turn occurs when you place the canoe as close to the feature as possible, crossing the sharpest portion of the eddy line. Here, the two opposing currents will spin the canoe into the eddy, sometimes with significant force.

Plan for the Group
In group travel, eddies that cannot hold all of the boats comfortably should be considered carefully—they may be useful for a temporary pause for only one or two boats at a time making communication difficult. Small or flushing eddies can result in boats being pushed backward into the current, create nasty traffic jams, or even cause collisions. You can split up the group if there is a series of nearby eddies, or stagger the entry into a single eddy so that some boats are moving downstream as others are entering. A boat should have enough time to move downstream and out of the eddy's "sweet spot" before the next boat enters. Tandem pairs in important boat

roles, like the lead boat and the safety boat (discussed below), should not be blocked in, as they often need to exit the eddy quickly to keep in front of the group or assist another boat.

FRONT FERRIES

To conceptualize a ferrying action or maneuver, it is helpful to picture the old style of river-crossing barges, or ferries, that are still used in some parts of the world. A cable is hung across the river and attached to the boat or barge to keep it from being swept downstream by the current. The bow of the craft points upstream, and the pilot angles the bow toward the opposite shore with the use of a rudder or large oar. No mechanical power is needed. The force of the oncoming current works on the exposed and angled side of the barge and pushes it across the grain of the current to the other side without losing ground downstream.

Ferrying in a canoe follows similar ideas and principles. The boat-handling principles of momentum, angle, and tilt that structure eddy turns are also relevant in ferrying, though with slightly different emphases.

Momentum. The canoe is pointed upstream, with the bow paddler providing the lion's share of forward momentum *if needed*. More often than not, a well-executed ferry needs little to no forward power applied by the paddler. Experimenting with ferrying maneuvers done with no forward strokes can be an enlightening exercise. If a perfectly lateral ferry is required and the canoe is being pushed downstream, however, you can apply forward power.

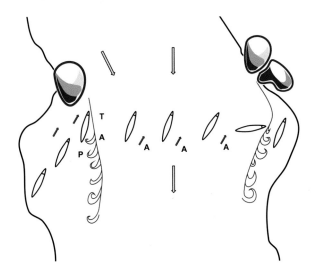

While momentum and tilt are important features of a front ferry, angle is the key element.

A front ferry need not constitute a direct lateral move across the river. This group is ferrying in sequence to a downstream eddy on the Big Salmon River in Yukon Territory.

Angle. The canoe is angled toward the opposite shore or other destination, with the stern paddler maintaining that angle. The angle used should be determined by the angle and speed of the current and your movement across the river. If you are not moving fast enough, open the angle; if you are losing the ferry angle entirely, close the angle. This allows you to adapt to changing angles of current. The best way to gauge the angle you need is to watch the opposite shore and judge your movement across the river. The danger in having too little angle to the current is that the canoe will stall and not move across the grain of the river, as no water is pushing on the exposed side of the boat. Alternatively, if you have too much angle to the current or an improperly controlled angle, the canoe will be exposed to too much force from the river and will spin out.

Tilt. While tilt is not strictly vital in ferrying actions, it makes the maneuver much easier and more stable. The boat should be tilted toward the destination, with the raised gunwale and exposed chine pointed toward where the canoe started, and the lowered gunwale and engaged chine toward the opposite shore or destination.

Crossing Eddy Lines While Ferrying

The challenge with aggressive ferrying maneuvers is that they are often executed from an eddy on one side of the river to an eddy on the other, so in addition to performing the ferry itself, you have to cross two eddy lines, effectively making this a compound maneuver with three significant parts. Leaving the starting eddy, maintain the canoe's momentum and tilt while

In this sequence, the paddlers are successfully beginning their front ferry, but their angle is a bit wobbly due to changing currents and oversteering on the Desolation Canyon section of the Green River in Utah.

keeping the angle of exit much smaller than that used in a peel-out, as the objective here is to *resist* the turning force of the opposing currents rather than utilize them—the boat needs to cross the eddy line while still pointing upstream.

As you leave the eddy line behind, employ the techniques described above for a front ferry to cross the river. When you are closing in on the eddy line near the opposite shore or other midriver destination, the key is to open the angle and change the tilt of your canoe at the last minute. The tilt—left or right—required to ferry is the opposite of the tilt required to cross an eddy line, and the angle is opened at the last minute so that the boat does not bounce off the eddy line, but instead is pointed at it sharply enough to punch through.

Practice

In many cases, proper setup, tilt, and angle can mean that no blade needs to touch the water for the canoe to ferry across even very wide rivers. In strong currents, this may not be the case, but it is worth practicing ferrying with a minimum of forward and steering strokes as a way of emphasizing boat control through tilt and angle-focused body movements.

The goal of all ferries and river maneuvers in general should be to complete them with a minimum number of strokes and use the current to maximum advantage. Areas with strong currents are often better for this because they have more defined troughs that you can use to your advantage. Faster currents also mean faster ferries, with minimal strokes needed. The more you can use river currents, and the less power you need to make moves, the better your paddling becomes. Loaded tripping canoes can be heavy and unwieldy, so you should use every bit of help you can get from the current.

BACK FERRIES

Many of the same principles behind a good front ferry also apply to the back ferry, one of the more challenging maneuvers commonly used in whitewater canoeing. The main differences in appearance and execution are that the bow is pointed downstream, so the current must be overcome with back strokes rather than forward strokes, and the bow paddler takes on maintaining the angle and steering.

The most common uses of the back ferry are to move laterally while navigating through rapids in order to avoid significant obstacles; to cross the grain of the river out of wave trains or into eddies; or to slow the canoe down in large waves so that it does not punch through them, thus lessening the water taken on. While a skilled tandem pair can use a back ferry to cross a river, the front ferry is easier and more effective for lateral moves, especially very long ones like those executed in crossing an entire river.

Ideally, the bow paddler does all the steering and angle setting. The technically correct strokes for the bow paddler to use are the reverse J, reverse sweep, and extended bow draw. The stern paddler needs to moderate his back stroke so he doesn't overpower the bow paddler's corrections.

Back ferries are also effective in entering very small, marginal, or shallow eddies where a full eddy turn would not work. Here, you slow down and tilt the canoe slightly, and then use back and steering strokes to back the canoe into the eddy with little dramatic spinning or punching.

S-TURNS AND C-TURNS

S-turns and C-turns are both compound maneuvers that are executed by linking up a series of moves. The S-turn achieves a similar goal to a front

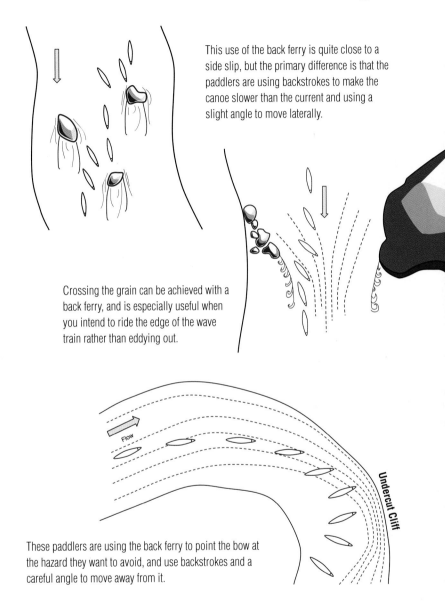

This use of the back ferry is quite close to a side slip, but the primary difference is that the paddlers are using backstrokes to make the canoe slower than the current and using a slight angle to move laterally.

Crossing the grain can be achieved with a back ferry, and is especially useful when you intend to ride the edge of the wave train rather than eddying out.

These paddlers are using the back ferry to point the bow at the hazard they want to avoid, and use backstrokes and a careful angle to move away from it.

ferry, in that you are moving the boat from one spot to another across the grain of the river, but the setup and order of operations are different. An S-turn is simply three known moves put together to form something new: it starts with a full peel-out, followed by crossing the grain, and ends with an eddy turn at the destination.

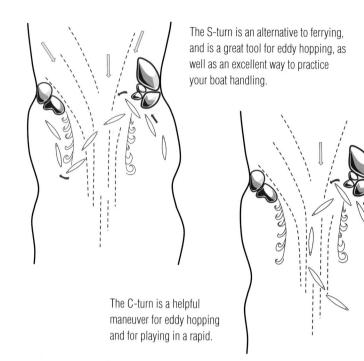

The S-turn is an alternative to ferrying, and is a great tool for eddy hopping, as well as an excellent way to practice your boat handling.

The C-turn is a helpful maneuver for eddy hopping and for playing in a rapid.

Sometimes a front ferry will turn into an S-turn, either by accident or by design. If you encounter a huge ledge that takes up half the river, for example, you may execute a front ferry from the eddy above the ledge to the river center, and then spin downstream and drive into an eddy on the opposite shore. Alternatively, a drifting front ferry can have the same role as an S-turn: you initiate a front ferry, but then let off the power or momentum, and the canoe moves across the river as it moves downstream.

The C-turn is simply a peel-out plus a downstream move back into the same eddy or a downstream eddy on the same bank. The maneuver traces a large C-shape and is perfect for eddy practice, playing the river, or near-shore eddy hopping down big-water rapids.

SURFING

Paddling a loaded expedition canoe onto a standing wave or hole and keeping it there is a fun and instructive challenge. In the right feature, the canoe is simultaneously pushed downstream by the current and held in place as it moves upstream down the face of the wave. You have a wonderful feeling of weightlessness and the opportunity to carve back and forth across the face.

Surfing isn't often strictly necessary for downstream travel. Once you are in the feature, it is easy to get carried away or lose a bit of control, and you risk burying the bow in the oncoming water or capsizing on the edges of the feature. Still, it is a good way to begin to feel the nuances of boat control, and in the right spot, it can inject some much-needed fun into the business of moving downriver.

You can either approach the feature from the sides and ferry into it or paddle up and into it from downstream. Another alternative is to position the canoe so that it floats down into the feature, but this is less effective, as the boat may be at a bad angle or have too much momentum to catch it effectively. The bow paddler can place steering strokes in a front surf, but these will rarely be as functional as those placed in the stern; the bow paddler is more a source of power for attaining the wave, and the stern paddler a source of steering forces. The next step on a particularly good wave is to slowly carve back and forth across it through subtle changes in steering forces. You can also back surf by backing or back ferrying the canoe onto the feature, but this is a much harder move in a loaded boat. Practicing surfing in unloaded boats can provide great learning with less consequence in the event of a capsized canoe.

Large and heavy tandem canoes need forgiving waves and smaller holes to effectively surf. Before attempting this maneuver, it's important to take account of any downstream features and potential consequences and to have a safety boat whose team is keeping an eye on you, as swamping or capsizing on a wave and being swept into nasty or unavoidable obstacles with no one watching or ready to rescue would be a bad outcome for a simple pleasure. You should not attempt to paddle any rapids or features on an expedition unless you are willing and prepared to swim, and this fact is worth remembering when contemplating a beautiful, glassy standing wave downstream.

WAVE BLOCKS

River waves are not only obstacles, but also can be used to move the canoe across the grain and around the river. When a wave threatens to splash the side of your boat and push it off course or dump water inside, you and your partner can work together to position the hull so that the wave bounces off. You can do this in one of two ways, by changing either the angle or the tilt of the boat. If you set up the boat to quarter the wave, paddling into the wave at a slight angle, the force of the wave will hit the slanted side of the boat and slide astern, rather than hitting full-on and washing both sides of the boat. Tilting involves raising one gunwale to block the wave by executing a snap of the hips and a shift in pressure on the control surfaces—knee pads, thigh straps, and seat. The bow paddler often will be the first to see the wave coming and can initiate the block, basically just a momentary tilt of the hull.

PLAYING THE RIVER

The objective of river travel on a canoe expedition is to move up- or down-river while managing risk as effectively as possible. Doing it in good style and with skill growth in mind are important aspects as well. Playing the river is the idea of using the moving water and the features therein to practice, play, experiment, and challenge yourself and your team.

This necessitates a change in viewpoint. The massive boulder in the center of the river, for example, ceases to be an obstacle to avoid and instead becomes a feature that you and your partner can drive for and eddy out behind, using the maneuver to access the other side of the river. The only viable route might be on the other side of the river, and eddying out behind that boulder might be the only way to access it. In such cases, you are playing the river in order to navigate downstream. Looking at it this way, playing the river for fun is preparation for more difficult moves required just to move downstream.

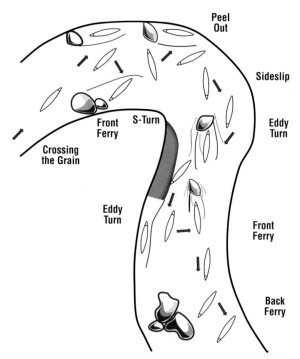

The red arrows trace the path of the canoe through a variety of maneuvers done in quick succession. This is sometimes called playing the river, and it is an excellent way to practice skills and have fun; in more difficult water, being able to quickly execute linked maneuvers becomes vital.

Although playing the river may represent a slightly higher risk in the short term, it reduces your overall risk over the long term, because aggressively practicing in forgiving water, as well as trying new things under the right circumstances in what may be less forgiving water, fuels growth like nothing else can. The key to becoming a competent Class III canoeist is to start by reliably making Class III moves in Class II water, and this accomplished, starting to make those same moves in Class II+ and III water.

In addition to skill development, playing the river is fun, and having fun is part of why we go on expeditions. You will become a more creative creature, thinking up and styling new lines and moves as you grow and improve all the way to the last eddy before the take-out.

Another important tool in growth is playing the river to the point of failure, capsizing or swamping your boat. This should be done in a manageable environment with appropriate safety measures, but nothing else can as effectively teach you the how water interacts with your boat and paddle than challenging a feature until you fail and wind up taking a swim.

Structuring River Strategy

From initiating the planning process to negotiating the first set of rapids to reaching the take-out, the basis of sound river strategy is to build a flexible structure of skills, gear, expectations, knowledge, and judgment. Important parts of your group's strategy include a pretrip safety talk, forms of communication that everyone will understand when on the water, and assignment of boat roles.

SAFETY TALK

Before your group gets on the water for the first time, it is imperative to have a discussion or presentation of pertinent safety topics. Even if team members have paddled this route before, conditions may have changed, and it is rare to paddle with exactly the same group time after time. There will likely be an information and experience gap among members, and this moment of communication is an effort to get everyone on the same page and make expectations crystal clear to all. Not only is a safety talk a good idea, but in many places, it is mandated by law or by institutional risk management requirements. On an institutional expedition, much of the safety talk will be taught or delivered. On a team expedition, some of it will require the group to make decisions and revisit structures, answering questions such as "What are we going to do if . . ." and "What do I do when . . ."

A comprehensive safety talk should cover several areas: any new conditions and information, such as the water level and flow, whether there are downed trees or any of the rapids have shifted recently, any problems with animals or seasonal wildlife issues, and closed campsites or portages; use, fit, and care of equipment and gear use, including helmets, PFDs, and rescue and safety gear; personal care, such as proper clothing and footwear, staying fed and hydrated, and personal risk management; objective hazards like undercuts, strainers, holes, rocks, waves, and any other groups or users that will be on the same water; managing and reacting to hazards, including swimming, pins and broaches, foot entrapment, self-rescue, and use of throw bags; group travel communication and signals; boat roles; and the location and use of medical and rescue kits. If you are paddling with friends, you may omit some of the more obvious notes above.

COMMUNICATION AND SIGNALS

One of the most important factors in having a successful and enjoyable expedition, both on the water and off, is your ability and willingness to communicate with other group members. Communication or a lack thereof can bolster or make useless a rock-solid technical skill set and can lead to the success or failure of an entire expedition. It is also a key risk management tool.

When on the water, your team needs a way to communicate without words. The roar of a river easily obscures the sound of one person's voice and can even silence a well-pitched yell from a few feet away. Signals are simple nonverbal commands or expressions of information that have meanings understood by everyone using them. These must be discussed and agreed upon ahead of time, but a signal system is flexible and should meet the needs of the group. In the heat of the moment, the value of being able to immediately interpret the situation of someone who is just a tiny red speck on a rock in the middle of the river becomes quite clear. Signals are commonly made with paddles, hands and arms, and whistles.

Paddle Signals

The keys to effective paddle signals are to give them clearly, without much movement or change, and to wait until they are given back; only then do you know for sure that your signals have been received and understood. When a signal is being given while on the move, especially when it is being passed from the sweep boat forward from boat to boat or when the distances are great, it is helpful for the whole group to get in the habit of making a unique, high-pitched sound when a signal is received and before passing it along; a shrill "WHOOP!" carries well.

The following paddle signals are internationally recognized across the boating community, but they may be used slightly differently from group to group or place to place.

Go. Hold the paddle vertically above your body, with the blade pointing toward the sky and the power face facing the recipient.

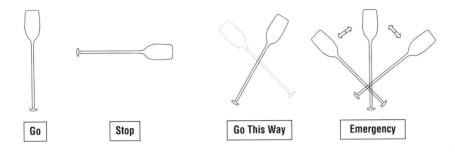

These basic signals are understood throughout the boating community, but small differences in interpretation exist, so it is a good idea to clarify what you mean with each before getting on the water.

Stop. Hold the paddle horizontally above your head with one hand, with the power face facing the recipient.

Positive pointing. Holding the paddle at a 45-degree angle off of straight vertical, point it left or right *toward your intended direction of travel.* This signal is used when your intended path is different from the one the lead boat is taking because of an unforeseen obstacle, or if the following boats have gotten off an agreed-upon line. Do not use this signal to point at hazards or lines to avoid.

Emergency. Hold the paddle in the same position as for the *Go* signal, and wave it back and forth from 10 o'clock to 2 o'clock. It is helpful to decide ahead of time as a group what constitutes an emergency and who can give this signal, especially on an institutional trip.

Hand and Arm Signals

All of the above signals can easily be done with your arms held out and elbows locked; however, your arms are much smaller and harder to see than a paddle. The *Go* signal is one arm held straight up. *Stop* is both arms held straight out to the side. *Pointing* is done in the same way, with a straight arm in place of the paddle. For the *Emergency* signal, wave your arms over your head with the hands out.

There also are two important signals that cannot be done with paddles:

Eddy out. Usually done by the lead boat to signal that the group or pod will be eddying out, a paddle cannot be used for this signal because it would look too much like the *Emergency* signal. Face forward and extend the arm on the side of the river the eddy is on. Bend the arm at the elbow and trace a few circles in the air with your index finger and hand, and then point directly at the eddy. The arm used should be on the same side as the eddy; if you point across the chest with the other arm, no one will see it.

I'm OK. This signal is actually a question-and-answer system to assess swimmers' condition, gauge readiness, and get a sense of an individual or group. The first person asks, "Are you OK?" by patting himself on the top of the helmet with his fist and making eye contact with the subject, and potentially yelling the question as well. The subject responds with the same motion, essentially answering, "I am OK!" If she does not respond, unless she is not paying attention, the first person knows she may be injured or unconscious.

Whistle Signals

Every paddler should have a whistle on the PFD, and these can be used to indicate needs or situations by agreeing on what a certain number of blasts means. However, even a very loud whistle like the Fox 40 can be drowned out by the white noise of very large rapids and significant distance. Generally, multiple and continuous loud blasts mean there is an emergency. Your group can designate meaning to one or two short or long blasts if there is a significant need on a river with lots of blind corners. Whistles are also great for lost portagers or swimmers to indicate their whereabouts.

Signal Use

Signals can be used to communicate subtly different messages, and if all team members are not on the same page about the meaning of each signal the group will use, this can easily end in disaster or decreased functionality. For example, say the group is eddied out on river left at the base of a cliff, with few scouting or portaging options, and there is an obscured and loud rapid just around the next bend of the river. The group decides that the lead boat and one buddy boat will ferry to the other, much mellower shore to gather more information. Once they reach the other shore, they give a *Go* paddle signal, but the rest of the group has no idea whether that means they should go downstream, ferry to the lead boat, or that all is clear. Deciding what a signal will mean beforehand in a specific situation prepares the lines of communication to function. If the options are too numerous or the plan is anything but simple, it is best not to commit to a situation where detailed communication will be difficult and perhaps even irreversible, if the boats cannot get back together.

ASSIGNMENT OF BOAT ROLES

The free-form pod formations that occur organically on gentle flat water can be dangerous in rough lake conditions or on moving water. On an institutional expedition, it is appropriate for the designated staff to paddle in the lead and sweep boats, with some variation for teaching and risk management purposes. On a team expedition, your group should agree on assigned

Often, your peers are the best source of coaching to improve your technique. Hess River, Yukon Territory.

boat roles and the order in which they will travel based on the skill, experience, and leadership ability of the paddlers.

Lead Boat

The role of the team in the lead boat is to make the hundreds of tiny decisions that must be made throughout the day and to set the group up for making the larger, more important, and higher-risk decisions, as well as potentially guiding those processes. The designated leader of the day or the expedition is often in this boat or very close by. The lead boat need not stand alone, but because it is the first boat in each situation, on the river or lake, its team must react before everyone else most of the time.

The paddlers in the lead boat thus have the most responsibility in the group, and while they can be a mixed pair in terms of skill, the weakest paddlers or least functional pair should not be in the lead boat. Take turns being the lead boat day to day.

The only special gear that those in the lead boat should consider carrying is a throw bag, and especially on rivers, possibly a second throw bag rigged as a towing system (discussed in chapter 11). Having a full suite of navigational aids—maps, compass, and guidebook—means the lead paddlers can reliably go in the right direction, with the backup of other paddlers checking their work and following along.

The lead boat can have many responsibilities, including setting gathering points after a rapid and watching each boat for signs of distress. Hyland River, Yukon Territory.

Sweep Boat

The standard role of the sweep boat—in an unchanging boat order—can be a relaxing and enjoyable one, but it is not without responsibility. Its job often includes maintaining good spacing in the pod, regulating the flow out of eddies and down rapids through verbal and paddle signals, and occasionally performing rescues. Because it is almost always the farthest upstream of all the boats, and because of its role, the sweep boat must have one of the stronger and more self-sufficient teams of paddlers in the group, as helping or rescuing those in the sweep boat can be very difficult and sometimes even impossible.

The rescue kit is often located in the sweep boat so that most resources will be upstream of a potential pin and can be paddled down to an incident rather than carried or moved upstream. However, if the entire rescue kit is in the sweep boat, and that boat pins, the group will not have access to potentially needed rescue items. An alternative is to spread the contents of the rescue kit among the other boats in the group, adding a few more throw bags with static line. This will make the group more flexible in dealing with rescue situations anywhere in the boat order. The downside is that in an emergency situation, the necessary gear may have to be gathered from several boats and might not add up to a full system, so some thought should be put into where things are located beforehand, depending on group members' skill levels and the needs of the river.

Adequate spacing allows the safety boat to respond to trouble. Clarence River, New Zealand.

Safety Boat

The safety boat's role is to be in the position in a set of rapids where assistance or rescue will be most likely needed. Sometimes this is a fluid placement and other times it is a deliberate spot, such as behind a pin rock or in a midrapid eddy, that affords the most options for rescuing swimmers or boats. Typically, one boat fulfills this role throughout the day, meaning that one or two people can be relied on to be in the appropriate mindset and to catch eddies or pause in dangerous places spontaneously to support, cover, and assist. Alternatively, your group might designate a single boat as the safety boat before entering each set of rapids, while a safety plan is being formulated, or on an ad hoc basis in the heart of a deteriorating situation.

On flat water, the team in the safety boat might take up a position on the side of the group away from shore to gauge incoming swell and distance from the shore, as well as to serve as sentries on the outside of turns while rounding points. They can also consider carrying a throw bag rigged as a towing system, the medical kit, or both, assuming the role of a tugboat or medical frigate.

Buddy Boats

Buddy boating is a group travel technique in which an even number of boats are split up into pairs that have ultimate responsibility for one another. The two teams of paddlers in each pair look out for and check in with each other. This is most useful with large numbers of canoes or in river environments that are very narrow and where no one can see all the other boats for long. Buddy boating can also be a boon when lining, wading, tracking, or portaging for extended periods of time, in that two extra people will be nearby to help with stuck boats or difficult moves. In downriver travel, lead, sweep, and safety boat responsibilities can be divided in a buddy boat setup. In one scenario, the buddy boat follows the lead boat into a set of rapids, the two teams set running safety for each other—positioning the boat to perform a rescue if needed—and they both stop below to wait for the rest of the group to follow. This provides some coverage and support for the lead boat.

Pod Travel

Alternatively, your group can travel in pods of three or four boats each. This is most useful in mild to medium flat water or river conditions when covering distance or if teaching in an institutional setting is the goal. If there are three experienced paddlers or teams, and a total of nine boats, then it is easy to form three pods with someone experienced in each one. One-on-one attention is possible in this system, as is a close management setup. In anything more than easy water, the group should probably be functioning as a single organism for management and communication purposes. If there are more than nine or ten boats on the expedition, pod travel can be somewhat unwieldy.

Leapfrogging

With experienced teams, having the lead and sweep boats leapfrog can be more efficient and offer better safety coverage. The team in the lead boat descends a set of rapids or length of river and sets safety, letting the other boats join them and watching the sweep boat descend past them to become the lead boat and continue downstream. This is best suited for longer stretches of read and run moving water (water that is easily boat scouted).

Reading the Water

Reading and interpreting water well is not an art, it is an attainable skill that must be practiced and honed like any other. Highly experienced paddlers might naturally see barely noticeable lines and subtle differences in currents, whereas novices might not be able to put the pieces together and may not even be aware of their ignorance. Growing the skill of reading water is about understanding water environments on a scientific, observable level, but also about developing a feeling for water, particularly moving water, through experience. Paddling with more experienced people who can

Analyzing water is like learning to read a new language: learn the characters (eddies, holes, waves), start small and simple, and practice. Seagull Creek, Yukon Territory.

guide, teach, and point things out is a helpful step in bridging the theoretical and the kinesthetic. Scouting is an important first step to reading the water, and a tool set for scouting rapids follows.

SCOUTING

Scouting—the act of choosing a line down a set of rapids—can be broken down into nested steps or tools that will help a group of paddlers manage risk as they are moving downriver. It is worth being systematic so as to support the sound communication and decision-making that are required for managing risk. On institutional or educational expeditions, the value of structured scouting is paramount.

A key element of scouting, in any form, is communicating what you see to other people. Some may not have been present to see the same things you did, but even those who were will not interpret what they see the same way. It is vital that everyone on an expedition use the same language for the same things. It helps to agree upon the terminology for certain structures and features in advance, like calling the right side of the river when looking downstream "river right" and the left side "river left." Whether the group calls a recirculating feature a hole or a hydraulic does not matter, as long as the whole group uses similar language and everyone knows what the word refers to.

There must be a group culture of encouraging folks to elucidate exactly what they intend to do, both to help them clarify their intentions and to let the group know of their plans. "Rebecca and I are thinking about paddling down and hitting the eddy at the bottom" is a poor way of describing a line. Compare that to saying, "Rebecca and I are going to start left, run right of center, finish right, and then wait for the group in the eddy by the big willow tree." Clear, detail-oriented communication is vital.

Blind corners, cliffs, and bends can make scouting difficult, but getting to the bottom of a rapid is key, so there are no surprises. Bonnet Plume River, Yukon Territory.

Tool Set for Scouting Rapids

There are four steps to scouting rapids, each of which answers an important question: How are we going to scout this set of rapids? What is going on in the rapids? Are we going to run the rapids? If so, how are we going to run the rapids?

1. The view from the lead boat: How are we going to scout this set of rapids? The lead boat should decide whether to scout from the boat, "read-and-run," or whether to stop and scout from the shore. Paddlers can recognize several factors that indicate the need to scout a set of rapids. First, the rapids should be scouted if the paddlers cannot see the bottom of the rapids or a place, usually an eddy, where they are positive the entire group can gather with little notice; rounding a blind corner, especially with obvious whitewater present, is a recipe for disaster.

Second, if the paddlers can see or sense significant and obvious hazards such as undercut rocks, large holes or wave trains, water pushing into sharp rocks or cliff walls, or strainers, scouting is a good idea. Third, if the paddlers can see that this set of rapids quickly flows into another set, or that the run-out is not long or calm enough for a rescue to be easily performed, more in-depth scouting should be attempted. Part of judging the run-out is making sure there is an obvious place at the bottom of the rapids where the whole group can gather; if there is not such an eddy or beach, get out and scout to find a place where all the boats can meet up after running the rapids.

In situations where it is necessary to get out of the boats to scout, the leaders need to find a place where the entire group can gather above the rapids. The paddlers in the lead boat need to make sure that the other boats will not drift into the rapids. A large eddy, beach, or low shore makes an ideal pausing place. The site should be chosen well upstream of the drop so as not to commit the group to any mandatory line down the rapid. For example, if you choose an eddy on river left below a cliff that will make portaging or lining difficult or impossible, then the group's only options will be to run the rapids or ferry to river right. If the eddy chosen is too far downstream to safely ferry from, the group may be forced to paddle a difficult line down the rapid.

Scouting positions can include the following, ranging from those that take the least amount of time and commitment to those that take the most: boat scouting by slowing down above a drop to analyze it and possibly standing up to increase depth of field; pulling over to scout but not getting out of the boat; getting out the boat to stand up and maybe walk up the bank; sending two people down to scout and either come back with a plan or call to bring down the whole group; or taking the whole group down from the start. Often scouting may involve a combination of these options.

Boat scouting is an efficient way to process information and execute a plan, so long as the water is straightforward and well within your and the group's ability. Desolation Canyon, Green River, Utah.

Scouting from land, like here on the Bonnet Plume River in Yukon Territory, can be time consuming in some cases, but is often necessary if the difficulty and complexity of the whitewater and skill of the group warrant.

When scouting from on land, scout from the point of best visibility or from several different points.

Tie up the boats securely if you get out to scout on land. Getting to a good scouting spot in time to watch an empty canoe run the rapids is an experience many paddlers have had, but it is easily avoided. Tying each boat's painter line individually and tightly to a tree or rock with a bowline, three half hitches, or mooring hitch takes just twenty seconds and gives supreme piece of mind. Pulling the boats up onshore while loaded can cause damage or the potential for water leakage, but it is sometimes the only option in an environment with no ready anchors.

Scouting very long, multipart rapids or gorges can turn into full-on day hikes without much warning; it can be helpful to treat them as such by packing a daypack with food, water, and layers. Even a short scout gives you enough time to eat and drink to restore your functionality, and even an easy scout probably warrants having your helmets and PFDs clipped and zipped. Also take along at least one throw bag in case someone ends up in the water. Maintain structure from the outset. The number of factors involved in scouting even a small and short set of rapids can be staggering.

Sometimes you have no choice but to clamber over rocks and up to some promontory to see around the next bend or get a better angle on a

Scouting from Above

I once observed a tourist in a Starter jacket gaze carefully over the edge of the 90-foot (27-meter) cliffs that make up Class V Rip Gorge on Maine's West Branch of the Penobscot and casually remark, "Honey, isn't Class V the biggest? It doesn't look too bad from here."

This demonstrates an important point: it is not a great idea to scout from on high. Looking down on a set of rapids from an elevated position flattens out its hydrologic features, and you lose the depth of field proportional to the distance from the object. This misperception might lead you to make a poor decision.

Scouting from high above a rapid can flatten or obscure its features, but is often the only way to scout gorges without committing to running them. This rapid is the Ripogenus Gorge on the West Branch of the Penobscot River in Maine.

chute on the other side of the river. Still, scouting is best done from river level and, if possible, complemented by an overview later.

2. WORMMSS: What is going on in the rapids? There are various methods for gathering and organizing the information that everyone sees while scouting a set of rapids. The acronym WORMMSS represents one simple method that can also serve as a checklist to make sure the group recognizes and plans for all the parts of a descent. First and foremost, it is an aid for reading water and should not be viewed or used as a decision-making tool.

Water. Where is the water going? How much water is there, and where is the current moving (e.g., where will the river carry a floating stick)?

Obstacles. What obstacles are present in the rapids? Is the water pushing into them?

Route. What lines exist in the rapids?

Moves. What moves or maneuvers are necessary to execute those lines? Can all of the paddlers make those moves reliably?

Markers. Are there clear features in or beside the rapids that can help paddlers stay oriented while negotiating the length of the rapids? These might include rocks, trees, holes, standing waves, or eddies. On longer or more complicated rapids, markers can be a great help in pacing moves. Features within the rapids are much more useful as markers than ones beside the rapids.

Swimming. If any boats swamp or capsize and paddlers end up in the water, where are they going to swim to get out of the rapids? Or will they ride out the length of the rapids?

Safety. Where should the expedition's rescue resources—throw bags and safety boats—be placed? What are the options for self-rescue?

Over time, experienced paddlers will internalize these steps and will not need to think through the whole process, but with novices, a mixed team, or people that have not paddled together before, it is often helpful to fully verbalize these things to make sure that everyone is on the same page and speaking the same language. Applying the WORMMSS tool to a set of rapids gives a good sense of what information has been gathered and what each paddler is seeing, but it does not actually make the decision of whether or not to run the rapids.

3. Decision-making with four questions: Are we going to run the rapids? Asking four simple questions will provide structure to the decision-making process and help your group decide whether to run a set of rapids. It helps to directly verbalize the following questions and the ideas behind them: Can we see a navigable line or route through the rapids? Can the entire group make the line? What are the consequences of not making the line? Are these consequences acceptable or is the risk involved too great?

The bottom line is that your group should not run a particular set of rapids if you cannot see a navigable route or line through the rapids; if any paddlers cannot reasonably be expected to make the line based on their experience, skill level, or current physical state; or if the consequences of not making the line would constitute unacceptable levels of risk.

Realize that no one has to run anything. The social or institutional pressure to run a set of rapids or paddle out of cover on a rough lake can be immense. Everyone needs to know that whether to take a particular risk is a personal choice and that there are always other options besides running the rapids. Some people can paddle and some can walk; the ones that paddle can even tie up and help out. The correct answer to the question "Is it OK if our boat doesn't run this one?" is yes. It can be worth mentioning this to the group as a whole, depending on its makeup.

4. Making a plan: How are we going to run the rapids? If, after scouting and analyzing the water, your group has decided to run this set of rapids, the final step is to make a plan for how the boats are going to descend the rapids. Most elements of the plan are actually already there; they just need to be put together. A line has already been chosen, and if anyone is going to deviate from the obvious line, everyone knows about it and has acknowledged it; a safety plan has been made, with a safety boat or two designated, throw bags installed if deemed necessary, and swimming and self-rescue options identified; and all the paddlers have a good sense of where they need to be in the rapids and what moves are required, and they feel confident in following through. All that remains is establishing an order of operations and communication protocols.

The lead boat usually descends first, after the rest of the boats are ready to follow. How the other boats follow the lead boat can vary, depending on the skill of the group and the significance of the rapids. It is sometimes

Positioning your team to scout the intended route is important; if the intended route changes, move to a new location or side of the river to scout, if necessary, as these paddlers are doing on the Gray Canyon of the Green River in Utah.

helpful to number the boats or have a set and known order of some other kind. There are three common organizational structures:

Boats follow one at a time. Each boat starts out when the boat in front of it has reached the final eddy or gathering point safely. Simply seeing the boat reach that point is often enough of a signal to start, but if the distance is great, a paddle signal works well.

Boats follow with spacing. After a boat has gone a set distance or has passed a certain point, usually after the most important or difficult move, the next boat begins its run. The distance between boats can be as much as ten boat lengths to give the upstream boat plenty of time to maneuver or eddy out if the downstream boat runs into trouble, but three boat lengths may be enough in straightforward, clear rapids with no chance of getting hung up or swamped.

Boats follow on signals. The next boat in line starts when a paddle signal is given and returned. One person in the starting eddy should be designated as the sender and another at the gathering eddy as the receiver. The sender should look for a signal from the receiver and be able to determine that the rapids are clear and all the boats are in good positions before sending the next boat down. On long rapids with numerous bends, where the starting eddy is out of sight of the gathering eddy, members of the expedition can be spread out to pass along the signal.

Travel Tactics

SPACING

Adequate spacing between boats is a consideration not just in rapids, but in all kinds of water on the expedition. Agreeing on and maintaining appropriate spacing from the beginning of the trip will help prevent collisions and give upstream boats sufficient space to maneuver to avoid any hazards the leaders point out. Most important, it gives the following boats time to back ferry or charge out of the way if the lead boat runs into trouble or gives a stop signal because of unforeseen hazards. Two boat lengths might be acceptable on flat water, but on moving water, more is better while still keeping close enough to maintain contact by sight or communication.

EMERGENCY STOPS

On narrow, continuous, or fast-flowing rivers, hazards can appear quite quickly, and the situation can rapidly deteriorate. In an emergency situation, maintaining good spacing means that upstream boats will not run into the pinned boat or crowd the lead boat as it is back ferrying to shore. Ideally, someone will recognize the incident or downstream hazard—a horizon line,

On a river with continuous runnable whitewater, like on Seagull Creek in Yukon Territory, the group can sometimes get spread out. If a significant hazard suddenly presents itself or a boat gets into trouble, the whole group might need to stop abruptly.

Breaking gorges and long continuous rapids down into smaller sections with large easy eddies between them is a helpful strategy, but stay aware of downstream consequences and committing a group to a series of must-make moves. Seagull Creek, Yukon Territory.

a capsized or swamped boat, rapids that are unexpectedly challenging and warrant a new plan—and give the *Stop* signal. Most of the time, those in the other boats will not have seen the reason for the stop, but they do not have to see it—they only need to stop immediately upon receiving the signal.

This calls for a rapid response and is not a suggestion—all boats should immediately move to shore even if it is not an ideal spot. It is necessary to exercise good judgment here so that no additional

Scouting a long rapid or gorge, like this one on the Bonnet Plume River in Yukon Territory, can be very slow, so secure the boats well and consider bringing daypacks. At a certain level of complexity, it may be simpler to portage.

boats are lost and as many boats as possible gather in the same spot, or at least on the same side of the river. Often an adequate eddy will be nearby, but it may be easier if each boat simply moves to the same shore, rather than trying to group up in one eddy, which might be unworkable. If there is no eddy or only a flushing one, the bow paddler will have to jump out and anchor the canoe as it spins in to shore, or both paddlers may have to grab onto vegetation or trees to hold their boat in place. There are risks involved in an emergency stop, so when one is called, it should be for good reason.

EDDY HOPPING

In long or continuous rapids of a certain acceptable level of difficulty, it is possible to link up a series of eddies to slow and control the flow of the group through that set. In some situations, it is a wonderful endeavor for play or practice; at higher risk levels, it is a way of sneaking down one side or another, pausing to reassess at each eddy. Use care in choosing eddies, regarding both size and level of commitment.

RUNNING LONG RAPIDS AND GORGES

The problems noted above with scouting long sets of continuous rapids or gorges are just the beginning of the challenges in such river environments.

Staying focused on the water can sometimes blind you to the changing landscape. Watch out for new rock types and closing hills and cliff bands that might indicate you are entering a gorge, like here on the Tungnaá River in Iceland.

Remembering all the features and hazards in a large, continuous 2.5-mile (4-kilometer) set of rapids is impossible, as is adequately setting safety for a pod of loaded boats that will be running these rapids. A canoe flipping on an eddy line in Class II rapids is usually a minor and easily remedied incident, but if such an incident occurs in the entrance rapid to a continuous gorge, the boat and swimmers may be carried downstream before they can execute a self-rescue or be rescued. Worse, the paddlers in a safety boat may have to decide to chase them into unknown and unprepared-for waters, putting themselves at significant risk and splitting up the group. Packing boats to be self-sufficient is great preparation on such remote, continuous, or exploratory rivers.

The first step in analyzing a long set of rapids or a gorge is to determine whether it is committing and, if so, the level of commitment. That is to say, once the paddlers begin the stretch, will they be able to get out any way other than by paddling to the bottom? There are different levels and types of commitment. Consider whether there are options to line or portage, camp along the shore, how steep the sides are, how flood-prone the river is, and whether a helicopter can access the gorge if necessary.

Determine if this stretch can be run in digestible stages with clear markers and good eddies or pausing places. Broken up into stages, trickier sections can be lined or portaged and easier ones paddled, with the boats waded through on the inside beaches of large bends. Eddy hopping can work well, as can hugging close to one shore the whole way. One side of the river may be committing while the other is not; your group should take this into account on a particularly wide or hard-to-cross river. The options are many and depend on the paddlers' experience and skill levels, as well as the local river environment.

CHAPTER 8 | TRAVEL SKILLS

Ideas and techniques for canoe travel in moving and open water, on the ocean, over land, and in ice, including using lines and poling

Open-water travel, lining, tracking, poling, ice traveling, portaging, and a variety of other expeditionary skills were honed over thousands of years by indigenous North Americans in bark and skin boats. These skills developed in response to the need to move through seasonally marginal environments quickly, safely, and with significant loads. The same need forced Europeans to adapt and modify them for commercial and exploratory pursuits.

As you travel through some of the same environments on your own expeditions, you will come to recognize the utility of these skills. Many of these are niche travel skills, however, in that most paddlers will not use them most of the time. Getting by without them is possible on many routes, and plenty of paddlers will not have the need to use these skills or see the need to practice them. However, incorporating flexibility in your traveling methods and risk management structure offers a great sense of accomplishment, well worth the investment of time and energy.

Well-rounded expedition paddlers practice a variety of skills and employ a range of tools. They may focus on the ones they will use the most, but each new skill or tool makes possible new avenues of exploration. Expedition paddlers should seek to learn from those with skills and specialties different from their own. Some paddlers have prejudices against flatwater newbies, sit-and-switch racers, or creek-focused OC-1 open canoe paddlers, for example. But if you keep an open mind, you can learn something from other paddlers with different skills: the efficiency of a river guide, the biomechanics of a flatwater racer, the control of a slalom racer, the risk management of an instructor, the lining and portaging skills of the traditional guide. All these paths lead to accessing new environments and experiencing new joys.

Mastering a variety of skills will make you a well-rounded expedition paddler, and you should treat each skill with the same respect as simple flatwater paddling or complex river running and view it as having similar value. They are all tools you can add to your toolkit.

The Use of Lines

Lining is like being an acrobat and a puppeteer at the same time.
—Robert Perkins, *Against Straight Lines: Alone in Labrador*

Lining refers to the act of moving a canoe downstream with the use of lines, but it is sometimes used to describe *tracking*, the act of moving a canoe upstream with the use of lines.

The use of lines on a canoe expedition opens up a whole world of possibilities in ascending and descending rivers. Lining is dual in nature in that you must manage your canoe in a dynamic liquid environment and a static solid environment simultaneously, dancing with your partner onshore while flying a 400-pound (181-kilogram) "kite" in the river. Multiply this by as many as twenty expedition members and ten boats, and throw in upward of 500 feet (152 meters) of line, and you have some idea of the complexity and potential hazards of this technique. The act of lining is a technical skill that requires significant practice and management, and because you are working in two environments, it is arguably more complex than paddling. Under the

Lining is a basic skill for river travel. North Branch Big Salmon River, Yukon Territory.

Lining through challenging water or terrain, as on the Desolation Canyon of the Green River in Utah, requires teamwork and communication.

right circumstances, however, the use of lines to descend or ascend a stretch of moving water is a vital skill in the expedition paddler's toolbox.

Lining is an art honed through practice, and it has much to lend in developing your general river sense and canoe handling skill, as it relies on the same knowledge of the movement of water and its friction on a boat's hull. When lining, no one is in the boat, so it can be spun and maneuvered countless times in rapid succession, and thus you think of its orientation in terms of an upstream and a downstream end, rather than bow and stern. It occasionally relies on the natural ferrying behavior of a canoe in current to provide control.

It is easy to underestimate the risks and challenges of lining, especially because most people feel somewhat safer onshore, and this can result in complacency, which can be dangerous. Things can go wrong while lining, and when they do, they happen just as fast as when paddling, so it is important to stay focused.

DECIDING WHEN TO LINE

What makes a good or bad lining environment is complicated, but it is usually a function of the quality of the footpath onshore and the river path in the water, combined with the consequences of something going wrong. In general terms, you have three propulsion options when faced with moving water: you can paddle, line, or portage. After evaluating the hazards of a given piece of moving water, you can make a generalized decision as to whether the section is runnable, marginally runnable, or unrunnable. In many cases, an ideal lining opportunity is a marginal paddling opportunity, and an ideal portaging opportunity is a marginal lining opportunity. The options might look something like this:

	Paddle	**Line**	**Portage**
Runnable	ideal	good	good
Marginally runnable	marginal	ideal	good
Unrunnable	poor	marginal	ideal

In reality, the situation is usually more complex, but the above tool is a helpful starting point, especially if you are a novice liner. If you are contemplating lining, always consider efficiency in your decision. It may be faster and safer to portage, depending on the environment.

When making the decision whether to line, a thorough evaluation of both the river and shore environments is necessary. The scouting model described in the previous chapter still largely applies. A decision not to paddle a set of rapids implies the recognition of a potential level of risk of injury or equipment damage that still exists in the lining scenario. Scouting using structure and critical analysis and observation are still a part of scouting for lining.

LINING PRIORITIES

Establishing a set of priorities can provide a helpful hierarchy when dealing with something as complicated as lining and line use. To a lining novice, this is a helpful structure to refer to.

Personal

Wear your PFD and helmet while lining and remember that your first priority is yourself. One of the only rules in lining is not to put knots or wraps in the line because they can get caught on a body part or stuck on a rock underwater. A natural tendency is to wrap the line around your body or hand in order to get a better grip. This is dangerous. Under sudden tension, the line will seize around the body part and could potentially cause injury or drag you into the water. Know when to let go of the line. When the ferry angle of the canoe has been lost and the leverage of the current against the upstream line is threatening to flip the boat, it is time to let go. The canoe will hopefully float right side up down the rapids and can be collected at the bottom. In high-speed and high-consequence drops, it might make sense to sit down and belay the canoe with another person ready to anchor you.

Making a Butterfly Coil

When facing the direction of travel, one personal system is to have the shore-side hand storing the rope in a neat butterfly coil and the river-side hand acting as a brake that occasionally passes line into the butterfly coil or takes it out again. The butterfly coil in boating is a variation of the one used by climbers to carry ropes when not in use. One hand is outstretched, with a bight lying across it. Lift the line running to the ground and lay it across your hand, forming a second, matching bight; this forms the wings of the butterfly. Repeat the process on alternate sides until the rope is coiled. The advantage over a normal round coil is that tension on the line will pull it out of, rather than around, your hand. Start with the end farthest from the canoe, so that the line is stacked in your hand and can pay out easily.

Your Boat Partner

After yourself, your boat partner is your next priority. Constant communication—even to the point of overdoing it and asking for confirmation and clarification—is critical when lining. Each of you should know in advance what your boat partner intends to do and when. With the roar of moving water sometimes only a few feet away, the importance of making eye contact with your partner while communicating cannot be overestimated.

The Group

After considering what is happening around yourself and around your boat partner, your next priority is group awareness and communication. What are the other members

Your priority in lining is to yourself first, and then to your boat partner, to the group, to your boat, to the group's boats, and to other group's boats, in that order. Desolation Canyon, Green River, Utah.

The liner is stationary while making an easy but high-consequence move on the Clarence River in New Zealand. The river side hand is a brake, and the shore-side hand holds the unused line.

of the team doing? How are they progressing? Where are they placing themselves, and are they in the way?

See how the individual team members fit in and in what ways they can be most helpful to the group's mission. The emphasis here again is on communication.

The Boats

The canoe is less of a priority than managing the expedition's human resources. You must remember your priorities—if the swamped canoe is going to pull you into the rapids, then let go. Your personal safety is more important than your pride or any gear that might be lost.

Before lining begins, all gear should be firmly secured, ideally below the gunwales, with water bottles clipped in and paddles tied or jammed in below the gunwales (paddles tend to grab line when they extend above the gunwales). In other words, the boat should be truly "rigged to flip." If the expedition will be doing extensive lining, adjusting boat trim can be an energy saver. The canoe is weighted downstream whether it is being lined or tracked. This brings the upstream end just out of the water and makes lining easier and safer by decreasing the pressure the water is capable of exerting on the upstream end of the hull.

Often you may need to anchor your boat to allow your partner to jump ahead and help another pair with a difficult move. Or, you may need to coach and inform other boat teams as they move through a tricky spot.

When only one line is engaged, one person is freed up to assist other boats, or just relax and move downstream. Clarence River, New Zealand.

LINING STYLES

The skill level of the liners and the complexity and consequences of both the river path and footpath dictate which style of lining is best. Following are a few different styles, from simple to complex.

One Line: Walking the Dog

Best suited for slower-moving water with few obstacles or novice liners on even, clear riverbanks. Also helpful when an expedition is lining continuously for several days at a time, as team members can take turns to conserve energy.

The simplest form of lining involves taking the upstream line and walking the dog along shore.

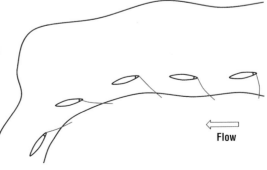

Flow

One person controls each canoe with a short upstream line, holding the upstream end of the canoe close to shore while the current moves the boat downstream.

This method has the advantage of freeing the second boat partner for help on hard moves, in station lining, as a spotter or support person for the liner, or for scouting ahead. It has the disadvantage of putting just one person and one line in control of the boat, with that person moving over potentially uneven terrain.

One Line: Leapfrogging

Best suited for fairly straightforward water with an uneven footpath or a river path that requires avoiding an obstacle.

One person controls the canoe with the upstream line, pushing the boat out into the current and then letting it pendulum back to shore downstream, where the other team member catches the boat and takes control of the upstream line. Then the first person moves downstream to catch. The advantage of this technique is that while moving along shore, you can focus on the footpath and not worry about the stationary boat; only a person or the boat is moving at one time, allowing you to focus on one or the other.

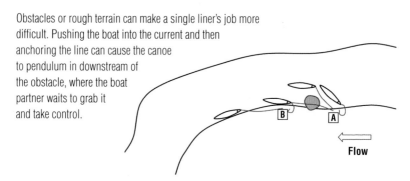

Obstacles or rough terrain can make a single liner's job more difficult. Pushing the boat into the current and then anchoring the line can cause the canoe to pendulum in downstream of the obstacle, where the boat partner waits to grab it and take control.

Flow

Two Lines: The Puppet Show

Best suited for competent liners in faster-moving water with clear, open riverbanks, especially if there are obstacles near shore that need to be avoided.

Two people control each canoe with upstream and downstream lines. The downstream person does much of the steering and route finding, while the upstream person acts as a brake and maintains the angle. If no obstacles exist, the upstream end can be held close to shore while the downstream end is let out a few feet. If obstacles must be navigated, the upstream end is let out while the downstream end is snugged in so as to create a ferry angle.

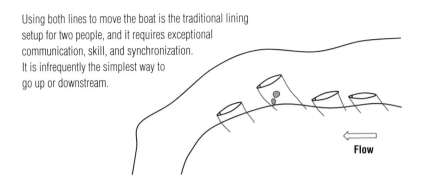

Using both lines to move the boat is the traditional lining setup for two people, and it requires exceptional communication, skill, and synchronization. It is infrequently the simplest way to go up or downstream.

Flow

The canoe wants to ferry away from shore, which puts tension on the lines, giving you the control to move the boat around obstacles.

Two Lines: Leapfrogging
Best suited for rocky, uneven terrain or big, higher-consequence water.

With both boat partners engaged, you have the ability to leapfrog and pass the lines. The upstream line is pulled in and held close to the boat, while the running end is coiled and tossed to the downstream liner. The downstream liner puts his line in the boat and takes the upstream line, allowing the boat to move one boat length downstream. The upstream liner then moves around to become the downstream liner. This has the advantage of eliminating the need for each individual to manage lines, boat, and self simultaneously while moving over the ground; the boat is stationary while a person moves, and vice versa.

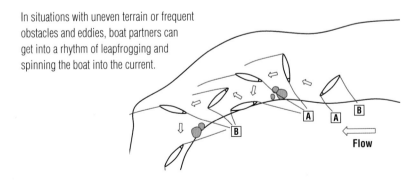

In situations with uneven terrain or frequent obstacles and eddies, boat partners can get into a rhythm of leapfrogging and spinning the boat into the current.

Flow

Station Lining, or Stage Lining: The Assembly Line
Best suited for very uneven or hazardous riverbanks next to higher-consequence rapids.

In station, or stage, lining, the group spreads out along the rapid, building an assembly line and then passing each boat through it. A variety of hands-on or lining moves might be involved. San Juan River, Utah.

The group is spread out along shore in stationary locations, and the canoes are passed through one at a time from person to person, entering at one end and being moved through to a clear collecting point.

This has two primary advantages. First, each member of the system is akin to a factory worker on an assembly line and becomes competent at one specific move in one hydrologic situation, repeating the process with each boat. Second, the hazards of the static environment—the riverbank—are reduced by not requiring individuals to navigate along a footpath, as they remain in fixed positions. More skilled or experienced group members can be placed on harder moves, allowing each member of the expedition the appropriate level of challenge. One larger theme that station lining hits on is the idea that when faced with an increased risk level, it can be managed in part by making a dynamic situation into a static one. The move is simplified and easy to manage. It has the disadvantage of being slower than other styles, but this is often outweighed by the advantage of exposing the paddlers and boats to less risk.

Hands-On
Best suited for heavily obstructed or shallow sections, or where access from shore is easy and secure.

Station lining in rapids that have swift currents through the intended lining route, as on the Desolation Canyon section of the Green River in Utah, often requires the liners to be quite close to the boats, or even have their hands on them, to better control them.

This variation is used where the riverbank is such that it is possible or even necessary to move the boats with little or no use of the lines. With the paddlers keeping their hands on the gunwales, the boat is moved either by partners or by the group in a station setup. This allows a larger measure of control, but only in specific shore environments.

Obstacles such as shallow water, tree strainers, or heavy water can necessitate taking the hands-on system a step further. Most of the boats are secured, and eight or more people use good lifting technique—bending the legs and keeping chins up—to move a single loaded boat at a time around or, more often, over the obstacle. Establishing a single move leader who can set up other roles and communication systems for this method is helpful.

Long Lining

Best suited for clear, open rivers with uneven or heavily vegetated banks or for clean, open, big-water rapids with clear banks.

Long lining refers to the use of a very long length of line to skip past significant shore and river obstacles, either to move more efficiently or because there is no other lining option. Throw bags can be used and can be turned around to prevent the bag from getting caught along shore or in the rapids. This technique can be repeated in a cycle to line long distances.

If you encounter steep, obstacle-free, big-water rapids with a nasty or dangerous downstream run-out, lining may be a good, if time-consuming, option. One canoe at a time can be pushed hard out into the current, while the person in control of a 50-foot (15.2-meter) or more line is standing onshore halfway down. The canoe bobs and floats down, light enough not to swamp or punch large waves, and is pendulumed into shore at the bottom. All the boats pass quickly through the system.

Alternatively, your group might make the decision to line while descending a gorge or section of river with continuous rapids that cover a long distance. Unfortunately, the shoreline has dense, overhanging trees and brush, and no one can reach the river without getting into deep, moving water. In this situation, your group chooses sending and receiving spots onshore, and then collects the boats upstream. One at a time, the boats are thrust into the current and floated or pendulumed down to the receiving spot.

Combinations

In reality, moving a canoe expedition downstream or upstream often requires employing a myriad of techniques, sometimes simultaneously. For example, on a canoe run through Lodore Canyon, an expedition was faced with descending the long, multistage rapids called Hell's Half Mile, which takes the river around three bends, over a falls, and past islands and cliffs. The expedition portaged the initial falls; had partners use two lines to cover the open-shored middle; set up a station line on the rocky, cliff-bound section; and finally, paddled out the bottom.

Tracking

Tracking is best accomplished with the upstream person one boat length ahead of the boat and the downstream person around the center thwart. This maintains a ferry angle that creates tension on the ropes and allows the trackers to just walk upstream without the canoe being pushed into the shore. The advantage of this method is that upcoming hazards will be obvious before the current puts boats or people in jeopardy.

More often than not, the finesse of moving upstream is lost on small or steep creeks or in areas with obscured banks; this is mostly the case when going upstream on small, steep rivers or streams to help access larger watersheds. Progress is made with lots of wading, dragging, and hauling rather than the fancy tracking that is possible in deeper water.

Tracking with a Bridle

Best suited for experienced liners tracking in deep water for extended periods with riverbanks clear of obstacles.

One other tracking option, albeit a time-consuming one, is to fabricate a bridle that is placed on just the upstream end or both ends of the canoe. It consists of two long loops of webbing or rope that pass under the seat and create an attachment point for the painter line, which is actually under the boat. This angle of pull has zero leverage on the gunwales, and no matter how hard you pull, the canoe tends to shed hull drag and not capsize; in deep, big, pushy water this is a great asset. The disadvantages are significant, however: the bridle tends to snag on rocks, the rope creates drag in the water, and it is time-consuming to put on and take off the bridle.

LINING AND TRACKING MOVES

Keeping the Boat Snugged In

In very rough water with few obstacles close to shore, it is often best to ensure that the boat is snugged in while lining. Keeping the upstream end almost onshore allows the current to keep the boat snugged in close to shore and out of nasty water. This tactic is not always pretty, and it can be hard on boats, but it is simple and fast.

Spins

A spin, when the boat rotates 180 degrees, may or may not be intentional. An intentional spin is a powerful tool for moving around significant obstacles that would hamper the movement of boats, lines, or people. The downstream partner anchors, and the other partner pushes the upstream end of the canoe into the current. The boat peels out into the current and is brought back to shore downstream, rotating around its human anchor.

An unintentional spin usually occurs when the ferry angle gets too big for the strength of the current, and the upstream end of the boat starts to turn downstream. You or your partner may be able to correct the spin out by holding the upstream line, but more often than not, if the angle is too wide, the water will push one way and the line will oppose it, causing the boat to capsize. Before that can happen, the upstream partner needs to let go of the line and should be communicating with the other partner all the while. The downstream liner should let the current spin the boat around while securing the line and letting the boat come parallel to shore. Now the upstream end has become the downstream end, and the partners switch places.

On some riverbank types, an expedition may find that the only effective way to line is to "rollerball" the river—that is, to spin dozens of times in a row and have partners leapfrog, or station spin. This technique can be fast and effective.

Ferrying
Much of advanced lining involves simply putting the canoe into a nonlateral ferry angle and maintaining this angle as the boat moves downstream, or upstream in the case of tracking. Lateral (across the river) ferrying is also possible. This requires that the boat partners communicate while slowly, steadily letting out line, maintaining their angle as the current pushes the boat farther out, possibly to pass around an obstacle.

Eddy Turns
In lining an eddy turn, the boat has no paddlers in it to generate tilt, and generating momentum is possible only in some circumstances, so angle is the key here. The two partners work together to position the boat and get the angle they want above the eddy line. Next, the downstream liner moves his tensioned line close to parallel with the canoe and pulls, while the upstream liner throws her line into the boat or river. The boat crosses the eddy line and swings into the eddy.

Eddy Turn into a Spin
Without people, the canoe is vastly lighter and rides higher on the water, reducing the current's pressure on the hull because of the lower surface area. Fast moves between tightly packed rocks now become possible. Two liners can start an eddy turn but let only one-third of the boat enter the eddy. The current spins the boat, and as the liners pass their lines, they maneuver the new downstream end of the canoe into a chute between two rocks that was inaccessible before.

Efficient Travel

Having efficient habits, tools, and structures eliminates many small chunks of wasted time that can quickly add up in camp and on the water. Efficiency also involves taking care of yourself on a basic personal level—eating, drinking, staying out of the sun—in order to remain capable of contributing to the group.

Travel lighter to travel faster. Lighten the load as much as possible by limiting what you take to the essentials and finding things that can do multiple jobs. With fewer pieces of gear, packing and organization are easier.

The secret of covering long stretches of water has little to do with fancy strokes, space-age canoes, and ultralight gear setups. The best way to cover more distance is simply paddling longer. And to paddle longer you need to practice good technique and use efficient body movements.

Open-Water Strategy

Open-water travel includes large rivers, lakes, seas, and oceans. (Ocean travel is discussed in a separate section later in this chapter.) The harsh truth of open-water paddling is that in some circumstances, the consequences for a group can be higher than on a river. On moving water, most incidents involve only one boat and tandem pair. On a large, open body of water, however, it takes only a few relatively minor poor decisions to expose an entire group to nasty consequences, which can be particularly bad in cold water.

Strategy begins with route planning, when good choices are made before the trip in building a route that minimizes exposure on open water as much as possible and provides enough flexibility that you never feel forced to paddle in inappropriate conditions. Initial route planning is followed up in the field with daily planning that supports risk management by minimizing exposure, observing conditions, and constantly communicating. In rough water, interboat communication is extremely challenging.

Of accidents in rough, cold water, sea kayakers like to say that the first thing you will lose is your formation, the second thing you will lose is your ability to communicate, the third thing you will lose is control of the situation, the fourth thing you will lose is your boat, and the last thing you will lose is your life. This can happen even on small lakes, particularly in cold water.

Lakes should be respected and not feared, however. With ample planning, conservative decision-making, and the application of a few flatwater tactics, the risks can be managed.

OPEN-WATER TRAVEL TACTICS

On open water, the direction that the wind originates from is called *windward*, used to refer to the side of a canoe or island that the wind is impacting. The opposite, more protected side is called *leeward*. This is helpful terminology in understanding the three key tactics for open-water travel: stay close to shore; pay attention to the weather; and make informed, conservative decisions about whether to make particular crossings, as knowing how to handle rough water is secondary to knowing to avoid it.

Staying close to an accessible shore is a key tactic on the open water of the Spednic Lake in Maine.

Stay Close to Shore

In the majority of instances of canoe lake travel, the easiest way to manage risk is to stay close to shore. The benefit is twofold: there is usually more protection close to shore, either from points, trees, or the land itself, and in the event of a capsize, the distance a boat and people need to be towed or swim is short. The rougher or colder the water, the closer to shore you should be, under most circumstances. Which shore you choose to paddle close to is important. The wind will blow an unpowered boat onto a shore lying on the leeward side of the boat, called a *lee shore*, and if there are significant reefs, breaking waves, or other hazards, this may be dangerous.

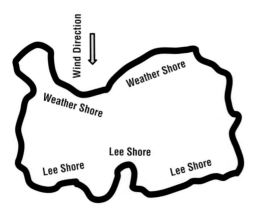

The lee shore is the one toward which wind and waves are moving. The weather shore is the more protected shore where they are coming from.

If conditions are producing a lee shore that is dangerous to a canoe, perhaps the risk is too great and your canoe should not be on the water at all.

The idea of avoiding a lee shore is most helpful on small and medium lakes in a situation like the following: A group enters the lake and can see the outlet directly across the lake. Conditions have deteriorated, with wind blowing perpendicular to the intended direction of travel, and crossing is deemed too high a risk. Both shores would be the same distance to the outlet, but the lee shore is being pummeled by wind and waves. The windward shore, often referred to as the *weather shore*, is calm and protected and provides the easiest and less risky path. The loss of efficiency in hugging the shore can be frustrating. For example, your campsite or portage may be only 1.2 miles (2 kilometers) across the lake, but because the afternoon wind has kicked up whitecaps, your group will hug the shore, adding 6.2 miles (10 kilometers).

Pay Attention to the Weather

Knowing and studying local weather patterns before your trip is only the beginning; on the expedition, it is necessary to constantly assess the conditions, including wind speed and direction, and wave height and period. On a larger scale, following barometric pressure changes and watching the sky can give clues as to weather changes over the next twenty-four hours. Cloud formations, evidence of high-altitude wind, clear evidence of fronts moving in—all these and more can be clues as to expected weather. Carrying a weather radio in large bodies of open water is a good idea, but outside of the United States and southern Canada, reception and coverage might be spotty. A VHF radio can both transmit and receive.

The most common weather event on lakes in the United States and southern Canada is a localized increase in wind that occurs in the afternoon in summer. By that time

Large storms, like this one on the Peel River in Yukon Territory, can move in in minutes, quickly changing the conditions on which you might have made an earlier decision.

of day, the sun has had a chance to heat up the atmosphere. Lakes change temperature slowly and remain colder than the surrounding land, so a temperature difference occurs between the shore and the water, and this causes a pressure difference, resulting in sometimes very strong and dangerous wind. By evening, the heat source has disappeared, and the pressure differential dissipates. Avoiding this localized lake-effect wind is easy, for risk management or efficiency or both: paddle in the morning and be onshore or in a protected spot before the wind starts.

Make Conservative Crossings

The highest risk period of lake travel is in crossing from one shore to another, which can involve paddling from point to point, from mainland to island, or clear across the lake. Crossings are never truly necessary—you can adjust your route to follow the shore all the way to the intended destination and avoid islands. But in many cases, crossings will save enormous amounts of time, sometimes cutting out huge distances of shore-tracing toil with a short, rapid jump.

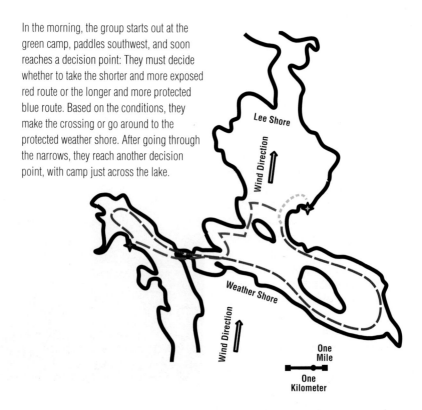

In the morning, the group starts out at the green camp, paddles southwest, and soon reaches a decision point: They must decide whether to take the shorter and more exposed red route or the longer and more protected blue route. Based on the conditions, they make the crossing or go around to the protected weather shore. After going through the narrows, they reach another decision point, with camp just across the lake.

The problem is, lakes can quickly go from calm water and clear skies to whitecaps and rain. So if you choose to cross, look for the narrowest point at which to cross, watch the weather, and don't deviate from a straight course as a way of limiting the exposure.

For a longer crossing, setting a turn-around distance in case of building conditions is a good idea, but far from shore, it can be difficult to judge distances. One trick is to establish your average group speed on flat water by timing distances marked on a map or with a GPS, and then using that information to know where you are in the crossing. Usually if you have reached the halfway point, it is just as easy to keep going, provided there is a clear point of protection at the destination, so choosing a turn-around point one-third of the distance across is best.

EXPOSURE AND PROTECTION

In planning an open-water route, during either route or passage planning, you can identify places of exposure and places of protection with an eye toward moving from one identified point of protection to another by making short, fast passages through areas of exposure. The amount of time or potential consequences associated with traversing each area of exposure is sometimes referred to as the level of commitment.

Exposure refers to a passage in open water that is laid open to risk, usually because of a significant hazard. Exposure is a feature of crossings, rounding points, and island hopping, for example, but it can occur even quite close to shore. Depending on the wind direction, a capsize could

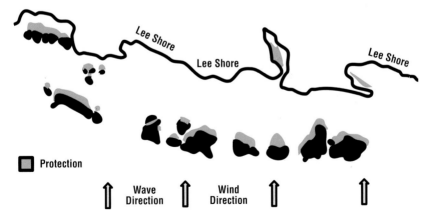

Small spots of protection exist along the exposed shoreline of this large lake, both behind islands and in small bays. Linking them together can provide a route, depending on the conditions outside of the protection.

Take note of points of protection as you go along, and of potential campsites in case you need to backtrack. Also consider how accessible the shore is—could you get off the water? Georgian Bay, Lake Huron, Ontario.

easily result in you and your canoe being blown away from shore, leaving you with a very long swim. Recognize that the distance to the lee shore has a big effect on exposure.

Protection refers to a location during an open-water passage where wind and waves are blocked or that somehow offers less risk. The leeward sides of islands and points are often points of protection, as are bays and windward shores. Shifting conditions can decrease the level of protection of certain features. An ideal point of protection also has a good landing zone and potential campsite; noting such features as you travel along a shoreline gives you key information in case your group has to backtrack in an emergency.

For stretches of very short exposure, such as when making a short crossing between two islands, it is possible to build a system of limited exposure in which only one boat crosses at a time. Be sure to come up with agreed-upon signals and boat order, as well as contingency plans in case of capsize.

FORMATIONS

In open water, it is easy to lose any order. In small ponds or calm conditions, there is nothing wrong with that, but in any kind of exposure, a tight

Making crossings in formation, like here on Spednic Lake, Maine, is one way to prevent getting spread out and losing the ability to communicate. The sweep boat can be in charge of maintaining the formation, and the lead boat in charge of pacing.

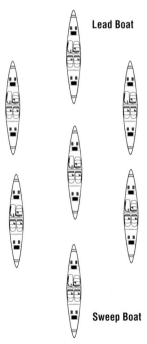

and organized pod is important. Conditions can change in a matter of minutes, and the formation of the pod must be able to sustain communication and safety. Paddling in a diamond formation is one way to keep the group closer together.

In the diamond formation, the lead boat sets the pace, while the sweep boat brings up the rear and keeps the pod together. In between, boats might be two or three abreast in one or two rows, all with a boat length or two between them. If waves begin to build, there is a danger of two canoes getting pushed into each other; rougher conditions might warrant a little more sea room between boats, as long as communication is not severed among the pod. If boats are getting surfed, it is too rough to be out.

The diamond formation for a seven-boat group, showing the positions of the lead and sweep boats.

HAZARDS

In addition to the interactions of wind, water, and shore discussed above and in the previous chapter, you need to be aware of a few other hazards of open-water travel and how to deal with them.

Lightning

Lightning is a significant hazard on the river and on open water, and in some areas it is deadly and common. As a canoeist on open water, you are the highest thing around, and water will conduct electricity some distance from the strike. Far-off rumbles could necessitate looking for landing spots and protection. Visible or close strikes make it imperative to immediately exit the water. Tie up the boats or quickly bring them onshore, and then follow typical lightning protocol once you are on land.

Other Boats

On some routes, you may encounter fishing boats, ferries, motorboats, or large ships. Technically, the unpowered boat has the right-of-way, but in reality, most pilots of motorized craft have trouble seeing a paddler far enough ahead of time to stop or maneuver to prevent a collision. In Maine, commercial vessels refer to canoeists and sea kayakers as "speed bumps."

Good ways to minimize the risk from other boats are to keep the pod out of high-traffic areas, give larger vessels the right-of-way, wear bright and obvious clothes, and notify ships of your plans in advance. Before open crossings with any expectation of ship traffic, consider making a VHF call announcing the details of your crossing and advising other vessels of it. If a ship is in the vicinity, announce your position on a common band.

The wake from these larger vessels can be more of a hazard than the boat itself. Watch the boat go by and track the oncoming wave—it can be larger, longer, and more uniform than natural waves.

Limited Visibility

In certain regions, fog and mist are very common and can be a significant hazard, particularly to navigation. You run the risk of paddling in circles when away from land. You can still travel along shore, particularly if there are obvious features on the map, but crossings might not be a good idea.

A more common limited-visibility situation for canoeists is paddling at night, either by choice or because you cannot find an appropriate campsite. The stress of paddling in ever-darkening conditions, particularly on a river, can be immense. The truth of the matter is that pushing into the night is rarely necessary. What looks like a nasty camp from the water often turns into one of the more memorable spots in the morning light. Paddling at night by choice is a different matter; a moonlight paddle on open water to

Navigating in thick fog can be very difficult, especially without solid landmarks, as on the Danube River in Romania.

a known campsite or out from the beach after dinner can be nothing short of magic. Wait for the stars and moonlight, turn off your headlights, let your eyes adjust, and enjoy. River travel in the dark, even in mellow moving water, requires clear visibility, and even then it should be approached cautiously.

PADDLING IN WIND AND WAVES

Along with learning how to avoid rough conditions, you also need to learn how to paddle in them, as you may get into situations where it is necessary. Practicing in rough conditions is a worthwhile exercise; not only is it the only way to prepare for situations where you are forced to deal with wind and waves, but it also can be very fun.

A good place to practice is near a lake campsite that has some protection for landing and launching, along with water that has wind exposure and waves. Warm air and water conditions, sun, and warm layers and hot drinks onshore make the exercise safer and more bearable. The key feature, however, is a very close, mild, and accessible lee shore, where a capsized boat will drift to shore and be easily rescued, rather than be carried out into the open water by the wind and waves.

Wind speed and wave height are hard to measure. As a general rule, if gunwales in neighboring boats are disappearing in swells, the waves are about 1 foot (30 centimeters); if PFDs are disappearing, the waves are about 3.3 feet (1 meter). If whitecaps are forming in cool water, the wind is at about 15 knots.

Just as on moving water, if you want to have power, control, and stability in rough open-water conditions, you need to be on your knees.

Headwinds

Paddling into 20-knot headwinds is almost impossible, and even 15-knot headwinds make it a slow and tiring process. From a risk management perspective, wind is usually less of an issue than the waves it creates, making it mostly a frustrating efficiency killer. Planning a passage with little exposure can negate the problem of headwinds, but this is not always possible. Paddling 6.2 miles (10 kilometers) out of the way to stay in protection might be faster, more efficient, and safer than paddling a 1.8-mile (3-kilometer) exposed stretch in strong wind.

Knowing the prevailing wind direction as well as the timing and presence of diurnal wind cycles can help you time group travel to fit into certain windows. Waking up at 3 in the morning and paddling from 4 a.m. to noon is a common strategy, as is pushing hard during windows of calm.

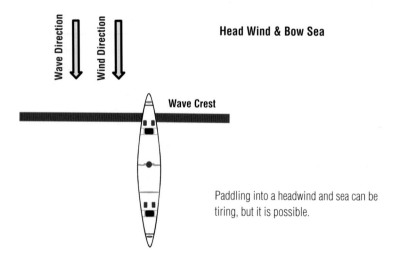

Paddling into a headwind and sea can be tiring, but it is possible.

Turning on a Wave

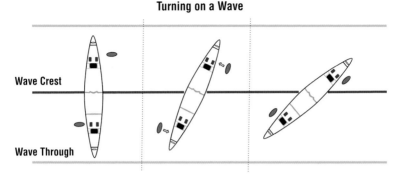

Turning the canoe 30 degrees or more in waves can be difficult. Using the wave crest to take the ends of the boat out of the water provides a good opportunity to change directions.

The canoe can be most efficiently paddled into a headwind if the centerline is parallel to the wind direction, making the profile, or sail area, of the canoe as small as possible.

On large, flat rivers with significant flow and no obstacles, upstream wind can quickly create large waves, including standing waves.

Bow Waves

Paddling into bow waves of any size can be a challenging exercise, in both the risks and the fatigue that it can entail. The goal is to paddle forward, but paddling forward too aggressively can cause the canoe to punch through an oncoming wave, potentially getting water in the boat, rather than rising up the face of the wave and letting it pass underneath. Boat design plays a role in this, but more important is your ability to control the speed and angle of your boat. One strategy is to angle the canoe between 20 and 45 degrees off parallel to the wave direction, causing the two crests to lift the boat up at the same time, rather than one crest sending the boat down at a steep angle. The slope of a wave face is much shallower when your boat goes across it rather than straight down. In some focused flatwater canoes, particularly solo canoes, this can cause a brief, wobbling instability as the pivot point is lifted up, potentially out of the water entirely.

Another trick is to employ a good wave block: abruptly dropping one knee and lifting the other can tilt the boat for a second, lifting one gunwale and keeping the wave out of the boat. If you have to do this frequently, however, the conditions are probably too big for safe canoe travel.

Tailwinds

Racing along in a good tailwind without using much of your own energy is one of the joys of canoe travel. Rigging sails, whether they are actual sails

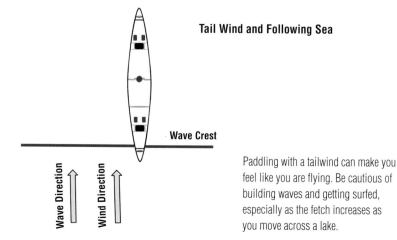

Tail Wind and Following Sea

Wave Crest

Wave Direction   Wind Direction

Paddling with a tailwind can make you feel like you are flying. Be cautious of building waves and getting surfed, especially as the fetch increases as you move across a lake.

or umbrellas or simply a kitchen tarp between two paddles, can be a fun way to make miles without much effort. While this might give you a good afternoon of travel, the primary benefit is in its novelty, as tailwinds just do not last. Building a catamaran can also be a fun way to travel in a tailwind, but with wind there is the chance of waves, and canoe catamarans fail quickly and spectacularly in waves. Never tie two canoes together in a way that they cannot be quickly released.

Following Waves

Following waves, or seas, are often a cause for joy as the canoe is rolled along, accelerating briefly with each pulse of wave energy. The challenge with following waves is not fatigue or a lack of speed, but rather too much speed. As a wave rises under the stern of the canoe, it lifts up the boat. If the boat is moving slightly faster than the wave or even at the same speed, it can start to surf down the face of the wave, accelerating and losing stability as it does. A loaded expedition canoe will not continue to surf for long, and the wave will pass under the boat after a moment of acceleration.

In mild conditions or on waves with a long wavelength, this can be a fun and easy way to move quickly, but on larger and steeper waves, the canoe will be more likely to surf down the face and either broach or punch its bow into the next wave, with sometimes disastrous consequences. You need to keep aware of the tendency to broach and punch forward in large following waves, as the tipping point can be hard to see coming.

As when paddling into oncoming waves, holding the canoe at a slight angle to the direction of the waves is helpful in maintaining control.

Getting Surfed in a Following Sea

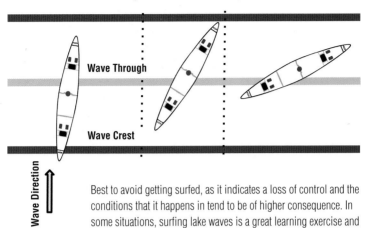

Best to avoid getting surfed, as it indicates a loss of control and the conditions that it happens in tend to be of higher consequence. In some situations, surfing lake waves is a great learning exercise and can speed up travel.

Quartering Winds

The real challenge comes when the wind is over the bow or stern quarter, causing it to exert a significant steering force on the boat. Paddlers expend so much energy in correcting for this force that their headway is impeded. The wind attempts to turn the boat so that it is blowing right into the side, and the paddler, particularly the stern paddler, has to maintain control. It is usually easier for the stern paddler to have his on side to leeward, allowing him to do J-strokes or, more likely, strong stern pries to keep the boat from yawing and broaching.

A quartering wind and sea is a gift and a curse. It can be difficult to control the boat, as the conditions want to force it perpendicular to the wind, but it also allows the boat to bridge the waves with more stability. In the stern, consider keeping your on side to leeward.

Quartering Waves

When the waves are moving in a direction about 45 degrees off the center-line of the canoe, they are said to be quartering waves. They can be hitting the bow or stern to the left or right, meaning there are four kinds of quartering waves, all basically variations of the above types. In paddling in following or oncoming waves, one of the methods described above is to position the boat at an angle to the waves. If the direction of the waves or the canoe means that the boat is already at that angle, you are one step ahead. Quartering waves, as well as the often attendant wind, exert a steering force on the canoe that the paddlers must overcome, or else the boat will turn off-course or broach.

Beam Waves

When a canoe turns parallel to the waves—perpendicular to their direction of travel—it is said to have *broached*, or turned sideways. Turning a canoe in waves requires passing through this position, which should be done as quickly as possible. If you keep your hips loose and maintain a flexible separation of your upper and lower body, it is possible to roll with the swells as they go by. If the waves are breaking, or if you cannot roll with the waves, a capsize, swamping, or water over the gunwales is imminent.

Beam Winds

When the canoe has completely broached, also called being *beam-on*, the whole sail area of the canoe is being pressured, and the steering force the wind is exerting becomes ineffective—it cannot turn the canoe anymore. In a strong or gusting wind, the canoe can be capsized; more likely, it will be blown downwind, sometimes quickly. A fully loaded canoe will resist this force because the hull extends farther below the surface, but the wind will

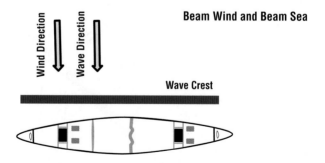

Beam winds and seas can be dangerous when sufficiently large, but knowing how to maintain stability in them is valuable.

still move the canoe. All wind wants to turn a canoe into this position, no matter what angle the wind comes from.

Wind Ferry

On a front or back ferry on the river, the current applies a force against the hull that, at the right angle, will push the canoe laterally across the current. On a lake, wind—and potentially waves—can apply similar forces and move the canoe in a wind ferry. Angle is most important, with some momentum needed to arrest backward drift. Tilt is less important, as the fluid medium moving the boat is mostly the air, rather than entirely the water.

It is harder to see your progress in a wind ferry than in a front river ferry, and it is a slightly less effective maneuver overall. Playing with wind ferries in different conditions can help you learn about wind forces and potentially save energy. In suddenly very big conditions, using this technique may be your last hope of reaching shore without broaching.

Tacking

Wind and wave action can cause your boat to drift off course, so when operating close to shore, it is often necessary to paddle deliberately off course or at an angle to your true course to correct for this. When waves are big enough that you need to avoid being abeam to the waves and wind, this can mean paddling at a 90-degree or greater angle to the intended course.

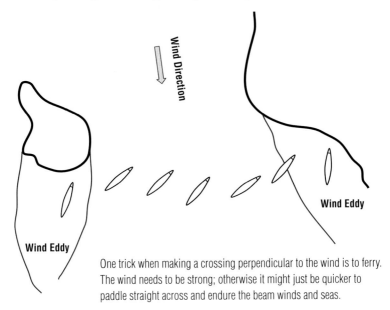

One trick when making a crossing perpendicular to the wind is to ferry. The wind needs to be strong; otherwise it might just be quicker to paddle straight across and endure the beam winds and seas.

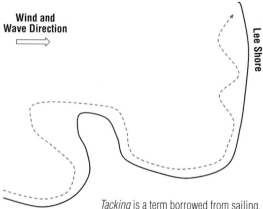

Wind and Wave Direction

Lee Shore

Tacking is a term borrowed from sailing, and in a canoe involves rounding points pointed into the wind and then turning abruptly, as well as zigzagging along lee shores.

Imagine rounding a point, for example. While you are running along shore to round the point, the wind and waves are pushing your canoe toward shore. To round the point without getting pushed into it, you need to turn into the wind and waves, paddle out 100 feet (30 meters) or so, and then turn downwind around the point. Another situation where this tactic can be helpful is when paddling along a lee shore in rough conditions. If you tack repeatedly, your canoe will trace a zigzag course, thereby both making headway and avoiding the shore.

LAUNCHING AND LANDING IN ROUGH CONDITIONS

When no significant protection is available, it is possible to land or launch in waves and rough seas. Most of the time, if large waves are breaking onshore, the conditions farther out will be more manageable but still too rough for open canoe travel. You should avoid landing in rough conditions by getting off the water *before* the waves build to a dangerous point. Even in perfectly calm weather, your team should be constantly assessing the shore for landing points, protection, and campsites. If caught out in the open when conditions change, however, it might make more sense to stay in even swells rather than risk navigating large breaking waves to reach the land.

Sometimes rough-water launches or landings will still be necessary. Landing in breaking waves can be an exhilarating challenge, but waves much larger than 2 feet (61 centimeters) give you a very low chance of success. In most cases, this is considered an emergency situation on a canoe expedition. If the waves are spilling onto a low-angled shore, it is much easier to land, as the height and steepness of the waves will not be

Even with no obstructions, bays can have very different conditions than the middle of the lake, making it hard to fully judge from shore. Lake Huron, Ontario.

outrageous, and the run-out onshore will be long. If the waves are dumping on a steeply angled shore or onto underwater features, however, swamped boats will probably result.

The ideal beach, then, is low-angled and sandy. If the waves are moving along shore or at an angle, it will be fairly straightforward; waves moving perpendicularly in to shore will be more challenging but potentially more predictable. The key is for the team in each boat to stay in control by not surfing, moving slower than the waves, keeping the boat perpendicular to the waves, and ideally paddling through the breakers during a lull in activity. One boat can move through the hazard at a time, ideally with signals. Helmets are a good idea in this situation. Avoid being in the path of a loaded canoe, whether or not it is under control or swamped. Try to choose camps with multiple facets or undulating shoreline when possible, as no matter which way the wind shifts, there will be areas of protection and exposure.

In the event of a capsized canoe, one strong team should land, with the paddlers removing their boat from the equation and helping the swimmers out of the water. The swamped canoe may be allowed to drift in, or a throw bag attached to it can be thrown to shore, and the boat is then pulled in. As the other boats come in, they are quickly unloaded by the team or suitcase-carried out of danger (see the section on the suitcase carry later in this chapter).

Ocean Travel

Ocean travel in a canoe is quite possible and should be treated like any other open-water canoeing on a large body of water, as described above, except that you cannot drink the water, and the weather systems and wave sizes can be vastly bigger and more dangerous. The likelihood and consequences of a capsize or other open-water incident are much higher on the ocean. This is a function of the complexity of ocean currents, wave and tidal forces, and the power that ocean waves can have.

Expeditioning on the ocean in small, open canoes for any significant distance might not be feasible due to exposure. Tandem and solo canoes are not designed for this environment, and if used, they must be employed conservatively and paddled only in protected waters. Ocean canoe voyages are carried out by experts in large, oceangoing canoes, boats with outriggers, expedition rowing shells, or sea kayaks.

Most of the techniques and ideas in the section above on Open-Water Strategy also apply here, but you should use a decked boat built for the purpose, like a sea kayak, if you are planning to travel long distances on the ocean.

Travel Over Land

One thing that sets a canoe apart from other craft is the ease with which it can be carried from one body of water to another. This unique versatility gives the canoeist the ability to travel over land faster and more efficiently than those using any other human-powered craft, save perhaps the packraft. Bicycles need roads or trails, but all a canoe needs is water and someone to carry it.

PORTAGING

A portage may be undertaken to bypass a set of rapids or difficult section of water or to connect two waterways. Many rivers have obvious trails on the side with the shortest path, usually on the inside of a bend well away from the rapids or falls.

Good portaging technique is simple, safe, and efficient. Portages are easily the biggest time burglar on a canoe expedition. The more complicated the plan or system, the longer the portage will take, so keep it simple. With good habits and technique, most team members should be able to scout, derig, unload, and start across the trail within five minutes of the decision to portage.

How you should pile up your gear depends on the terrain and whether there are other groups vying for the space. Ideally, individual paddlers or

One of the defining aspects of the canoe is its ability to be carried over land in a variety of ways. North Branch of the Big Salmon River, Yukon Territory.

teams move their gear from one isolated pile on the starting shore to a second isolated pile across the portage. Mixing gear is a recipe for losing things, so people should help others only after they are done with their own gear. Always know where your gear is, and check it after the carry. Small pieces of gear, like water bottles and helmets, should be packed on the *inside* of a pack or duffel bag. Use the packing ideas in chapter 1 to make easy-to-carry loads. I like taking a huge duffel bag for all the tiny pieces on a portage; it conforms easily to the top of a pack or barrel and can be held with one hand.

Hundreds of pounds of sometimes large and awkward gear moving over uneven terrain on a portage trail can make for a high-risk environment; musculoskeletal injury and lost persons are the biggest risks, as, to some extent, is lost or damaged gear. Practice good lifting technique and know your limits. If necessary, ask one or two other people to help; a common safety mistake is to carry too much weight. It is also better to make multiple trips than to do one backbreaking single-carry.

The group tends to find the path of least resistance during a portage, like this logging road in northern Quebec along the Mistassini River.

Scouting and structure can reduce the risk of someone becoming lost. Taking a side trail or missing a turn is shockingly easy with sweat dripping into eyes and fatigue setting in; avoid this by using a buddy system or team portaging and having everyone carry a whistle. In grizzly or jaguar country, paddlers may portage gear in teams of four or five.

Everyone should carry an *equitable* amount of weight, not an *equal* amount of weight. People vary in size, strength, and abilities; thus different people should carry different weights. A rough target for flat trails

Carrying crushing loads isn't always the most efficient method. Seagull Creek, Yukon Territory.

Consider looking around for the easiest and safest footpath. Boulders and dense vegetation can turn an ankle and end a trip. Desolation Canyon, Green River, Utah.

and short distances is 40 to 50 percent of a person's body weight, but what each person can safely carry will vary. On long portages and rough terrain, smaller loads are encouraged.

For maximum efficiency, avoid taking breaks. Hit the beach, immediately carry to the end, take sixty seconds to drink and splash water on your face, and then take it easy on the return load-free walk. Near the end of a long expedition, with the crew well honed in portaging and the packs a bit lighter, the process should be fun and done with style.

With proper carrying style and technique, you can avoid fatigue and pain. The keys to fatigue-free portaging are to avoid using your arms, have a good load-carrying system, and move steadily with few or no stops; pain-free portaging focuses on padding, balance, and good load creation. Preventing damage to gear usually entails simply putting things down softly and under control; portaging to the point where you have to throw the load off in pain means you've pushed it too far.

Portaging a Canoe

The canoe can be the preferred load or the torture rack, depending on the person, the canoe, and the technique. Taller people tend to have slightly more trouble portaging a canoe, possibly because a longer spine has less support from abdominal and torso muscles. The canoe is easiest to carry when it is balanced front to back and the carrier does not have to continually pull down or lift up the bow. If the bow and stern are the same distance from the ground, without being seesawed by the carrier, the boat is probably balanced.

Painter lines are best run to a seat or thwart and made fast, as even the tightest deck bungee can drop a line on the trail—bad rope care and a tripping hazard. Stern throw bags are best taken off and carried separately. Depending on the individual, some paddlers may carry a daypack or light pack or barrel in addition to the canoe. Padding the yoke with a rolled-up shirt, piece of foam, or screw-on yoke pads made for this purpose will cut down on point pain in the shoulders, at the cost of a slight loss of control and potential slippage.

There are a few ways to carry a canoe, including the specialized-use suitcase carry described below. More often, it is carried by two people with the bottom facing the ground for very short distances or by one person,

upside down over the head, for a carry longer than a few hundred feet. For moving boats, such as during loading and unloading, it is easier for two people to carry two boats side by side, with a deck handle in each hand, than for two people to carry one boat at a time; with a boat in each hand, the carrier can stand upright and balanced, despite the weight being doubled.

Picking up and putting down the canoe for solo carrying can be achieved in two main ways: the *tripod*, also known as *rangering*, or

Portaging in a small group is sometimes the most efficient method, as people can switch loads easily. Here on the North Branch of the Big Salmon River in Yukon Territory, two canoes are "rangered," or tripoded, while new people switch in.

Backpacks and hiking boots make this 10-kilometer mountain portage near Seagull Creek in Yukon Territory safer and more efficient.

the *solo flip*. In the tripod, two people face each other at one end of the canoe and hold their hands out in front of them with palms touching. The touching hands closest to the boat drop to the near gunwale, while the other set reaches to the far gunwale; at the same time, the two people roll the canoe and lift with their legs until one end is above them with the other end resting on the ground. One person then holds the canoe with arms straight above her like a tripod, while the other moves into position to stand up into the yoke, taking the weight of the canoe.

Alternatively, one person can flip the canoe solo. He positions himself beside the canoe just forward of the yoke and faces the boat. Bending the knees, he grasps the near gunwale and pulls the boat up so the bottom is on his thighs and the chine on his midsection. In one motion, he rolls the boat onto his shoulders. To do well, this method takes some practice and good technique, as well as upper-body strength, and you risk injuring your back if you do it with a jerking motion or incompletely.

On the portage itself, carrying a boat can become intensely painful or fatiguing to the point where you might need to take a break or switch carriers. Significant energy has been expended to get the boat into the air, so it is best to keep it there. Look for a tree just off the trail with a horizontal branch or V-shaped notch. Jam the bow in the notch to just past the deck plate, and then, crouching, slowly make your way out from under the boat.

Paddles
Portaging paddles can be a surprising headache; they are not very heavy, but groups of them are awkward to deal with and almost have to be carried in your arms. Other options include lashing them in canoes; having each person carry one paddle per trip; or running them, blade to the air, through the handles of a barrel. They are easy to lose on the trail, as they do not have a specific home unless you give them one.

Tumplines
A type of carrying strap that is used to sling a load and incorporates a wide band that fits just up from the forehead and forward of the top of the head. The strap, usually called a tumpline in North America, is typically made of fabric, rope, or leather, and either tapers from the forehead band to two 5- to 10-foot (1.5- to 3-meter) tails or comes back together to form a sling.

Keeping gear neat and organized is a time saver, and helps to eliminate losing important items.

The tumpline is best used in conjunction with a modern pack with shoulder straps, especially on rough terrain. Tumplines also exist for canoes.

Novices do not have the thick muscles girding the upper spine that the longtime tumpline user does, and if they are approaching this skill, they should do it slowly with smaller weights. Tumplines can be initially uncomfortable and can be dangerous if used for a significant weight.

Special Cases

Carpenters have a saying that you can do something fast or you can do it easily. So it is with portaging in tricky situations. There are tips and tricks and a few principles that can help, but portaging in cases like those described in this section will always be tiring, hard on the body, and slightly dangerous, especially if it is done quickly.

Off-Trail Portaging

Portaging off-trail or through dense brush can be immensely frustrating and exhausting, especially with a canoe. The first steps in mitigating this problem are to scout a route with a map and establish an easy-to-find end point. The group should move in teams, possibly with one person in a pair guiding the bow of a canoe through thick trees or brush. Whether to improve the path of a portage is a tricky question. This conversation has deep roots; people may go on a canoe expedition to get away from evidence of civilization, and a cleared portage that has been improved with feet and ax can detract from the feeling of wilderness for people that follow. On the other hand, most of the time we are not really traveling in a wilderness at all, but in a park or, more likely, a place that has been inhabited for thousands of years, with many existing portage trails. If there is an obvious trail that is now impassable, improving it with a light hand is probably acceptable. In truly wild lands, spread out your impact and leave things as they are.

Crossing into a new watershed or doing a long carry out of sight of the river, above treeline, presents an interesting challenge. In the eastern North American Arctic, you may find few features to navigate by, and the portage might be just a field of tussocks a few kilometers long. In such situations, portaging is more a matter of route finding than anything else. Some people prefer to drag their Royalex ABS canoes over the soft tundra in cases like this.

Firelines

Similar to station lining, a fireline can be used to move large numbers of small and medium items over short distances. The group lines up with each person about 3 to 4 feet (.9 to 1.2 meters) apart, and pieces of gear are passed from person to person to a pile at the end of the line. This technique, often used on rafting trips, is particularly effective in unloading an expedition's worth of boats in a tight area or moving around a steep, rocky, or uneven piece of terrain.

Encountering Bears

In grizzly and polar bear habitat, it is imperative to portage as a group, especially because the dense brush and roar of a river can lead to a sudden, unexpected encounter with a bear. Portage in balanced groups of four. (For more details on dealing with bears, see the discussion in the Wildlife section of chapter 4, as well as *NOLS Bear Essentials.*

Encountering Other People

On most canoe trips—especially in parks and popular canoeing areas—you are likely to run into other people on the portage trail. This can be a messy situation, with two or more teams trying to efficiently move down the trail with hundreds or thousands of pounds of gear. When you hit the unloading spot, quickly unrig and move your gear off the beach to a consolidated pile separate from the other group's gear. It is good style to stay out of each other's way and to keep your gear off the trail and off the beach.

When portaging through cities or towns, be protective of your gear; there is usually little reason to worry, but it is best not to risk having a hard-to-replace paddle, cart, radio, or camera go missing in a place far from home. Unload and load in a secluded place, and move gear in stages, keeping everything in sight while keeping your passport, wallet, and electronics on your person or close at hand.

The Suitcase Carry

Where the portage is very short—maybe 15 feet (4.5 meters)—and the footing is clear and consistent, cutting off the bends will save significant time and can be done easily with a suitcase carry. You may encounter multiple portages like this, such as in the headwaters of a river in thick brush with swift, shallow current and many strainers blocking the flow. To do the suitcase carry, from six to twelve people, depending on the weight of the boat and size and strength of the people, line up on the gunwales of a single boat. They lift the canoe with their inside hands on the gunwale, and transport the boat to the new location. Use good lifting technique (leg use, chins up).

Beaver Dams

Ascending and descending beaver dams is a common effort on expeditions in North American, Eurasian, and, select Patagonian forests. Beavers were once the impetus for European exploration and were nearly hunted and

The suitcase carry is fast an efficient, but requires a good even footpath and several fit people. North Branch Big Salmon River, Yukon Territory.

trapped to extinction. Populations have rapidly rebounded, and they still dominate stretches of water across the Northern Hemisphere. They can be a gift and a curse for canoeists: beaver dams can raise the water level of small rivers and creeks, making them navigable but at the cost of forcing you to travel over or around them.

Well-rigged, good-condition Royalex ABS canoes can basically be thrown up or down most beaver dams without much worry; moving them with control will help prevent the rare occurrence of a sharp stick puncturing the hull. The real hazard in this move is a boat falling on someone, either on the way up or on the way down. Having a setup with people on top of the dam and off to the sides below or midway down the dam is helpful. This is a situation where having on rugged footwear is a good idea. Damage to the dams is inevitable during this process, but beavers can easily fix most accidental damage.

In high water, when there is significant volume going over the top of the dam, your group should treat it like a whitewater feature.

Long Carries

When circumstances dictate carrying boats and gear on foot for more than 2.5 or 3 miles (4 or 5 kilometers) of road or trail, or for smaller distances over terrain that is slow or difficult to portage, it usually makes sense to break up the carry into shorter units. A group strung out over long

A portage is often all it takes to reach a new or otherwise inaccessible watershed. A long carry can save the money of a plane flight as well. Consider breaking longer portages down into shorter, more approachable sections. Seagull Creek, Yukon Territory.

distances is an invitation to lost people or gear, and it can be inefficient and hard on morale. The group also runs the risk of having to cut the portage short toward the end of the day without having the necessary gear all in the same place.

When planning to access a remote watershed on foot, you should consider the percentage of walking to paddling in deciding what footwear and carrying systems you will employ. Backpacking packs do not work well as canoe packs, but they will make a 6.2-mile (10-kilometer) hike vastly more comfortable and can be crushed down and jammed between the canoe packs and the sides of the canoe while paddling.

THE TRANSPORT

At NOLS, the transport drivers are some of the most dedicated and professional risk managers we have, and for good reason: the drive to transport the canoes and gear to the put-in has a high actual risk but a low perceived risk—we drive all the time and perceive it to be safe.

Well-maintained, well-chosen transport equipment lays a foundation for safe driving principles. There is no one right way to load a vehicle or run a transport, and every expert will have a slightly different take, but there are generally accepted methods that encompass the idiosyncratic—

Transporting canoes with a large truck and canoe trailer allows you to move a lot of boats and gear on back roads to your put-in.

Poorly secured canoes are easily blown or bounced off a trailer or vehicle; unexpected wind can even flip a canoe trailer—all the more reason to secure gear and boats well.

and time-tested—methods of outfitters and base managers. The bottom line is that legally as well as ethically, it is the driver's responsibility to check the load and recheck it often. Let one acknowledged person lead and coordinate the loading and unloading processes, have others check them, and when on the road, stop every hour to stretch, check the load, and retighten straps. Securing everything well and consistently is key.

For moving a large expedition's worth of boats and gear to a put-in, a personal car just does not have the capacity. A four-wheel-drive vehicle is helpful at some of the trickier put-ins, and a truck is especially useful for

Poling

Poling is a niche skill that has almost died out in mainstream expedition use. Most active pole users probably like it that way, wearing their niche skill as a badge of honor. Using a pole instead of a paddle, canoeists stand up in the boat and push off the riverbed in order to maneuver. This skill is particularly used to ascend shallow creeks and rivers less than 3 feet (.9 meters) deep, can be quite effective, as the pole connects you with a stationary platform to push off of. Poles are made of a number of materials, but the best are made of straight-grained ash wood about 10 feet (3 meters) long.

moving large numbers of packs and hauling a trailer. For a smaller group, a large car with a strong rack system might be able to handle three canoes for a short trip down the road, but you should not load more than two canoes on a car rack for a long-distance transport.

To load the canoes, one way that works well is to place them with the gunwales down on the bars of the rack or trailer, roughly centered. Loop a cam strap per bar around them and then lay this flat over the hull of the boat, with the cam buckle up and hanging on the chine of the hull, usually about 1 foot (30 centimeters) from the bar. Next, take a half turn around

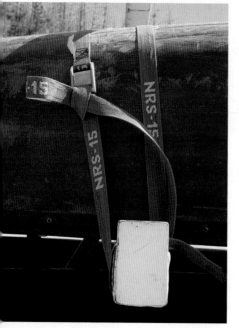

the bar with the working end and pass it through the cam buckle from the boat side, and then hold the buckle in place while taking out the slack and tightening the strap to the point where the canoe, when shaken, does not move front to back or side to side.

Woven 1-inch (2.5-centimeter) polypropylene webbing rated between 1,300 and 2,000 pounds (590 and 907 kilograms) stitched onto a metal cam buckle will hold the boat, but it should be tight and backed up; wash the straps when dirty and retire them when worn. The painter lines, or other tie-down ropes, can be laced through the

Cam straps are a simple and effective way to secure a canoe to a roofrack or trailer.

Making a pole in the field is one option for a short section of difficult upstream work, but it is useless without a relatively complex set of skills to back it up.

boat's grab loops and then secured, bow and stern, to the vertical posts as a redundant measure in case the straps fail.

Two straps per boat are enough. Tying in the bow is more important than the stern, but having a system for securing both is a good idea. Test every boat once both straps have been put on. Avoid having the boats in contact with one another, as the jostling that would occur on a long drive could cause deep friction burns.

Ice Travel

To the casual canoeist, this discussion might seem a bit crazy; the use of canoes seems to imply warm weather and open, liquid water, so why would a summer sport be concerned with a winter element? When venturing into certain environments in certain seasons, however, the expedition paddler will encounter ice and must know how to deal with it. Ice in any form is a significant risk and impediment to travel, and one that is often poorly managed. However, when you manage, prepare for, and embrace ice travel, it can also be exciting and fun, and it adds an element of challenge and adventure to what might in summer be a mild route. Also, in areas where ice is present, your group usually will not encounter any other people.

RIVER ICE

Traveling on a frozen or partially frozen river is usually a bad idea. Using whitewater terminology, the ice on the river is essentially one giant undercut that, even with negligible current, can flip a boat and put people under the ice with little chance of rescue. Approach large ice sheets on moving rivers as though they are one of the most dangerous river features you have ever seen—they are.

In spring, two things happen to frozen rivers, potentially at the same time. The water level rises as the runoff increases and the freshet begins, and the sun and air temperatures start breaking the bonds that hold the ice sheet together. This results in an unstable mess, and usually the pressures build over a few weeks and break in one flood of debris, water, and ice that

The early stages for ice formation can look like small stellars, or even angel wings. This lake on the Boundary Waters in Minnesota was open the day before, and the ice is about ⅛-inch thick and is fairly easily paddled through.

can heavily disturb riparian habitats. Paddling a river after ice-out can be a humbling experience—bark is ripped off trees, entire trees are torn out of the ground, islands can be plowed out of existence, and banks are covered in massive plates of rotten ice and slush. It is an important disturbance for the ecosystem but probably not one that a group of canoeists would want to travel in.

An intermediate stage occurs in late winter, when there is open current in the river but the banks are built up with large and potentially overhanging bluffs of ice. Travel is possible, but you might need to scout even mild stretches. Imagine the overhanging and undercut ice as rock, and treat it like a river feature.

LAKE ICE

Ice forms unevenly, meaning there are significant regional variations. It will form first in shaded bays, protected areas out of the wind, and then along shore. The last places to freeze will be inlets and outlets, as well as the center of the body of water, areas in direct sunlight, and narrow regions with current. Shallow ponds, bogs, and lakes will freeze before deep bodies.

New ice is vastly stronger than old or thawing ice. Because of horizontal bonds, new ice has an elastic quality to it—it may sink a few inches under your weight without breaking, and when it does break, cracks will appear and large intact plates might break open under you as your weight is transferred horizontally.

In the spring, the increased average temperature works with the sun to shift the mechanical bonds in the ice from horizontal to vertical. The ice becomes almost opaque and breaks easily into sharp, candle-shaped pieces. This old ice is extremely weak, and at certain stages of thaw, it can appear very solid but then break quite suddenly when weighted, no matter how

One clear, calm night in late fall is all it takes to start the freezing process. Boundary Waters, Minnesota.

thick. When it does break, bonds will snap vertically, meaning the only pieces of ice moving down under you might be two in the shape of your boots. Old ice is weaker because the bonds are weaker, have less shear strength, and cannot transfer weight outward. New ice might give you a little warning, but old ice will not.

It is easy to be misled by the diurnal melt-freeze cycle: new ice can form between and on top of old ice, but the weaknesses are probably still there.

Rotting lake ice often breaks into candle ice on Lake Auburn in Maine. Candle ice is narrow sharp splinters of ice that tingle as they rub against one another.

TRAVEL IN ICE

What do you do if you encounter ice after your expedition has begun and your group has committed to the route? The options are many. Your group can portage the lakeshore or get to shore with lines and drag from there, potentially setting up drag systems on a point. Even very thick sheets of ice

In spring, many northern lakes, like the Forked Lake in the Adirondacks of New York, have a melange of slushly candle ice, thin new ice, foot-thick sheets, and open leads, all shifting with melt and wind. Navigating through them can be a fascinating and frustrating experience, as well as dangerous if you are trapped far from shore.

often have 5 feet (1.5 meters) of open water along shore that canoeists can use to sneak past. With weak thin ice, one of the more effective methods is to paddle aggressively toward the ice to break a path. Ice is very strong, however, and if it is more than ¼ to ½ inch (0.5 to 1.3 centimeters) thick, it will stop the canoe cold and could potentially damage it. A better idea is to act like an icebreaker: instead of ramming the ice, paddle and pull the canoe on top of it; the weight of the boat and paddlers will break it, and you can then repeat the exercise. However you decide to negotiate the ice, expect it to take a long time and be exhausting to move a short distance. It is important to test the ice constantly and even then never fully trust it.

Sheets

In early season travel on thick, consolidated sheets, it is often possible to get out of the canoe and push it along like a bobsled start. Once the initial friction between ice and boat is broken, especially with a Royalex ABS boat, it will slide smoothly along. The ideal position is close alongside the boat, with your hands on the gunwales or deck and weight over the boat; in the event of punching through, you ideally will fall on the boat and not fully submerge, and at the very least you should be able to self-rescue by pulling yourself out with the boat as an anchor.

With more confidence in the ice, paddlers can act as sled dogs, dragging the boats over the ice with painters rigged as harnesses. If you expect to do significant ice work on an expedition, consider taking along microspike lightweight slip-on crampons, which are lightweight and will make this process much more energy efficient. A dry suit is almost a must-have in these conditions.

Whatever method you use, actively watch the ice for changes, as there can be significant regional variations in the sheet. Even then, this kind of travel is still risky, because weak spots and frozen-over leads can manifest with no sign whatsoever.

Leads

As the ice sheet candles and begins to break up, open water leads will appear. These might spiderweb out to isolate individual pieces of the ice sheet and can range from the size of a doormat to the area of a basketball court or five football fields. Wind will grip these sheets and move them around, opening and closing leads all day, sometimes in a matter of minutes. Overnight, cold temperatures can grow new fall-style ice between two sheets, temporarily gluing them together.

In consistent wind, loose sheets of ice will be blown downwind and compressed on the lee shore. A canoeist trying to paddle an open lead that is closed by wind can get trapped in ice that cannot support a person's weight. Usually the two sheets push the boat up onto the surface, but in a nightmare scenario, the boat could be overturned or crushed. Either way, leads are fickle and can be a godsend or a curse, and they rarely go exactly where you need to be.

Working through a refrozen lead can be tough work. Raquette Lake, Adirondacks, New York.

Working through ice—mixed spring ice or new fall ice—is made much easier with a traditonal tool sometimes called an ice hook. This one used on the Fulton Chain of Lakes in the Adirondacks of New York is a repurposed garden tool.

Mixed Travel

More often than not, lake ice that is preventing easy travel includes a variety of different elements, and the best way to navigate through it is by using a combination of ramming and breaking ice, following leads, pushing and pulling, and going over a sheet.

Sometimes, there is a final step when the lake is filled with small unconsolidated plates and huge quantities of candle ice. Travel in this environment is usually easy and always surreal—it sounds as if you are paddling through a field of breaking glass. This material also dampens wave action to a point, though wind and waves can quickly push the entire mass onto a lee shore. When the lake finally clears, it usually does so in one significant wind event, leaving piles of candle ice, plates, and slush on the beach.

NAVIGATION

A survey of backcountry navigation as it pertains to river and lake travel

Determining your position in the world is a process often made to appear mysterious and complex. It need not be so; staying found and moving through the landscape rely on two key skills—terrain association and deduced reckoning—and these along with a few other simple clues allow the navigator to make a position fix. Beyond these interrelated skills is a universe of party tricks and expensive gadgets for rare and special cases. However, simply watching the terrain and keeping a good map in front of you is the most reliable and functional option for expedition canoeing.

Navigating on a canoe trip shares the same basic principles with navigating on land, but it is simplified by having clear borders on at least two sides. The lakeshore or riverbanks bound you in, and this means that you need only navigate within a given plane, one that is free from obstructions of view. Conversely, you cannot get up high and look down during canoe travel as you can in the mountains; your depth of field is basically limited to two dimensions.

Your tools in this environment are your eyes, your brain, and your maps. The real world is projected on maps by cartographers, meaning that some information is not included, while some cannot be represented. A giant pillar of rock on the banks of a river might not be on the map if it is "hiding" between contour lines, and some apparent channels might have shifted or may be only seasonal. The farther you go off the beaten path or into highly variable environments, the less accurate the maps tend to be.

This chapter deals with a few key principles of navigation and some tricks specific to the water environment. For more information on navigation principles and practice, see *NOLS Wilderness Navigation*.

Terrain Association

The simple truth of backcountry navigation is that all you really need is a good map and a rock-solid ability to associate terrain with map features. Other tools, such as compasses, triangulation, and Global Positioning System (GPS) units, may occasionally be useful, but most of the time terrain association is the key. *Association* refers to the process of reading real-world terrain and matching it to the representation of that same terrain on a map or chart. These two skills—reading terrain and reading maps—are interdependent.

Terrain association is best supported by constantly referring to the map as you travel. If you have not been following the map, fixing a position is difficult or nearly impossible. When someone asks, "Where are we?" you should be able to look around and update your at-most five-minute-old fix and point to your new location. More important, you should be able to back up your fix by sharing three or more obvious features that you used to determine your approximate fix. When communicating your fix to the rest of the group, avoid saying a definitive "We're at such-and-such a position," but rather use "I *think* this is where we are."

READING MAPS

The primary, and arguably only, tool needed for navigation on a canoe expedition is the map. Paired with eyes and brain, it is all that is required for the majority of environments and situations. (For detailed explanations of river and lake map types, as well as where to find them, see chapter 1.)

Imagine a map as being a piece of writing composed in a language that you do not know. It has something to tell you, and with time and practice, being able to read it will become easier. Eventually, when looking at the map, you will cease to see a foreign language of colors and shapes and instead will be looking at the actual landscape. At that point, you can scout ahead through the terrain just by looking at the map; this can be a vital tool both while on expedition and in prior planning. Learning this language involves using a translation guide—the legend—as well as getting out and practicing reading maps in conjunction with terrain, linking them to the real world.

The map represents terrain using colors, lines, labels, and symbols; the guide to what each variation means in real life is located in the legend. If a legend is not included on each map sheet, you may want to include one that fits with your map. Over time, however, you might be able to identify the parts without a legend.

Colors. Colors on a map usually represent vegetation cover and water. Green traditionally indicates an area that is forested or densely brushy and white represents open or lightly forested ground. Blue indicates a body of water; sometimes a darker blue is used for deeper water.

Lines. Lines of various colors and thicknesses most often represent changes in elevation, the borders of watercourses, roads, and trails. Changes in elevation are represented with contour lines and indicate slope. Contour lines are the key aspect of a topographic map's representation of terrain and run perpendicular to the slope of a landform like a hill or mountain. One contour line follows a set elevation all the way around the feature, be it a small hill or a mountain. Widely spaced lines indicate a gradual slope, while closely spaced lines indicate a steep slope or cliff. Contour lines are usually black or brown, small creeks and streams are blue, roads are black or red, and trails are black dotted lines.

Labels. Labels indicate given known elevations or features. A peak might be labeled with a name, as rivers and lakes usually are, and elevation or depth is ordinarily given in either black or brown numbers.

Symbols. Symbols may represent features too small to otherwise show up on the map, such as large rocks, pingos, submerged reefs, buildings, or direction of flow. They can also be used to indicate terrain types, like swamps or shallows. The particular symbols used for different features can vary from one brand of map to another.

READING TERRAIN

Becoming familiar with different terrain features takes time. Estimating slope angles, gaining a sense of how far away things are and how terrain changes in space and over time, are all part of this landscape language that you will eventually learn to translate from what is printed on map.

The first step in learning how to read terrain is to explore these features on foot and in a boat and build a spatial awareness of landscape. This is usually a by-product of expeditioning, but you can do it in any situation. The second step is to practice matching or associating things you are seeing with what you are reading on the map. The only way this process is possible is if you keep the map right in front of you all the time. If your map is tucked in your daypack or you do not look at it for a period of time, even as short as twenty minutes, this can break the process of transferring information from the real world to the map and back again—especially on the river.

Deduced Reckoning

Also called dead reckoning, deduced reckoning is the idea that with a little bit of information about how and where the group is traveling, you can make a good guess at where you are. This relies on having a known position fix in the past and is a function of speed and direction. For example, if your group is paddling steadily along a monotonous shoreline in a fog, you might have trouble fixing your position. If you know that you are moving roughly east along shore (direction) at 2.5 miles per hour (4 kilometers per hour) (speed), you can estimate that after twenty minutes, you will be 0.62 miles (1 kilometer) from your last known position, in a line from that position in the direction of travel. In this example, direction is determined roughly as being east or along shore, but it can be determined much more specifically by using a compass to shoot a bearing.

Over longer time spans on the water, the math can get fuzzy, and deduced reckoning is better used to check a potential fix. For example, after collaborating, the group members decide that they have reached a given island that was their destination for the day. Travel had been downriver all day with few landmark features, and the paddlers were paying little attention to the map. If the group paddled for ten hours at 3.7 mph (6 kph), and the island they think they have reached was 37 miles (60 kilometers) downriver from where they started the day, then chances are they are roughly correct.

Gauging speed can be challenging, but it can be accomplished to achieve a rough measure with a watch, map, and string. The string measures the distance between two landmarks, and the watch times how long it takes to travel between them. If someone in the group repeats this frequently, and additional values are estimated from the map during travel, a sense of how fast your group is moving can be ascertained. An expedition of six experienced tandem canoes can frequently achieve 1.8 to 2.5 mph (3 to 4 kph) on flat water and 3.1 to 12 mph (5 to 20 kph) traveling downriver under neutral conditions.

Fixing Your Position

The above tools can give you a rough idea of your position, but to accurately fix your exact position, more detail is sometimes required. When paddling up to a massive and isolated cliff clearly marked on the map or pulling over at the confluence of two major rivers, terrain association is probably all you need for a position fix. In many cases, however, deduced reckoning and terrain association will give only an approximate position, and it can be hard to pinpoint exactly where you are. There are various tools and tricks to help you fix your position, including using a compass, GPS unit, and certain methods of terrain observation.

LAKE NAVIGATION
When paddling along the shore of a lake, you know where you are along a linear path and have to determine where you are along that line.

Lines of position. You take lines of position off of terrain features using another terrain feature or a compass. Two lines of position can give a fix at their intersection, as can a solid line of position intersecting a shoreline or narrow river, though with less accuracy. When a line of position is taken by lining up two terrain features, such as a small island and a distant point, it is called a *range* or *transit* line; when it is sighted through the compass to a terrain feature, it is called a *bearing*. In busy shipping channels on lakes and in the ocean, artificial range lines are often created by buoys, lights, or other markers to indicate channels and passages.

Offshooting. If you intend to arrive at a specific point on a line, you should aim to the left or right of that point so that when you hit the line, you know which way to turn; this is known as offshooting. Aiming straight for the destination, missing it by a short distance, and turning the wrong way can be frustrating and get you off-course.

RIVER NAVIGATION

On a river, the linear nature of the environment makes determining your position and intended route both easier and harder. Rivers flow downstream, and as long as your group does not portage off-trail, you know where you are all the time—on a fixed line. But just where you are on that line is the challenge. In hiking, using a terrain feature like a river to keep track of where you are is often called a *handrail*, and on the river, paddlers have the best handrail of all.

Rivers with similar and repetitive features can become confusing when you are navigating; if you are not closely following the map, all the bends can start to look the same. Following subtle bends to establish your position can be challenging and requires an attentive eye.

One helpful trick for navigating on the river is to look at the map and determine certain points that the group will pass through that are dominated by obvious, unmistakable features. In backpacking parlance, these are called *stop-me features*, or *backstops*. They should be unique and obvious enough to help you and your group know exactly where you are when you reach that point so that you can make a fairly reliable fix. Islands, rapids, major confluences and creeks coming in, bridges, steep cliffs and banks, tributary valleys, and large point bars are all features that can fill this role.

While moving downriver, scout down the river with your map, picking out stop-me features every 550 yards ($\frac{1}{2}$ kilometer) or so to help reevaluate your position. Challenges can arise in stretches without any large and noticeable features, such as on a big, single-thread river on a flat floodplain. Finding smaller features will help, but in cases like this, deduced reckoning becomes more important. If your group passed the last stop-me feature thirty minutes before and is traveling downstream at 3.7 miles per hour (6 kph), you should be at a point 1.9 miles (3 kilometers) downstream.

On a branching or braided river, or when going upstream, this can be more challenging, as the unique feature that appeared so obvious on the map might be missed if it's on a side channel. Navigating braided rivers is usually not too difficult, as the braids tend to stay in the same general area and often have open ground between them. Branching rivers can be harder, as a branch might take your group off-course. Either way, modern, updated maps and perhaps satellite images can help in these fast-changing areas.

COMPASS

A compass is a useful tool in situations with low visibility, when making crossings on very large open bodies, or when navigating lakes with lots of small islands and similar redundant features. With good terrain association and a little deduced reckoning, however, most canoeists can paddle around the world without using their compass.

DECLINATION

The needle of a compass reacts to the magnetic field generated by heavy concentrations of metal at Earth's core. The *magnetic north pole* generated by Earth's core does not match *true north*, the point where Earth's axis of rotation meets the surface. The difference between these two points is called declination and is calculated by drawing lines from your position to each of the two points and determining the angle. Lines on a map that point north, like longitude, will converge on true north, while the compass will point to magnetic north, which is thousands of miles away. The locations where all north-south lines on a map converge are called *grid north and south*. All maps used for navigation should tell you the declination of the area you are in.

In the Northern Hemisphere, the closer you are traveling to the imaginary line running directly south from true north through magnetic north, the smaller the declination will be, all the way to zero when you are navigating right on the line. To the east and west of the line, you must correct for the declination. In the Southern Hemisphere, the declination is determined in the same way with the magnetic south pole and axial south pole.

GPS UNIT

Tiny, durable, waterproof GPS units have caused a revolution in navigation over the last couple decades, easing the movement of human-powered expeditions as well as the ships, planes, and troops it was originally designed for. As a tool in navigating on a canoe expedition, a GPS unit can be helpful in a few situations, but it is not a vital addition to your kit. Use of maps and

Landscape Change

When navigating, it is important to remember that the landscape does not remain static. Change is a fundamental principle. Water levels change from day to day and year to year, and even the shoreline of a lake or river might have been drawn on a map inaccurately or could have changed in a flood or storm. Many experienced paddlers have stories about mishaps that occurred as a result of landscape changes: they got trapped in a bay that should have had an outlet but didn't because it was low tide, or they were not able to find a portage trail because a beaver dam had caused the entire trail to be flooded.

eyes are vastly more important, and you cannot rely on GPS units as you can terrain association. In low visibility, however, whether from fog, snow, or the densely vegetated banks characteristic of some narrow upstream and downstream work, a GPS unit can be useful in fixing position.

A NOLS course scouts a rapid before continuing downstream. Seagull Creek, Yukon Territory.

This section touches on a few advanced expedition leadership topics, start-ing off with the NOLS leadership model, followed by chapters on canoe rescue and wilderness medicine, risk management and decision-making, and environmental ethics. These topics provide the leadership framework that allows all of the pieces of an expedition to support larger goals.

10 | THE NOLS LEADERSHIP MODEL

Leadership roles and skills to help you develop as a leader

NOLS defines leadership as "situationally appropriate action that directs or guides your group to set and achieve goals." This section looks at the roles you might assume on an expedition and then examines the skills that allow you to realize your leadership potential.

Four Leadership Roles

At NOLS, we break leadership down into four roles with different needs and responsibilities: designated leadership, active followership, peer leadership, and self-leadership. These four roles apply whether you are on a sports team, a wilderness expedition, or in the boardroom. While the designated leadership role, leading from the front, is commonly seen as being the whole of leadership, the three other roles are vital in effective group function, and you will find yourself in all of them, often simultaneously.

DESIGNATED LEADERSHIP
The designated leader holds the larger vision and can facilitate the group in making difficult decisions. The designated leader does not have to do everything; she just needs to make sure that everything gets done. She can also save the group time and energy by making many of the smaller decisions that few people have a real interest in. A leader is usually designated by the group or the sponsoring organization, but if not, one person often becomes the de facto leader

ACTIVE FOLLOWERSHIP
To lead, sometimes it is better to follow. Whether the group or the designated leader is making the decisions and crafting the visions, it is the role of the rest of the group to *actively follow*. Most often, this means supporting

and executing the decisions of the group or of the designated leader with enthusiasm, creativity, and engaged participation. Offering opinions, providing information, and asking for clarification are also ways to actively follow, as is occasionally dissenting on a significant point you feel strongly about, if done in a respectful, appropriate manner.

PEER LEADERSHIP

Demonstrating leadership among individual group members and outside of a hierarchical structure is called peer leadership. At its most basic level, it means having good expedition behavior, working hard in the group, and achieving short-term group goals without needing a designated leader. Good peer leadership is often demonstrated by working hard and being courteous in camp, in the kitchen and in the tents. The real challenge comes in higher-level peer leadership, when you need to teach, coach, or assist peers or have high-stakes conversations that include feedback and conflict management.

SELF-LEADERSHIP

Before you can excel in the other three roles, a foundation of self-leadership must be laid. Basic self-leadership involves the kinds of outdoor and personal care skills that everyone should be doing all of the time. These include meeting your physiological needs, like staying warm, dry, hydrated, clean, and healthy, as well as maintaining basic outdoor functioning, like keeping organized and stormproof, with all your gear dry, clean, and in good working order. Contributing to group work and processes comes next, and then personal growth in higher leadership skills.

Self-leadership means that you are consistently taking care of your basic needs and working toward achieving higher functions.

Seven Leadership Skills

NOLS identifies seven skills necessary for good leadership. These skills work synergistically with each other and constitute an integral system.

EXPEDITION BEHAVIOR

For individuals, expedition behavior is a key leadership skill. It refers to how we act in the group and helps form the basis for how others receive our forays into leadership. At its core, good expedition behavior involves a simple prescription: work hard and be nice.

Good expedition behavior is a basic requirement for a functional group, and in the close quarters of an expedition environment, it is all the more important. Serve the mission and goals of the group, and treat everyone with dignity and respect.

COMPETENCE

Developing competence in expedition canoeing has been a key theme throughout this text. While it often starts with technical skills, this skill goes far beyond knot tying and paddle strokes. It involves a heavy dose of self-leadership, creating habits of learning and awareness to grow your competence in everything from technical skills to risk management to communication. Set personal goals, make action plans, and follow through.

COMMUNICATION

Communication is a basic skill and is a key element in an expedition. Even when all the other elements are in place—strong technical skills, all the right gear, perfect conditions—a lack of communication can sabotage an expedition. In adverse situations where those elements are not in place, effective communication becomes even more important.

This leadership skill does not mean simply communicating well, but rather involves *communication skills*, employing tried and true structures and tools that support effective communication. Some of the tools that NOLS commonly teaches are structured feedback and conflict managment. Let your group know what you expect of them and what they can expect from you. In giving feedback, be timely and growth oriented.

JUDGMENT AND DECISION-MAKING

Much has been said in this text about developing judgment and the ability to make good decisions on a canoe expedition. Guided and reflected-upon experience and technical competence together help you build judgment, which allows you to make good decisions. Still, even those with a lot of experience and good judgment use structures to help them make good decisions and avoid mistakes. Some of these are obvious structures or tools, like WORMMSS for rapid scouting or the decision-making graph, while others are heuristics, which are more subconscious tricks of the brain (see chapter 12). Use situationally appropriate decision-making styles, and develop a range of different styles.

TOLERANCE FOR ADVERSITY AND UNCERTAINTY

One facet of expedition travel is the adversity and uncertainty that come along with it. Frequent physical and mental challenges of some level are standard fare on most expeditions, and a sense of not knowing exactly what will come next pervades the experience, despite all possible planning. Complaining or collapsing under the pressure will help no one. *Tolerance* for adversity and uncertainty is a basic expectation we should all have of our expedition mates, while the ability to *transcend* them is what we hope for in ourselves and others. Tolerance means voicing illness or injury, but perhaps not discomfort, and continuing to play your role in the group while maintaining self-leadership and active followership. Transcending means engaging and even defying your circumstances, thinking creatively and enthusiastically about solving the problems you can, and ignoring the ones you can't. In large part, it is a matter of attitude. Turn challenging situations into opportunities.

SELF-AWARENESS

Self-awareness is the ability to accurately gauge your skills and abilities. Many of the other skills here can come unhinged without self-awareness, as it is difficult to successfully exercise judgment or manage risk if you don't have a sense of your abilities, or to communicate your needs if you can't accurately say what they are. Knowing where you stand in the group and where your strengths and growth areas lie is a key part of effective leadership in all four roles. Seek feedback from others.

VISION AND ACTION

The same process is involved in crafting and executing a plan for anything from a fast meal of macaroni and cheese to a two-month expedition in Alaska. You build a vision that includes the steps and resources needed, and then you take action to make your vision a reality. If that vision is larger or has higher stakes, you may need group buy-in, adding the steps of communicating the vision to the group and securing their enthusiasm and support. Great leaders create an environment that inspires individuals and groups to achieve their full potential.

One Signature Style

Every leader is different, and so too is how you execute each of the seven skills in each of the four roles. Your signature style is the sum total of how you practice leadership and the tools, tone, and skills with which you perform best. Growth areas are not ignored, but your personality and natural strengths inform your signature style. High-functioning leaders each have a leadership style that works best for them and that they feel most comfortable with, but they are capable of changing and adapting to suit the needs of the group and the requirements of the goal at hand. Building a toolbox of experiences, structures, ideas, and tricks is a natural outcome of leadership growth. A canoe expedition is an excellent place to foster this growth and add to your kit for the next trip as well as for growth in other areas of your life.

CHAPTER 11 | RESCUE AND MEDICAL ISSUES

A quick reference to canoe-related rescue and medical tips and tricks

M uch of the book to this point has focused on prevention rather than picking up the pieces after a mishap, but a key part of competent leadership is having the judgment, skills, and experience to deal with the occurrence and aftermath of an incident, from a small cut on someone's finger to chasing a swimmer or unpinning a boat.

This chapter provides a brief survey of rescue theory and practice and some basics on treating medical issues on an expedition. It is not a definitive guide and is meant only to serve as a reference with some canoe-specific ideas. For more in-depth discussion on these topics, see *NOLS River Rescue*, a pocket-size reference guide for river rescue, and *NOLS Wilderness Medicine*, a comprehensive guide to first aid in the backcountry.

Canoe Rescue

As with most expedition skills, rescue and medical care cannot be learned simply through reading a book. Building competence in rescue skills begins with watching and aiding in rescues and being a resource in a group where rescues are taking place. Before you take on a designated leadership role on a canoe expedition, in either an institutional or a team setting, you should complete a formal swiftwater rescue course. The progression of training, experience, and practice working toward developing judgment applies here.

For guides, instructors, or those planning to undertake large expeditions in remote environments, it is worth considering taking a professional-level Swiftwater Rescue Technician course. Designed for the team member or for leaders on shorter trips in significant but not extreme conditions, this recreational-level sixteen-hour course deals with a variety of craft and situations and gives extended practice in real rescue environments.

Most Swiftwater Rescue Technician courses use rafts and kayaks, and some will let you bring your own craft if there is a downriver segment of the course. Few offer canoes for use, and even fewer deal with canoe-specific rescues and management. Call ahead and ask what the focus will be and what kind of water the course will take place on. This will help the sponsoring organization or instructor set up for your needs; even a course without a canoe in sight will give you a basis in rescue skills and practice that is easily transferred. Organizations such as Paddle Canada and the American Canoe Association include a rescue component in their canoe-focused skill courses, and companies like Rescue 3 International and Espirit often run rescue trainings.

RESCUE THEORY
The primary step in the rescue progression is recognizing and avoiding hazards (see chapter 6). Identifying hazards, understanding how water moves, and knowing how to control a boat to avoid hazards will all help minimize the need for a rescue, as well as the consequences of an incident if one does occur. These skills are the basis of prevention and avoidance, but a complete rescue strategy also involves several other components.

Leadership
After prevention and avoidance, the first key idea in rescue theory is how leadership fits into the situation. Leadership is the basis for group function, and in high-consequence situations where many things are happening at once with several people and boats in play, effective designated leadership, active followership, peer leadership, and self-leadership can be challenging. As the likelihood of an incident, the complexity of the situation, and the potential consequences increase, the need for directive and concentrated leadership increases.

In many cases, the guide or trip leader will assume control of the situation, unless this individual is the one in trouble. It is helpful to designate an incident commander in the case of a developing incident, if one is not already in play. This person need not command the group without input and feedback, but he should have an idea of what needs to be done and will be able to move the situation forward efficiently.

Priorities
The second key idea is that of clear rescue priorities that the group understands and adheres to in the heat of the moment. Knee-jerk reactions as boats are going over or getting pinned and people are swimming downstream can get the rescuer into trouble. You want to help, but there is always

The group begins to gather in a large eddy while the safety boat keeps eyes on in the Hyland River in Yukon Territory.

time to think before you act, even in very time-sensitive scenarios like foot entrapment (described later in this chapter).

The top priority is the safety of the rescuer and the rescue team; creating more patients and losing more gear would only complicate the situation exponentially. The next priority is the safety of the group not engaged in the rescue, who may be waiting in an eddy or preparing a camp with food, hot drinks, and shelters; taking them out of play but keeping them nearby in case they are needed as resources is a helpful strategy. The next priority is any persons requiring rescue, referred to here as the patients, which may involve freeing them, bringing them to shore, and assessing their condition and needs. Once these three people-centric priorities have been dealt with, or plans have been put into action to deal with them, the rescuer or rescue team can then turn to the equipment—boats and gear. In some rescues, the patient may become a victim, and the end goal then shifts from rescue to recovery of the body. Recovering the body is important, but in an expedition setting, gear may be vital to the group's survival. In a recovery, you have more time.

The unwritten risk in the above order of priorities is that gear is viewed as expendable in favor of the patient, especially on a fast-flowing continuous river or in rough conditions with lots of exposure downwind. The patient's life *is* more important, but in some cases an uninjured swimmer can self-rescue, while the swamped canoe is much harder to bring to shore and must be chased. Judgment is key in situations like this.

Time Element and Available Resources

The third key idea is assessing the time element involved in the particular rescue and what the resources and options are. The time element to a rescue can vary widely. A bad foot entrapment or an unconscious swimmer must be dealt with in a matter of minutes, whereas a fully wrapped canoe probably is not going anywhere. The trip leader or incident commander should have a good sense of the group's carried resources, and a quick survey of the scene can determine the presence of any local resources.

Start Simple and Increase Complexity

The fourth key idea is that of using increasingly complex techniques, starting with the simplest and fastest method and moving through the steps to more complicated methods. Start by shouting at the boat's occupants (or former occupants) and encouraging them to perform a self-rescue, which is usually the best rescue in any situation. The next step is for the rescuers to attempt shore-based methods, like reaching out with a boat, paddle, or pole or throwing a rope or throw bag. If necessary, the rescuers then move on to water-based methods like paddling or swimming out. In cases where there is significant injury, a lack of resources, or high risk to the present rescuers, a professional rescue team or helicopter should be called in if possible, although this may not be an option in very remote areas. You can remember the stages of increasing complexity with the simple phrase "Yell, Reach, Throw, Go, Helo."

A throw bag should be rigged in the stern to aid the paddlers in a self-rescue. This particular bag, used on the Hyland River in Yukon Territory, has static SPECTRA line, making it an excellent component in a mechanical advantage system but potentially risky in a dynamic shore-to-swimmer rescue or self-rescue.

OUTFITTING FOR RESCUE

Various systems for river and open-water rescue are described below, but the basic outfitting recommendations detailed in chapter 2 can quickly become rescue resources. A canoe with all the gear secured and rigged in is vastly easier to rescue. Tying a throw bag in place of a stern painter will make self-rescue vastly easier if it becomes necessary. Close the bag loosely and put it under the bungee, with the open side facing the bow and the line running out of the bag under the bungee to the grab loop; tie it in there with a bowline or water bowline. Each morning, it is a good idea to take the stern throw bag off your boat, throw it, stuff it, tie it to the grab loop, and put it under the bungee. This quality control, while repetitive, means that you know the systems on your boat are solid and will work if you need to self-rescue in this way.

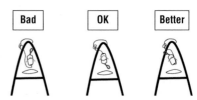

There are various ways to rig a throw bag for boat self-rescue, and some are better than others.

River Rescue

The river is by nature a dynamic environment, and the fact that water is continually moving downstream is a major factor in river rescues. Rescues may involve people, boats, and gear, and they can be either floating, usually downstream, or stationary.

RESCUING FLOATING PEOPLE, BOATS, OR GEAR

When people, boats, and gear are floating, the risk is not always where they are, but can be where they are going—downstream, out of sight, into rapids, against a strainer. Rescue is thus a matter of getting them to shore in a timely manner.

Swimming

Swimming in whitewater is a key skill for a paddler, and it is worth practicing under controlled conditions. Move downstream on your back with your head and feet out of the water, ready to push off of rocks or back ferry side to side. Keeping your feet up is important—foot entrapment is a real threat, especially in shallower, fast-moving water. When you see a calmer area you can easily get to, roll onto your stomach and paddle aggressively to shore, not standing again until your stomach is touching the ground.

A designated safety boat waits in an eddy and is ready to assist any boat that might get into trouble in the Desolation Canyon section of the Green River in Utah.

Sometimes an intentional rescue swimmer will attempt to reach a boat or person that in most cases has gotten caught up and is stationary and may, in the case of a paddler, have a line tied to a releasable rescue harness or belt. Rescue swimming is a more complicated skill and is one worth practicing in formal training or with paddlers with significant rescue experience. It usually should not be your first option in a rescue, however.

Self-Rescue

Self-rescue means that if a boat gets into trouble, its paddlers try to rescue themselves and their boat first. The consequences of losing a boat make self-rescue an important skill. It is the best option, when possible, as it is simpler than involving another craft and attaching the two boats together. If self-rescue is not possible, the group then becomes involved in the rescue.

If the boat is only swamped, the team may be able to paddle it to shore. If the boat capsizes, both people in the canoe slip out of their thigh straps, hold on to their paddles, and enter the water as the boat goes over. Breaking the surface, they make eye contact and ask each other, "Are you OK?" with hand signals and in words. They then pull themselves along the gunwales to the upstream end of the canoe, because if the boat pins a swimmer against a rock, the enormous force of the river against the boat can crush the person. If possible, they should roll the canoe open side up to make it easier to move and rescue.

Now the swimmers must decide whether they are capable of self-rescuing and if the river environment warrants trying. If the current is pushing the boat and swimmers into significant hazards, it may make the most sense to abandon the boat and swim to shore or, if they are in a set of rapids, to swim out the bottom of the rapids and then to shore. If they decide to self-rescue, the paddlers need to choose their position. Depending on the spot, they may have time and space to self-rescue in the rapids or may have to swim with the boat to the bottom and self-rescue there. Continuous rapids make this choice of position harder.

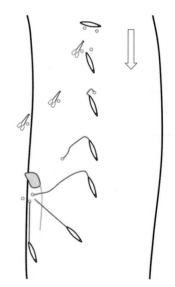

One paddler swims to shore with the paddles and moves downstream to assist, while the other swims the throw bag to shore and anchors it.

Next, one swimmer takes both paddles and swims to shore, while the other pulls the throw bag and follows. The swimmer with the paddles can have trouble making headway and might consider throwing the paddles to shore if possible; it's a good idea to practice this awkward act before the trip. The swimmer with the throw bag should not wrap the rope around a hand or the body, nor put a hand through the rope loop on the bag. The ideal spot for the swimmer with the throw bag to aim for is an eddy or an area of calmer water where she can easily exit the water and with a hazard-free eddy or calm spot just downstream for the boat to pendulum into. One trick for this swimmer is to swim downstream; if she can move aggressively downstream and toward shore, she has a better chance of making it to shore before the line comes tight.

Once onshore, the swimmer with the throw bag sits down facing downstream, with the throw-bag line behind her back and in each hand, effectively putting the boat on a hip belay. After putting the paddles down, the other swimmer can move to his partner, grab her PFD, and push down, backing her up as tension comes onto the line. In strong current, this backing up is especially helpful. The boat is now anchored, and it will swing, or pendulum, into shore. If the force is too great and risks dragging the paddler into the river, let go of the line.

Boat-Assisted Rescues

A rescue boat can bring swimmers to shore by having them hold on to the gunwale toward the stern and kick forward while the boat drags them to shore. Caution is necessary when nearing the swimmers, as a rescue boat charging in to pick up a swimmer can easily become a battering ram that knocks the swimmer out and under the boat. Swimmers can also upset the boat if they become frantic. Often it is easier to just have them swim to shore on their own.

Boat-assisted rescues of other canoes usually rely on towing the swamped boat to shore, as described in the next section. Alternatively, the rescue boat may be able to bump, or ram, the swamped boat to push it across the current and into an eddy. This only works in some cases, however, such as where the river is narrow or the boat is close to shore. If there are any swimmers in the water, the rescue team must be very cautious not to hit them or run them over.

Other variations can include clipping a tow system to the swamped boat's stern throw bag, making a double-length line and giving the rescue boat more time to get to shore, or tossing the towline throw bag to a swimmer and having him clip it onto the boat. If tossing a throw bag with a carabiner on it to a swimmer, the throw should be short, soft, and away from the swimmer's body but within reach, as the carabiner could

The beginning of a boat self-rescue. The paddlers capsize, move to the upstream side of the boat, one person pulls the stern throw bag while the other takes the paddles, and they begin moving to shore.

injure the swimmer. In any case, the swimmer should not become a part of a load-bearing system, such as holding a boat in one hand and a throw bag in the other. Other boats in the area can paddle out and collect paddles and gear, and bring them in to shore.

Towing

A very helpful trick for bringing swamped boats to shore, whether on a river or open water, is through the use of a tow line. There are several options here, but all involve connecting the two boats together, and they must be releasable. The advantage is that the rescue boat can ideally move all the way to shore before the line becomes tensioned. Then the rescuers can either haul in the swamped boat or anchor their canoe firmly and let the river pendulum the swamped boat to shore. This requires practice. When using any towing method, righting the swamped or capsized boat first will make towing easier, as the boat will rise up toward the attachment point and dump one-fifth to one-third of its water. Righting is not always possible, however, because of time constraints in the face of downstream hazards.

Improvised towing. This is a fast, easy option that is effective on very narrow rivers. Pull either painter of the swamped canoe out of its bungee, and put it over the stern thwart of the rescue boat and under the kneeling stern paddler's knee, ideally on her off side. The boats are thereby connected in a releasable system. The downside is that the painter is probably shorter than a throw-bag line, meaning you might have to get to shore more quickly.

Rigged to tow. A dedicated towing system can handle more force more reliably and is a better regular option for wider rivers and lake use. On the designated rescue boat, before launching each morning, clip a carabiner to the rope ring below the base of a throw bag, and place the bag within reach of the stern paddler—potentially on the seat next to her hip or on top of the stern thwart where it meets the gunwale. Take the running end of the throw-bag line out of the bag and run it through the stern grab loop, then back under the seat and to the stern thwart, attaching it there with a releasable thief's hitch. Ideally, the line and thief's hitch are set up on the paddler's off side so as to be out of the way when paddling.

It is possible to skip the grab loop and just run the throw-bag line under the seat, cutting out the friction of the grab loop, simplifying the system, and eliminating the small chance of the grab loop causing the towline not to release in the event that the rescue boat needs to be disconnected. The downside of skipping the grab loop is that if you change the angle of the rescue boat to the line, the line might resist the change and be pulled under the boat or across the stern paddler's back or lap.

The stern paddler clips the carabiner to the grab loop of the swamped canoe, places the throw bag in the water, and paddles aggressively to shore.

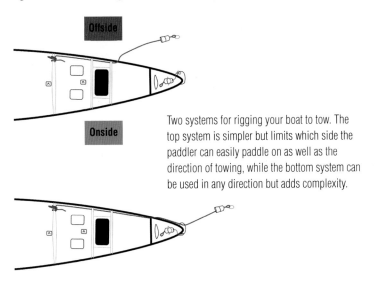

Two systems for rigging your boat to tow. The top system is simpler but limits which side the paddler can easily paddle on as well as the direction of towing, while the bottom system can be used in any direction but adds complexity.

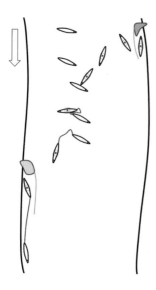

In this diagram, the rescue boat leaves an eddy and paddles to the capsized boat, bumping it and righting it. The rescue boat then clips in a tow line and paddles downstream to shore before anchoring the boat and letting the swamped boat swing in to shore.

Alternatively, she may clip the carabiner to the stern throw bag of the swamped canoe; this *double throw-bag tow* doubles the amount of line, giving the rescue boat twice as much length and twice as much time to paddle to shore. On a narrow river or in a situation with downstream hazards, however, the double throw-bag tow might get the rescue boat into trouble.

Two risks of this rigged towing system are that the rope might entangle the stern paddler if the rescue boat capsizes, and the thief's hitch might not release if the swamped boat needs to be abandoned. Both risks are somewhat mitigated if the paddlers on the rescue boat carry river knives on their PFDs.

In practice, especially on the river, other risks are not reaching shore before the line tensions, or reaching shore and being pulled back out before the rescue boat can be anchored. If the rescue boat team paddles downstream of the capsized boat to the full length of the towline, before they eddy out, they have effectively doubled the length of rope and gained more time.

An important key in towing operations on a river is to scout during the rescue, looking for a mellow eddy in which the rescue boat can stop and anchor, while taking care that the swamped boat is not pendulumed into a strainer or other hazard.

Shore-Assisted Rescue

On the river, unlike in open-water paddling, there will sometimes be people onshore watching, waiting, or better yet, setting safety, and ready to perform a shore-assisted rescue. This is occasionally possible by reaching out with a pole or paddle, by shifting a canoe from shore so a swimmer can grab on to it, or by throwing a rope or throw bag into the river for the swimmer to grab on to and be swung into shore. This kind of rescue is done only in the case of a swimmer that cannot swim to shore, as in the case of an injury, cold-water shock, or inability to swim. If the throw bag is being thrown to someone to get him clear of downstream consequences, the situation downstream should have been well scouted ahead of time.

For a shore-assisted rescue with a throw bag, the person onshore should find a stable spot on which to stand and make eye contact with the swimmer, tracking him through the current and looking downstream for hazards. When the swimmer is just upstream from her, the rescuer shouts the swimmer's name and yells, "Rope!" She then throws the bag underhand directly at the swimmer, while holding on to the end of the line with several feet of slack. The swimmer grabs the rope or swims to it. While

The rescuer is in a stable spot in calm, ankle-deep water and has a partner ready to act as an anchor. The swimmer may have to swim to the line.

After the swimmer is brought to shore safely, the rescuer can begin repacking the throw bag. Green River, Utah.

this is happening, the rescuer puts the throw bag on belay, with the rope going around behind her back and held with both hands in front of her body, and then sits down, ideally with a second rescuer to push down on the primary rescuer to prevent her from being dragged into the water. The rescuers should *not* wrap the line completely around their bodies or hands, which could put them in danger.

Meanwhile, the person in the water should be on his back and looking at the rescuer, watching for the line. When it lands on the water, the swimmer moves to and grabs the line, not the bag. The swimmer should hold the line on the chest in both hands, with the line running over his shoulder opposite the side the rescuer is on; this will create a slight ferry angle in his body. Again, the line should *not* be wrapped around the swimmer's hands or body. The rescuer then tensions the line, and the swimmer pendulums to shore.

To repack the throw bag after use, start with the standing end, and stuff it down into the bag rather than coil it. The last part is the running end, which is placed just inside the opening of the bag. This helps the rope come out cleanly when the bag is thrown.

RESCUING STATIONARY PEOPLE OR ITEMS
Stationary people or items are potentially in a higher-risk situation, as this means the current has pushed them into something and is holding them

A diamond formation of four, with a paddle or stick at the front, moves into knee-deep water by stepping together and communicating well on the Desolation Canyon section of the Green River in Utah.

there with potentially thousands of pounds of force. More complex systems often come into play in these rescues.

Wading

In shallow, fast-moving current over an even bottom, the most effective way to get resources to a stationary person or boat is by wading. In wading to a given location, the movement is usually lateral out from shore and has a lot in common with backpacking river-crossing techniques.

Rescues by wading can be performed in a variety of configurations. One person may face upstream and wade with a paddle in front of him that he leans forward on, creating a tripod. Other individuals can stand behind him in a line, circle, or pyramid. Practicing a variety of wading techniques under controlled conditions in training courses or before a trip is highly recommended, so the group can do them effectively and will be able to determine where they may and may not be helpful in a rescue situation.

A team of three finds that the channel is much deeper where the current is fastest and that it drops off abruptly and without warning due to the silty water of Desolation Canyon in the Green River, Utah.

A team of three moves into fast, waist-deep water and finds the limit at which they can keep their feet on the Desolation Canyon section of the Green River in Utah.

Two instructors demonstrate the mechanics of foot entrapment in dry land training.

Foot Entrapment

Foot entrapment refers to a situation in which a swimmer tries to stand up in moving water or is forced up, but one or both feet are caught underwater in a rock or debris formation. As the current pushes on the person's back, she is pushed underwater, sometimes gradually in the case of a conscious swimmer that can get one leg forward and lean on it, but sometimes very quickly. Foot entrapment can happen in water as shallow as 2 or 3 feet (60 to 91 centimeters) and is a common cause of death on the river. Prevention is the key, by training swimmers to keep their feet at the surface no matter what.

The time frame for rescue in this situation is critically short, and the options for effectively rescuing a stationary swimmer with foot entrapment are few. Practicing with snag lines and strong swimmer rescues are features of swiftwater rescue courses and should be practiced as part of the preparations for any river trip. For more information, see *NOLS River Rescue*.

Pinned Boats

The most common pin occurs when a canoe is paddled or pushed perpendicular to the current and hits a rock broadside; this is called *broaching*. If the canoe is held there, the water hitting the upstream side will try to force the chine and side underwater, eventually swamping the boat. The force of the current is vastly stronger than the hull and will cause the boat to start to deform, wrapping it around the rock. The paddlers may be able to self-rescue, but if the boat is broached and potentially pinned, then a system of

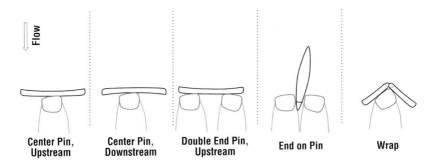

| Center Pin, Upstream | Center Pin, Downstream | Double End Pin, Upstream | End on Pin | Wrap |

A canoe can pin in a variety of positions, with an upstream center pin being the most common. Each position presents its own challenges in extraction.

removing it will have to be put in place. These are described below in order of increasing complexity.

Self-rescue. Self-rescue in this case involves the paddlers anticipating the impact and, as soon as it occurs, leaning downstream against the rock and trying to raise the upstream chine just out of the water. As they decrease the force holding them there, they may be able to push or paddle their canoe around the rock and downstream.

Hands-on. The simplest method involving other rescuers is hands-on. If it is possible to simply wade out to the pinned boat in shallow water,

A close-up of a common upstream center pin, with the two paddlers safely on shore by the Sunday River in Maine.

Another view of the above center pin, showing the force of the water bearing down on the hull and forcing it around the rock on the Sunday River, Maine. Moments after this photo was taken, the aluminum gunnel snapped and the hull tore down to the chines.

The angle of pull and the location of the attachment points are key ingredients in extracting a pinned canoe. Simply changing the angle and the attachment is often all that is needed to free the boat.

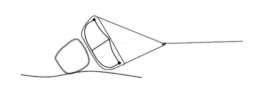

rescuers can push, pull, or roll the canoe out of the pin position. Although the current is pinning and potentially wrapping the hull, the rescuers must use the current or smartly counteract it to get the boat free. In some cases where the current is weak, rescuers may be able to force the boat loose with brute strength. Rescuers should use good lifting technique and anticipate where the freed boat will go so as to avoid being in its path. A tag line should be tied ahead of time so the freed canoe will not move downstream out of control and potentially pin again.

Attachment Points for Rescuing a Pinned Boat

When lines are being employed to free a pinned or wrapped boat, rescuers need to take care in how they attach the line to the boat. The simplest attachment, as used in the Boy Scout pull, is the painter or throw bag attached to the grab loop. More than four strong people pulling at once might snap the grab loop or painter line, however, and if they are in poor repair or the line is weak, they could snap more easily. Building an anchor on the canoe is the next option for increased mechanical advantage; webbing, spare line, or slack in the haul line is used, along with carabiners to attach to multiple different points. The thwarts, deck plates, and seats can be used, but D-rings are stronger. Wrapping the hull is stronger still; using a sling or girdle to encircle the hull is a great option, as it relies mostly on the strength of the webbing or line, rather than weaker parts of the boat. Most rope systems will fail with more than a 12:1 force being applied, either by people or through mechanical advantage.

Boy Scout pull (1:1). The next level of rescue starts with getting a painter or throw bag from the boat to shore, and then having three or four people pull on it. The rescuers should seek the most effective angle. If the boat is pinned with the rock close to the bow, the stern can be pulled downstream to use the water to force the canoe off, or vice versa. If four people are pulling with little effect on the boat, the angle should be changed or the method abandoned in favor of something more complex. Adding more people will only exert too much force on a relatively weak part of the boat.

Mechanical advantage. If the 1:1 Boy Scout pull did not work to free the pinned boat, the next step would be to use the haul line setup for the 1:1 and begin to build mechanical advantage systems of increasing complexity. While a good painter line or throw bag might suffice for a 1:1 pull, the forces present in a mechanical advantage system require a length of static

It is a good idea to practice extracting a pinned boat on dry land. Here, webbing is secured to a D-ring and a grab loop, then equalized with an overhand knot.

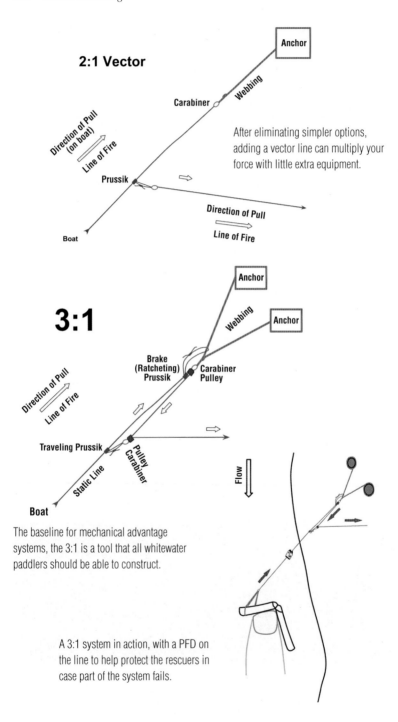

2:1 Vector

Anchor

Webbing

Carabiner

Direction of Pull (on boat)

Line of Fire

After eliminating simpler options, adding a vector line can multiply your force with little extra equipment.

Prussik

Direction of Pull

Line of Fire

Boat

3:1

Anchor

Anchor

Webbing

Brake (Ratcheting) Prussik

Carabiner Pulley

Direction of Pull

Line of Fire

Traveling Prussik

Pulley Carabiner

Static Line

Boat

The baseline for mechanical advantage systems, the 3:1 is a tool that all whitewater paddlers should be able to construct.

Flow

A 3:1 system in action, with a PFD on the line to help protect the rescuers in case part of the system fails.

Knots

The following knots are often required components in building rope systems and are important parts of general canoe travel and camp setup: water knot, bowline, water bowline, girth hitch, prussik hitch, butterfly, thief's hitch, double fisherman's knot, figure eight family, and trucker's hitch.

rope from the rescue boat or Spectra throw bags. The building of mechanical advantage systems, including anchor selection, slinging boats, and risk management concerns, is detailed in *NOLS River Rescue* and is worth practicing before and during an expedition. Below are a few common systems.

The above kit allows for the construction of all manner of systems, and training and practice with experienced paddlers and river rescue professionals can give you a basis in using these systems.

Pinned Swimmer

Swimmers rarely get caught in a boatlike pin setup; more likely this situation will arise when a paddler is caught in a pinned or floating boat. Canoes will usually dump the paddler in a capsize and sometimes during aggressive maneuvering. Things that can work against this tendency are

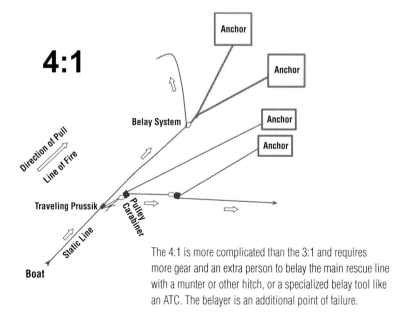

The 4:1 is more complicated than the 3:1 and requires more gear and an extra person to belay the main rescue line with a munter or other hitch, or a specialized belay tool like an ATC. The belayer is an additional point of failure.

low seats, very tight or high thigh straps, large feet or footwear, or gear inappropriately tied or clipped into the cockpit area. Freeing a pinned paddler is either a matter of self-rescue, potentially with a knife, or a rescuer getting to the scene as fast as possible.

Open-Water Rescue

Recovering boats and swimmers in open water is much simpler in technique and application than river rescue, but it is no easier, and the stakes can be just as high in rough conditions, cold water, and in areas with significant exposure. The options are few and usually involve towing or dragging boats, gear, or people to shore. The ideas of exposure, protection, and lee and weather shores presented in chapter 8 are keys to understanding your rescue options in open water and avoiding the necessity of a major rescue.

SELF-RESCUE

The best rescue is one in which no other boats or people have to become involved. If a canoe capsizes 200 feet (61 meters) from shore, for example, the swimmers may be able to self-rescue by swimming the boat closer and pulling the throw bag to bring the boat to shore, pulling hand over hand to get it into shallow water where it can be bailed. Flipping the canoe so that the gunwales are up makes it much easier to swim and pull. If the boat was gravity rigged, the gear will most likely come out and need to be rescued by other boats, with the potential that some could be lost.

BOAT-ASSISTED RESCUE

In cold water or if not properly outfitted, the swimmers can lose function quickly and may not be able to self-rescue. A safety boat rigged to tow can

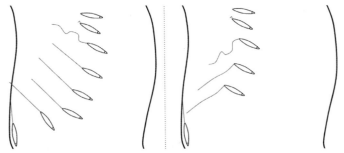

Two examples of open water self-rescue. The image to the left is incorrect because the rescuer is swimming upstream. On the right, the rescuer is correctly swimming downstream to the bank to avoid being pulled downstream by the boat until reaching shore.

The steps of a T-rescue (from left to right). Paddle up to the overturned canoe. Orient it perpendicular to your boat. Lift the bow or stern of the canoe onto your gunwale and carefully pull it over top of your boat. When all of the water is out, flip it over and push it back into the water right side up.

paddle in from upwind, allowing one paddler to reach into the water and flip the boat gunwales up if it is not already in that orientation. The boat is then towed in with a painter or one or two throw bags.

The *T-rescue*, also called *canoe-over-canoe*, is one of the most commonly taught canoe rescue techniques. It is effective and fairly easy to learn, but unfortunately, it becomes more difficult and less practical in environments where capsizing is likely. A loaded and rigged (tied-in) canoe that is swamped or capsized cannot be T-rescued without being unrigged (untied), making this technique less helpful in moving water, where tying in is the norm. On open water with gravity-rigged canoes, it is more useful, but in conditions where capsizing or swamping is more likely, such as in larger wind-driven waves, safely T-rescuing might be a challenge and could put the rescuing boat at risk.

Rescue Gear

HELMET

Paddling whitewater requires a helmet; if the water is white or you cannot see what it is about to do, put the helmet on. It is best to treat your helmet like your PFD: it is part of the wardrobe you put on every time you paddle whitewater. This way it will become comfortable and normal, and it will always be clipped in at arm's reach.

PFD

In paddling and scouting, the PFD provides insulation against the cold, protection against impacts and trauma, and flotation in the event of a swim. However, in rescue situations, even a well-fitted PFD will not necessarily keep an unconscious swimmer's head out of the water.

RESCUE KIT

Many of the rescues and unpinning techniques discussed here and elsewhere can be effected with the gear on the boat and on the rescuer. Most professional river canoe guides and instructors carry most or all of the rescue kit items listed in appendix A on their person or within arm's reach. Added to the painters and throw bags already on the boats, these items in the rescue kit and pin kit make many simple and effective rescue options possible. As the rescuer moves through the simple options without success, particularly in the case of a badly pinned boat, having a well-stocked and waterproof rescue kit in the group will vastly increase the options and give trained individuals the tools to build more complex rescue systems. The kit must be accessible during the travel day and include quality gear—not retired climbing gear—as a failure in a rope system due to old or worn gear can easily cause injury.

Wilderness Medicine

A full and thorough survey of the prevention and treatment of injury and illness in the backcountry is beyond the scope of this book. Building competence in wilderness medicine can begin with a formal course. The NOLS Wilderness Medicine Institute runs courses around the world all year long. For the recreationalist contemplating a trip fairly close to home and for less than a week, a Wilderness First Aid (WFA) course, usually sixteen hours long, is adequate. For longer and more remote trips, or for anyone leading or instructing a canoe trip of any length, a seventy-two- to eighty-hour

Wilderness First Responder (WFR) course is recommended. Other courses you might consider include Wilderness Advanced First Aid (WAFA) and Wilderness Emergency Medical Technician (WEMT).

Even for doctors or other medical personnel, the emphasis on improvisation, prevention, long-term care, and environmental medicine that the WFR course provides is a key part of backcountry practice. Training in cardiopulmonary resuscitation (CPR) is also recommended and is usually required by law for trip leaders. Some states and provinces also require further training, such as wilderness lifeguarding, river rescue, and various Occupational Safety and Health Administration (OSHA) related topics. One or more of these training courses is necessary for approaching and learning larger systems of patient assessment, long-term care, and general good backcountry practice.

What follows in this section deals mainly with a few common issues specific to canoe expeditions. Taking steps to prevent medical issues is key on an expedition.

PREVENTION
Similar to the attitude you should take toward rescue on the water, the best approach to backcountry medicine is to emphasize the structures, skills, and good habits that *prevent* the occurrence of medical issues and the need to treat them. Many expedition ailments and injuries are preventable, usually with little effort.

Self-Care
A key part of self-leadership is the ability to take care of yourself without anyone else helping or pointing things out. This means staying clean, organized, and timely, as well as warm, dry, fed, and hydrated. Slipping down into hypothermia, getting a cold injury, or losing function because of heat or a heat injury is often due to bad self-care. Good self-care is one of the foundational pillars that support a group in achieving far-reaching goals.

Sun Protection
Sunburn is a mark of the novice paddler; on the experienced, it is a mark of a lack of self-care. Sunscreen will help prevent sunburn and block some UV radiation when used in large quantities and frequently reapplied, but it does little to prevent the large loss of moisture and energy that exposed skin encourages. Wearing long pants and a long-sleeved shirt, a baseball cap or broad-brimmed sunhat, and sunglasses, and keeping your neck and face covered with high-SPF sunscreen, is the simplest method of staying cool, energized, and sunburn free. And don't forget SPF lip balm.

COLD INJURIES

Hypothermia

Throughout this text, there have been myriad references to avoiding hypothermia through gear selection, clothing, packing systems, and risk management. Prevention through these avenues is key, but your group must also know how to treat the condition, as full immersion in very cold water will almost certainly cause some stage of hypothermia. Water is an incredible conductor of heat away from the body: a person will cool twenty-five times faster when submerged in water than in calm air. No matter how strong a swimmer someone is, near-freezing water will rapidly deplete her energy, sometimes causing a person to drown when swimming just a few hundred feet.

Water under 65 degrees F (18 degrees Celsius) is dangerous, and water under 50 degrees F (10 degrees C) can be deadly. In the backcountry, you will not always know the water temperature, and the water is usually much colder than expected, especially in the spring and fall, in the mountains, and at high latitudes.

Mild hypothermia usually shows as a person begins to lose the ability to control her shivering and to perform fine motor functions like paddling, brushing her teeth, tying a knot, or writing her name. The "umbles"—stumbles, fumbles, mumbles, and grumbles—increase in frequency and severity.

Severe hypothermia usually shows as a significant change in mental status. The patient may have a normal level of responsiveness—alert and oriented to person, place, time, and situation—but she may be slurring her words, making inappropriate comments, or shivering violently, in spurts, or not at all. Additionally, vital signs may be unusual for that patient or changing over time.

Perhaps a more dangerous manifestation of hypothermia on a canoe expedition is that caused by slow-onset cooling. This form of hypothermia is hard to detect from outward appearances and easy to miss in yourself. Body and brain functions spiral downward so slowly that the condition is usually not noticed until it has crossed over into mild or even severe hypothermia. On very cold days, running ashore and doing group rewarming games and exercises is a great way to prevent this, as everyone can immediately see who is moving slowly or without enthusiasm. In rain or wind, it might be worth doing this once every forty-five minutes. Treatment is the same as for hypothermia from other causes.

Consider packing a 1,220- or 1,830-cubic-inch (20- or 30-liter) dry bag with extra clothes and warm gear, and perhaps a wet suit, as a "hypothermia kit," a small pack that is always accessible and has dry clothing for a person to throw on in an emergency after a swim.

Frostbite

Unless travel is taking place under extraordinarily cold and windy conditions, frostbite is not a major concern on a canoe expedition. When it does occur, it often hits paddlers that are not hydrated and adequately fed; this makes it easy to reduce your risk factors. More common in cold-weather and spring and fall travel is what is sometimes called *contact frostbite*, which is localized, usually superficial frostbite caused by contact with ice crystals or very cold metal. It typically occurs from grabbing a piece of frosty metal barehanded in the morning or, more likely, putting on frosty neoprene socks, gloves, or footwear. The common treatment consists of gentle rewarming and anti-inflammatory medication.

Cold Shock

When the body is suddenly and quickly immersed in very cold water, a variety of physiological reactions take place that can work against the swimmer. There is sometimes a strong, reflexive gasp of air that can bring water into the lungs, causing the swimmer to begin to drown. If his head stays above water, the swimmer will commonly begin to hyperventilate, lowering his function further, as hyperventilation reduces carbon dioxide in the blood, resulting in muscle cramping, chest pain, and anxiety. Hypothermia will begin to move in, but more commonly the above factors will cause the person to drown or lower his function to the point that he cannot swim to shore and self-rescue. In rare cases, sudden death from shock or heart attack is possible, usually in the case of someone with pre-existing conditions.

Nonfreezing Cold Injury: Immersion Foot

The most common nonfreezing cold injury occurs on the feet and is sometimes called immersion foot. This condition can occur anywhere on the body, but it typically affects the feet and sometimes the hands or butt. When tissue that is far from the core is consistently wet and cold, the body responds by localized vasoconstriction; if prolonged, this can result in nerve and tissue damage. As tissue is damaged red splotchy skin patterns will develop. It is important to be aware that this can occur in fairly warm water and air environments, and conditions need not be anywhere close to cold or freezing.

Prevention is easy. Having your feet warm and dry for eight to ten hours a day, including while sleeping, is the most important aspect, as is drying them out each afternoon and putting on clean, dry socks every night. Making sure feet are as warm as possible during the day is also key. Beware of constricting socks or footwear, as they can limit blood flow, potentially numbing part of your feet or legs and masking the onset of injury. Kneeling in a canoe is also a risk, as the hips, knees, and ankles are kinked in this position. Stretch frequently in cooler weather, and consider wearing boots to keep your feet functional throughout the day. Knee-high neoprene mukluks work well, as do loose Muck Boots or durable, well-made rubber boots.

SEASICKNESS

Seasickness is a form of motion sickness caused by the rolling and yawing of the waves on a large, open body of water, but it is rare on most canoe trips. On a freshwater canoe expedition, people are rarely affected by it unless they are very sensitive to motion sickness. In the rolling swells of the ocean, however, seasickness is much more common.

Seasickness is caused when the data being collected by the eyes does not match what is being collected by the inner ear and other senses; the brain interprets this as a defect in function and releases hormones that cause yawning, burping, fatigue, and dizziness at early stages, and potentially severe nausea, vomiting, uneven breathing, clammy skin, and sweating. Temporary or low-level treatments include focusing your eyes on fixed points like the horizon, eating dried or powdered ginger, and focused deep breathing exercises; beyond that, various medications are available for treatment. Easy ways to decrease the effects of seasickness ahead of time include eating only bland foods and staying well hydrated.

MUSCULOSKELETAL INJURIES

On a canoe expedition, the majority of preventable musculoskeletal injuries are caused by either overuse in travel or heavy lifting. Both can be minimized through good technique and awareness. Go slow in the beginning by calling the first few days early and portaging with light loads. Wrists, shoulders, back muscles—every part of your body—will function better if the demands placed on them are increased gradually, with periods of rest after periods of unusual exertion. Added to this, packs are heaviest at the start of the trip, making it more difficult to build up slowly. Using the body's strengths, such as in the case of supplying stroke power through torso rotation, can help prevent overuse and other types of injuries.

Wrist

The most common overuse injury for canoeists and kayakers is debilitating wrist pain caused by paddling-induced tendinitis. As described in the discussion of torso rotation, the arms—including the wrists—are power conduits for the back and core muscles. When the wrists are out of alignment—bent, torqued, or twisted any way but in line with the forearm—the force on them during even a mellow forward stroke is significant.

The muscles in the arm are attached to ligaments that help the wrist function and run through and around the bone. When these tendons are constantly being pulled and torqued out of line in repetitive motions like paddling, the friction between the tendon and the tendon sheath causes cell damage and inflammation. This swelling is where the real pain, numbness, and loss of function come from.

Repeated damage leads to a buildup of scar tissue and frequent swelling, which can put pressure on the nerves that run into the hand through the wrist via the carpal tunnel. Carpal tunnel syndrome is a long-term overuse injury and will not manifest from just a single expedition; the paddler probably knows he already has a history of the condition.

The easiest ways to prevent wrist overuse injuries are to keep the wrist in line, either through adopting new habits or using a wrist splint, and to maintain a loose, comfortable grip on the paddle. Almost every stroke and maneuver is possible without bending the wrist at all, except the J-stroke. Here, using a stern pry, with your thumb pointing up rather than down, as in the J-stroke, is the easy solution. In addition to keeping a neutral wrist, having a well-fitted paddle is key. If you use the J-stroke or have a history of tendinitis, consider using a more flexible paddle shaft for flat water, as well as avoiding scooped paddles outside of whitewater.

Treatment in the field is limited to the RICE method, which stands for rest, ice, compression, and elevation, along with anti-inflammatory drugs like ibuprofen. Light stretching of the tendons can help in preventing flare-ups, as can massaging the forearm to the elbow. In an extreme case, you can use taping and splints to keep the wrist in line.

Back

The massive and dense muscle groups of the back, core, and abdomen do not injure easily, but even minor tweaks can be incapacitating. Lifting heavy objects like canoes and food packs at awkward angles is the most common mechanism of back injuries. This can be eliminated in most instances by making a habit of using good lifting technique on an individual basis. The importance of good posture in preventing back problems cannot be underestimated. Walking around under a tarp bent over at the waist or sitting in a canoe with the spine in the shape of a question mark is not allowing the body to bear weight naturally, and even subtle movements and tweaks can pull muscles and shift discs. Don't be afraid to ask others to help lift heavy objects.

Shoulder Dislocation

The paddler's box concept is a key component of stroke technique for two reasons: power and prevention of injury. When you are applying force to moving water through the paddle, the system is also applying force on your hands, arms, shoulders, and back. When these parts of your body stay inside the paddler's box, your shoulders in particular are facing forward in a strong natural orientation. When your elbow is above or behind your shoulder and therefore out of the box, dislocating your shoulder, tearing a rotator cuff, or other injuries are possible.

With a shoulder dislocation, the injured person will have a high level of pain and be unable to raise or move her arm. Many shoulder dislocations occur in people who have dislocated a shoulder before.

Bringing the shoulder back into the proper position, referred to as *reducing* a shoulder dislocation, is within the scope of practice for a WFR operating in the wilderness, but the most effective treatment might be simply to let the muscles fatigue to the point that the shoulder reduces on its own. A weight can be tied to the patient's wrist to further the process and put an end to this particularly painful event. Shoulder dislocations should be evacuated even after the shoulder is reduced, as the tissue around the joint will swell quickly.

SUPERFICIAL WOUNDS

Surface-level wounds, particularly on the hands, are a common occurrence on a canoe expedition. The potential for infection is higher on an expedition, and some people report that in cold, wet condition, cuts don't heal as quickly. Here again, prevention of superficial wounds is key: avoid knives whenever possible, stick to careful kitchen habits, and wear gloves. Wearing gloves to protect your hands from sun, wind, and wet is a great start, as this will greatly minimize sun bumps (polymorphic light eruptions) and blisters caused by friction or sunburn.

RISK MANAGEMENT AND 12 DECISION-MAKING

Some canoeing-specific advice for managing risk and making decisions on expeditions

> *"We live in a society that tends to glorify risk, blithely airbrushing away the potential consequences. We laud risk when it succeeds and denigrate it as reckless when it does not. By definition, some risky ventures are going to fail. Managing risk is a balancing act between a desired outcome and the probability of achieving it. Knowing your goal is key because it is your 'yardstick for success' and helps determine how much you are willing to put at risk."*
> —Jill Fredston

In parts I and II, various skills, tools and structures were introduced that support managing risk on a canoe expedition. From cooking in the kitchen to running a set of rapids, in the field your team will constantly be forced to make decisions and manage risk to support your goals. This is one of the uniquely challenging and empowering aspects of a wilderness expedition—that your ability to manage risk and make decisions is tested constantly—and you receive feedback on your choices very quickly. An expedition is an excellent learning environment, and there are habits and tools you can employ to consistently make good decisions, from which paddle strokes to use to the best way to portage a canoe.

Decision-Making

In making decisions, your goal is to be able to gather sufficient information, analyze it, choose a decision-making style, apply it, and generate group buy-in. The key step is in analysis as the basis for making reasoned, fact-based decisions. Good decision-making can be learned, and you should question those that cannot give you the reasons and information they used to support their preferences and decisions.

In a situation where there is a consistent and appointed designated leader, it will often fall to this individual to decide what style should be used and sometimes to approve the final call. Using the appropriate style is a key step in achieving a good outcome in the decision-making process; choosing the appropriate style is a matter of weighing the necessity of group buy-in, the amount of time available to make the decision, and the importance of the outcome of the decision.

With small decisions, such as where to have a snack break on the river, group members do not necessarily want buy-in; they just want the decision to be made so that the outcome can be achieved. For a weighty decision, such as whether to paddle a challenging set of rapids, group buy-in becomes more important and must be sought.

DECISION-MAKING STYLES

The following broad categories attempt to cover the scope of strategies for making a decision.

Directive

The designated leader makes the decision, tells the group, and confirms that everyone understands.

Time. Very fast, assuming the leader makes the decision efficiently.

Group involvement. Very low, as the group has no say in the decision.

Consultative A

The designated leader decides, tells the group members, and asks for input and feedback on their decision, potentially altering or reevaluating the decision.

Time. Fast, assuming the leader makes the decision efficiently and does not revise the decision.

Group involvement. Low, as the group members will rarely challenge the proposed decision, but they may be able to alter it or voice their reservations about it.

Consultative B

The designated leader presents the options to the group, asks for input, and uses it to make the decision.

Time. Can be slow or fast, depending on how much input the group provides.

Group involvement. Somewhat high, as the group has an opportunity to provide input before the decision is made. The risk in this style is that a part of the group or an individual might argue for a decision the leader is not comfortable with, and then feel disenfranchised over the outcome.

Vote

The designated leader turns the decision entirely over to the group, perhaps with a preface about the options or the importance of the decision, and the group votes, potentially after debating.

Time. Can be slow or fast, depending on whether there is a lengthy debate. This method has risks in that one decision might not be the clear winner or one side may not accept the outcome. Public voting can have a social cost as well.

Group involvement. *High, as the group is actually deciding the outcome.*

Delegate

The designated leader delegates the decision to the group, a committee, or an individual, who then uses one of the other styles to decide.

Time. Can be slow or fast, depending on what style is used.

Group involvement. High or low, depending on the style.

Consensus

The group members discuss the decision until they come to a conclusion everyone accepts.

Time. Can be slow or fast, depending on the level of disagreement in the group over the best choice.

Group involvement. High, as the group is deciding the outcome together. The risk is that louder, more socially powerful voices can sway the decision in their favor, even if they are in the minority.

HEURISTICS

The human brain naturally works to speed up decision-making by creating neural pathways to deal with common actions or choices. These work to your benefit most of the time, as you don't really have to think about how to do a forward stroke while you are doing it. With experience paddling canoes and making decisions in the field, you get better and faster at them, but at a cost.

Occasionally these neural shortcuts can trip you up when unseen factors are present and you rely too much on your automatic response and not enough on analysis. Below are six common decision-making traps as identified by NOLS instructor Ian McCammon and his FACETS test, along with an example of a situation where you might experience each type.

Familiarity. If something about a situation is familiar, you might assume that it is less risky or that you have more control than you actually do. Approach all situations, even if they are very common or familiar, as opportunities for new analyses and decisions.

Acceptance. A group quickly develops a social culture of standing and respect. Sometimes your desire for acceptance in a group or respect from certain members of that group can blind you to the presence of certain risks to yourself or the group. In an effort to gain acceptance and earn respect, you may make a decision that does not take into account your skills and the risk present.

Consistency. In order to remain consistent, you stick to a decision despite the presence of new information. Reevaluate when provided with new information.

Expert halo. Someone that has achieved expert-level competence in one discipline can be mistakenly assumed to have expertise in another, with poor results. Self-awareness on the part of the expert can help avoid this trap.

Scarcity. If people are competing for a given resource or opportunity, then you might assume that this resource or opportunity is therefore more valuable. Because of this, you may be willing to endure higher risks or more likely to ignore or not notice certain risks.

Social proof. If others are doing something, you might assume the risk to be lower for yourself. This may lead your group to assume that the risks are low, because others have decided to do it, without gathering and analyzing information yourselves and making the decision that is right for your group.

Risk Management: Probability and Consequences

One simple tool in assessing and managing risk is to examine the intersection of probability and consequences in a given situation. First, you must accurately assess the consequences of things going wrong and determine the probability that you will encounter those consequences. This is a simplified model; the real world is more complicated. The consequences will actually exist on a range, with the worst-case scenario always being a possibility, but in most cases that possibility is quite small. Consider what consequences you are willing to accept, and know that while perfect accuracy in assessment is difficult, it will become easier and more precise as your judgment improves.

Low Probability, Low Consequences. If there is a low probability of an incident taking place and the consequences are low, then it is probably OK to proceed. This is a *green light* situation.

Low Probability, High Consequences. Where there is a low probability of an incident but the consequences are high, you should carefully assess the situation and determine how willing you are to expose yourself to the potential consequences. If the consequence is death, serious injury, or a major loss of gear, it is not worth it unless there is an extremely low probability. This is a *yellow light* situation. Example: At your turn-around point, one-third of the way across an open-water crossing, conditions have built slightly to rain and small rolling waves since starting out. You determine that the probability of the conditions growing to a dangerous level is low, but the consequences of losing a boat and swimming in the cold water far from shore are high. You decide to backtrack to a nearby point and follow a longer route along the shore of the lake to the other side.

High Probability, Low Consequences. With a high probability of low consequences, you should do what you can to lower the probability, but it is OK to carefully proceed. This is often a good learning environment, as you are likely to endure real consequences for mistakes, but they shouldn't hurt you significantly. This is a *yellow light* situation, perhaps a shade lighter than the above. Example: Your team rounds a bend on a hot, clear day and comes upon a short, steep set of rapids with large waves and a large, calm pool below with plenty of room for easy self-rescues. You scout it thoroughly and discover no holes or pour-overs, only deep water from start to finish. You assess the rapids as having a high probability of at least one boat in your group capsizing but low consequences. You decide to proceed and spend the rest of the day playing the rapids and practicing maneuvering in the large waves.

High Probability, High Consequences. With a high probability of high consequences, you should not proceed. This is a *red light* situation. Example: You are trapped on an island by a storm cycle, with large waves rolling in all day. After hours of waiting for a window, your team gathers on the beach to assess the conditions. You determine that given the high probability of getting surfed or swamping a canoe in the large breaking waves, along with the high consequences of losing a boat or a person in the cold, wet weather, you are going to stay put on the island.

ENVIRONMENTAL ETHICS

Effective Leave No Trace principles and practices for canoe environments and a brief overview of global and local water issues

When you travel in a wild place, you take some responsibility for that place in how you travel through it, the things you take with you, and what you leave behind. Being cognizant of this responsibility is an expectation paddlers can have of each other as well, and in many places Leave No Trace is becoming the law. On every trip—short or long, near or far—it is crucial that you walk lightly. Practicing Leave No Trace principles will enable you to do this.

Leave No Trace

Leave No Trace (LNT) is a code of ethics that informs responsible backcountry travel. The code is broken into seven principles that are continually refined, tested, and advertised by the Leave No Trace Center for Outdoor Ethics. The key thing to remember about LNT is that it is not a set of overarching rules, but an ethic of making science-based decisions before, during, and after a trip that minimize your impact in the backcountry. The seven principles represent a flexible structure of ideals that you apply in different ways depending on the environment you are in.

The bottom line with LNT is to be respectful of the ecosystems you are traveling through and considerate of other visitors to the same areas. More detailed information is available in *NOLS Soft Paths* and on the website http://lnt.org/learn/7-principles. You can contact the Leave No Trace Center for Outdoor Ethics at P.O. Box 997, Boulder, CO 80306, telephone 800-332-4100, or email info@LNT.org. The center conducts training sessions and offers free information on how best to apply LNT principles in your local area.

RIVER LNT

The way LNT principles are applied depends on the region you are in. Below are descriptions of the seven principles, along with a few notes on how to apply them to the rivers and lakes on your canoe route.

Plan Ahead and Prepare

Know the regulations and special concerns for the area you'll visit.

Prepare for extreme weather, hazards, and emergencies.

Schedule your trip to avoid times of high use.

Visit in small groups when possible. Consider splitting larger groups into smaller groups.

Repackage food to minimize waste.

Use a map and compass to eliminate the use of marking paint, rock cairns, or flagging.

This principle is covered in chapter 1 and is fairly simple. Research your destination thoroughly, take what you need to be self-sufficient in terms of both gear and skills, and minimize the number of people you will be traveling with.

Travel and Camp on Durable Surfaces

Durable surfaces include established trails and campsites, rock, gravel, dry grasses, or snow.

Protect riparian areas by camping away from lake shore and river-banks.

Good campsites are found, not made. Altering a site is not necessary.

In popular areas:

Concentrate use on existing trails and campsites.

Walk single file in the middle of the trail, even when wet or muddy.

Keep campsites small. Focus activity in areas where vegetation is absent.

In pristine areas:

Disperse use to prevent the creation of campsites and trails.

Avoid places where impacts are just beginning.

A canoe will have little impact on the water, which is also a durable surface. Of all the forms of outdoor travel, you may spend the most time on a durable surface when canoeing, but it is not without a few caveats. Paddlers concentrate their camps along lakeshores and riverbanks, rather than spreading out in the backcountry. This is the nature of travel on a river or lake, and it means that good camping places tend to quickly accumulate use. In heavily used areas, try to concentrate your impact in areas that have already been impacted, like designated Forest Service campsites. In pristine areas, disperse your impact. Gravel and cobble bars make great river camp-sites, as they are durable and are often swept clean each spring.

If you need to portage, do your best to find an existing portage trail rather than making your own new trail. When you do find one, stay on the trail even if you get wet and muddy; avoid walking on the margins or off-trail.

In the desert, avoid camping or even stepping on cryptobiotic soil, a crusty, living matrix of bacteria, algae, moss, and lichen that is a founda-tion of the desert ecosystem. Once crushed, it is highly erosion prone and can take decades to regrow.

Great campsites are found, not made. Avoid clearing sites for tents or kitchens. Before leaving the campsite, dismantle any woodland "furniture," shelters, and clothes lines, unless they are official installations of the Forest Service.

Dispose of Waste Properly

Pack it in, pack it out. Inspect your campsite and rest areas for trash or spilled foods. Pack out all trash, leftover food, and litter.

Deposit human waste in the region-appropriate place.

Pack out toilet paper and hygiene products.

To wash yourself or your dishes, carry water away from streams or lakes.

Take all trash with you when you go, keeping refuse off the ground and out of the water.

If you will be traveling on a desert river, take along an approved portable toilet, or groover, to carry out solid human waste, and plan on pee-ing exclusively in the river. The sandy soil usually cannot process urine, let alone poop, and desert campsites can quickly develop a urinal smell if your group does not deal with human waste properly.

Soap isn't really necessary for anything but washing hands and, if nec-essary, around small wounds. When using soap on your body, do it 200 feet (60 meters) from all water sources. To wash dishes, scrape every last crumb of food and speck of sauce into bowls to eat or trash bags to dispose of, and then rinse the scraped-off dishes with copious amounts of river or lake water. The food-particle-free wash water can be dumped in high-volume or desert rivers or very large pristine lakes, but in impacted areas, like many places in the Lower 48 and southeastern Canada, it should be dispersed away from camp and water. Before eating out of a bowl or pot cleaned in this manner, you should boil it or wash it with sterilized water.

Leave What You Find

Preserve the past: examine, but do not touch, cultural or historic structures and artifacts.

Leave rocks, plants, and other natural objects as you find them.

Avoid introducing or transporting non-native species.

Do not build structures, furniture, or dig trenches.

Minimize Campfire Impacts

Use a lightweight stove for cooking and headlamps for light.

Where fires are permitted, use established fire rings, fire pans, or mound fires.

Keep fires small.

Burn all wood and coals to ash, put out campfires completely

In northern woodlands, fires are a wonderful part of the canoe trip experience, but they are far from a necessity. Pack a stove and use it for most cooking. Where appropriate, you can use fires for heating, cooking, and ambience, but avoid bonfires in impacted areas. Burn any fires you do start to ashes before leaving the campsite.

If using an ax and saw, harvest only dry, dead, and down wood. If you will be camping in an impacted area, consider stopping a half hour before making camp to gather wood so that you do not strip a campsite's supply.

Use a fire pan or mound fire in the desert. In pristine areas with no existing fire rings, you might dig a shallow fire pit near the water on a seasonally disturbed beach, cobble bar, or gravel bar, where you can erase your presence the next morning; on these sites, all will be rearranged in the spring.

Respect Wildlife

Observe wildlife from a distance. Do not follow or approach them.

Never feed animals. Feeding wildlife damages their health, alters natural behaviors, and exposes them to predators and other dangers.

Protect wildlife and your food by storing rations and trash securely.

Control pets at all times, or leave them at home.

Avoid wildlife during sensitive times: mating, nesting, raising young, or winter.

Know what kinds of animals live where you are going, and research breeding and mating patterns. Learn how best to protect and, in some cases, avoid them. If you will be in bear country, take along appropriate equipment to protect bears from your food and vice versa (see the discussion on bears in chapter 4, as well as *NOLS Bear Essentials*).

Be Considerate of Other Visitors
Respect other visitors and protect the quality of their experience.
Be courteous. Yield to other users.
Take breaks and camp away from trails and other visitors.
Let nature's sounds prevail. Avoid loud voices and noises.

Lessen your visual impact by using darker-colored tents and tarps and setting them up away from shore in heavily traveled areas. Build flexibility in your trip and daily schedule so that you never have to camp with another group or even in the same area. Keep your voices down.

Conservation and Paddler Activism

While backcountry travelers are expected to follow Leave No Trace principles, many who travel in wild places come to appreciate them for their intrinsic and recreational value and go further in their efforts, working actively for their conservation and protection.

Paddlers have a role to play in the debate over how best to use our wild places, be they true wilderness, parkland, or an abused river down the road. And it is paddlers who often know a place best, with intimate knowledge that can aid in the work to conserve it.

PROTECTION OF PADDLING AREAS
The mid to late 1960s saw the beginnings of federal protection for special paddling areas with the designation of the Boundary Waters Canoe Area Wilderness, the Allagash Wilderness Waterway, and the creation of the National Wild and Scenic Rivers System. Countless places large and small have been conserved since then, but battles continue in North America and around the world. In Quebec, the Rupert River was lost to diversion dams, but the Great Whale River was saved. In Chile, the Futaleufu River appears to have been saved, but the Bio Bio River was dammed. In local paddling areas and distant wildernesses alike, houses, resource extraction, and other forms of development are planned and fought against. Learn what's going on in the places that matter to you, and lend your voice to the debate.

DAMS
The dam-building spree in the twentieth century helped win World War II and launch the United States to superpower status, but at a cost of the overwhelming majority of our wild and free-flowing rivers. The dam-building era in the United States appears to have run its course, as 2011 became the first year in American history where more dams were removed than installed. The pendulum is swinging in the opposite direction now, as even power companies realize that the economics of old and marginal dams no

longer make sense. In 2012, large dams on the Penobscot, White Salmon, and Elwha Rivers all came down, freeing rivers from long confinement and making them available for fish, wildlife, and paddlers.

This downward trend in dam construction is limited to the United States, however, as Chile, China, and Brazil, among others, charge ahead with massive dam-building campaigns. Dams are built for various reasons—to generate electricity, control flooding, or irrigate crops in arid regions—but they all have tremendous side effects. Land is flooded, forcing people to move, and the species that relied on the river tend to move or die off. Sediment that used to be moved downstream now piles up behind the dam, giving even the best-designed dams a useful shelf life of just a few decades.

Conclusion

There is a sadness at the end of any voyage, as you round that last buttress of rock and coast into the eddy by the take-out or pass under the bridge that signals a return to civilized country. In that moment, you know that in spite of all the hardships and going without, something special has occurred and is now coming to an end. A goal was set weeks or months before, and you are left with only a short portage yet to complete. The expedition was infused with the nutrients of communication and good leadership and supported with skill and judgment. You and your group flourished during the exploration, with a social unit of disparate individuals working hard together and experiencing wildness.

The sadness is only temporary, however, and as your group disbands with your goal satisfied, you realize the exciting truth: a dream or goal accomplished paves the way for more goals and dreams, and it will not be long before maps once more litter your living space and you again put blade to water.

Acknowledgments

This book would not have been possible without the constant support of those at the National Outdoor Leadership School, from trustees and directors to interns, who have influenced me as well as this book. The incredible river instructors that I have had the honor to work with over the years deserve tremendous thanks, as they have helped make me who I am. A consistent professionalism and a constant striving for excellence define this group, and I am lucky to have been able to call them teachers and mentors: Duck Murphy, Rebecca Raynor, Dave Pigott, Brianna Mackay, Jaret Slipp, Dale Shaw, and many others.

The constant support and encouragement of the NOLS community was integral to the success of this book. Publication managers Joanne Haines and Adam Swisher were always on hand to answer questions and provide structure and guidance, and curriculum director John Gookin sowed the seed that became this book. The senior faculty that worked to hammer this text into something respectable deserve special thanks: Jeff Carty, Briana Mackay, Brendan Madden, Nate Ostis, Pip Coe, Mark Hamlin, Tod Schimelpfenig, and Ken Olivier. The perspective they lent was invaluable, and while in the end this text was a group effort, any mistakes are my own.

My thanks go to Eliza for her drawings, constant support, and appreciating and encouraging a spirit of adventure.

Finally, I thank my students, for their eagerness to follow into the wilderness and for their eagerness to lead. I think that in the end, you have given me more than I have given you. This book is for you.

GEAR LISTS

The problem with any mandatory gear list is that it can't account for different environments, conditions, and times of year. Personal preference based on experience always leads canoeists to different choices. Below you'll find a list of the basic gear I take on every expedition, regardless of when and where, and then a few recommended additions for a variety of conditions. These are simple suggestions and should be adjusted to meet your personal and environmental needs.

BASIC:
EVERY EXPEDITION

Personal

Head
warm hat
sunglasses
sun hat or baseball cap
bandanna

Body: Top
2 long-sleeved synthetic or
wool shirts, midweight
fleece, midweight
wind jacket, uninsulated
rain jacket, uninsulated

Body: Bottom
2 long underwear bottoms,
silkweight
wind pants or synthetic, fast-
drying pants

Feet
3 pairs wool socks
wet shoes
camp shoes

Big Stuff
sleeping bag and compression
stuff sack
sleeping mat or pad
dry bag or barrel, 2,029 to
3,381 ounces (60 to 100
liters)
daypack, 676 ounces (20-liter
dry pack and/or pack)

Little Stuff
toothpaste and toothbrush
sunscreen
headlamp
bowl and spoon
water bottle, 34 ounces (1 liter)
lip balm
bandanna

Men's Specific Personal
2 pairs underwear, synthetic boxer-style or shorts

Women's Specific Personal
3 pairs underwear, cotton crotch
jog bra
tampons and/or pads
stuff sack with extra plastic bags (for trash)
optional extra bandanna
optional menstrual cup (bring backup tampons/pads)

Group

Shelters
tents or tarps with repair materials, cord, and pegs

Medical Kit

Repair Kit
multitool
Speedy Stitcher
needle and thread
pole splints
epoxy resin and putty
spare zippers and buckles
hose clamps
wire: 8-gauge and fine-gauge
patches for nylon, PVC, and mosquito netting
Seam Grip
spare bolts, seat parts
adjustable wrench/pliers
screwdrivers wit appropriate heads
spare p-cord
optional hand drill

Food and Kitchen Packs
stove and fuel bottle
pot and lid
fuel
pot grips
food and spices
water storage
water purification
lighter
turner/spatula
optional Fry-Bake pan and lid
optional spare pot

Communication Devices

Miscellaneous
trowel
optional beach duffel bag

Travel
outfitted canoe appropriate to use
paddles with 1 spare per boat
maps and cases
bailers
whistle

Common Luxuries
Crazy Creek style camp chair
books
fishing equipment
binoculars
camera
notebook and pen
music instruments

RIVER: EXPEDITIONS WITH WHITEWATER

Personal
    helmet
    rescue PFD
    river knife
    optional splash jacket or dry-
        top
    optional splash pants
    optional wet suit, top, bottoms,
        or Farmer John

Travel
    optional flotation

Rescue Kit
    knife
    folding saw
    whistle
    extra throw bags (personal
        waist bag or regular)
    $3/8$-inch (9-millimeter)
        cordelette (prussik cord)
    10 to 14 feet (3 to 4.3 meters)
        of tubular webbing, poten-
        tially looped around the
        waist as a flip line
    2 locking carabiners

Pin Kit
    150 to 200 feet (46 to 61
        meters) of static line or two
        75-foot (23-meter) Spectra
        throw bags
    locking carabiners, pear and
        oval
    climbing protection: nuts and
        stoppers

    $3/8$-inch (9-millimeter)
        cordelette in 4- to 5-foot
        (1.2- to 1.5-meter) lengths
        for prussiks
    1-inch (2.5-centimeter) tubular
        webbing in various lengths,
        8 to 25 feet (2.4 to 7.6
        meters)
    cam straps
    pulleys

WET CONDITIONS

Personal
    rain pants
    waterproof camp shoes or
        boots

Group
    kitchen tarp

COLD WEATHER

Personal
    rain pants
    warm gloves
    waterproof paddling gloves or
        pogies
    waterproof camp shoes or
        boots
    puffy jacket, synthetic
    extra base layers and socks
    neoprene socks
    optional river boots or mukluks
    splash jacket or dry-top
    splash pants
    optional dry suit
    optional fleece or neoprene
        skull cap

Group
    extra fuel

Travel
    optional hypothermia kit

EXTREME COLD

Personal
    waterproof camp boots
    waterproof river boots
    dry suit (river) and/or
        anorak/rain jacket and pants
        (calm water)
    waterproof mittens
    parka
    fleece pants
    puffy pants

Group
    extra fuel
    extra stove

Travel
    hypothermia kit

DESERT

Personal
    long-sleeved sun shirt, syn-
        thetic for all seasons, cotton
        OK for summer

Group
    kitchen tarp
    groover or other portable toilet
    water jugs and treatment
    waterproof dishes for butter or
        bottles for cooking oil

TROPICAL

Personal
    2 long-sleeved cotton shirts,
        collared and loose
    2 pairs long cotton pants, loose
    sun hat, wide-brimmed
    cotton or paddling gloves
    leather gloves
    bug tents

Group
    robust medical kit, including
        antifungals
    optional hammocks
    optional mosquito domes or
        netting

ARCTIC

Personal
    cold-weather gear

Group
    mountaineering tents
    optional bug tarp

EASTERN WOODLANDS

Group
    optional small forest ax
    optional bow saw

BUGGY AREAS
    mosquito head net
    optional bug jacket
    optional bug tarp

BEAR COUNTRY
    bear spray
    optional ropes for hanging
        food

FRONT- AND SIDECOUNTRY EXPEDITIONING

While rarely practiced at NOLS, frontcountry travel through areas easily accessed by vehicle is becoming more common, especially with small teams on long, continent-spanning voyages. In addition to enabling you to have fresh food, more frequent showers, and lighter packs, this type of travel brings you closer to the culture and history of a place. Civilization is centered around water, and a small, human-powered boat is often the best way to see it. From paddling among the chateaux on the Loire in France, to chatting with Romanian fishermen on the Danube, to passing Scottish castles on the Tay, to being invited in for supper off the Moose on New England's Northern Forest Canoe Trail, there are some things the backcountry can't offer. Depending on where the travel is taking place, however, it may not be all that different from a backcountry trip. The primary differences come in camping, provisioning, and portaging.

CAMPING
Paddling a frontcountry river might mean passing through small towns or even cities, as well as large tracts of farmland, pasture, and undeveloped forest buffers. Riverfront development is often much less common than you might expect, and you might find that stretches of rivers, more than lakes or ponds, are secluded places right in the midst of civilization because of inaccessibility, flooding hazards, or other factors. In many places, forest is allowed to grow up along the riverbanks to prevent erosion, and these buffer zones often are perfect places to camp. On state and federal land, open space near a boat ramp, fishing access, or BLM pasture can make for great camping. Be sure to practice LNT camping even in these areas, whether or not others are doing so.

Knowing whose land you are on is important, as is asking permission. In some places, constantly changing riverbanks and islands are public property, but in other places they are privately owned and you may see No Trespassing signs. If you wish to camp on large ranches, call ahead of time to ask permission, have the property owner's phone numbers with you as you go, and do your best not to break the law. Having a green or dark-colored tent is a good idea, as it helps avoid notice and lowers your impact, and camping out of sight and out of the way will increase your odds of not attracting unwanted attention.

Islands can provide safe, secluded campsites and are a great bet. They can shift and change on free-flowing rivers and in open river plains, however, and high water can cover features that are on the map, just as low water can expose things that are not. In some agricultural areas, especially in very rural areas or less developed countries, islands are sometimes used as natural animal pens, and you might have night visits from feral pigs, wild dogs, horses, or cattle, depending on where you are.

Generally, try to avoid camping in towns or cities, as you may not be able to find a good spot and you may worry over your gear. Only in the worst circumstances would your safety be compromised; more often, people will invite you in for a place to sleep and a meal to eat. Many towns have designated places where you can camp, often in municipal campgrounds or fairgrounds. As a last resort, stop by the police station, which will often be staffed all night in larger towns and may have a patch of ground on which you can camp. Canoe and kayak clubs are all over Europe and in a few places in North America; these can range from simple sheds to the yacht clubs of paddlesport, with showers, restaurants, beer halls, campsites, a repair shop, bunkrooms, and so on. Research ahead of time.

Campgrounds abound in the United States, Canada, Europe, Australia, and New Zealand but are less common elsewhere. Where you can find them, campgrounds are a great bet, as they often have hot showers and can be located right by the river or lake. In some rural areas, they seem to be nearly everywhere, but they may not be open year round. Some places prohibit tent camping, especially in oil and gas towns and areas with migrant labor. A quick Google Maps search and a few phone calls before your trip can give you a sense of what to expect.

No matter how strong your willpower or how empty your wallet, passing through a town by portage or paddle on a cold, windy, and rainy evening will get you thinking about a motel. In rural areas, they can be as inexpensive as $35 to $50 a night and are a worthy temptation. In small towns, a grocery store, library, and hardware store are often within walking distance of the motel. Look for the type of motel with rooms that open onto the street or parking lot so that you can easily move your boat into the room without having to pull it through the lobby. Non-chain motels and hotels may have a house or garage nearby for storage as well.

Couchsurfing (couchsurfing.com) is a free service that pairs up travelers with free accommodations around the world. Couchsurfing hosts often are happy to host a paddler—it is unusual and fun.

PROVISIONING

One of the best things about a front- or sidecountry expedition is that you often don't need to carry more than a few days' worth of food. This means your packs are vastly lighter, and you can eat fresh food every day and move faster with a lighter load. Google Maps can help give you a sense of where the grocery stores are closest to the river, especially in North America and Europe. It is a good idea to plan to hit these locations during business hours, and an even better idea to combine a portage with a run through town to pick up food for another two to four days.

Water can be tricky. You go through it fast, it is heavy, and on many rivers in more settled areas, the water you are paddling on may not be safe to drink. A 2.6-gallon (10-liter) MSR Dromedary hydration bag is a great piece of gear that can hold enough water to last two people about a day and a half in most conditions, if you are being judicious with your usage.

PORTAGING

Portaging plays a big part in front- and sidecountry trips, as dams and towns are more common in these areas, and your route will often connect multiple watersheds. For extended front- or sidecountry expeditions, or when connecting wilderness areas by human power, the distance and methods available add a whole new dimension, although technically, because you are transporting your boat and gear over land with your own energy, it is still portaging. The quantum leap forward in frontcountry expeditioning is in making long portages around dams, waterfalls, towns, or polluted streams, or overland carries, blissfully easy and fast through the use of a cart.

Your basic need here is a cart or set of wheels that is lightweight, durable, and has low rolling resistance. Portaging 200 pounds (90 kilograms) of boat and gear on a reasonably flat road or very good trail with a cart—in one trip—is as easy as walking. What you gain in efficiency, however, is lost in durability. Portage carts break, no matter what style, material, and wheel type—some quite quickly. They are not designed for rough terrain or for use with loaded boats, but many can handle them with a trade-off in life span. If weight is a concern, consider having the paddlers carry their own personal packs and take turns pulling the boat.

The cart should be placed on the ground; many have kickstands to hold them up, but these aren't strictly necessary. Then lower the canoe gently onto the padded supports of the frame of the cart, and secure the boat tightly in place with cam straps. The cart is best placed under the pivot point of the canoe, with whatever gear loaded such that it is balanced on the fulcrum of the cart. The supports can shift in use and put a wheel in contact with the hull. If this occurs, the friction generated can be immense and can burn a hole in a Royalex ABS boat; check if the cart becomes harder to pull. The more rigid the canoe is, the better it will take to a cart, as a softer hull will deform slightly on the focused points of contact where it meets the cart; this makes smaller Kevlar and carbon-fiber canoes slightly easier to portage with a cart.

Most carts have aluminum tubing and solid plastic wheels; these are easy-to-find options that cost under $100, but they are better suited for recreational use and will not last on an expedition, especially if the boat is loaded or partially loaded. Harder to find are carts with 16-inch (40-centimeter) pneumatic bicycle wheels, but these have minimal rolling resistance and are a joy to portage with. Thick mountain bike tires are best. The wheels can be under the hull, giving good clearance for light off-road duty, or off to the side, providing more stability and a lower center of gravity. The best type of cart has a heavy tubular steel frame and all-steel wheel attachments that allow the tires to fold in, forming a small, tight, if rather heavy package. This cart will last much longer, but the wheels, and especially the tires, will need to be replaced if used over great distances or rough terrain. This type generally costs $150 or more.

The bold will consider attaching the cart to a bicycle to increase the ease and mileage dramatically. The longest human-powered portage I have ever been part of was 450 miles (724 kilometers), and we did it in eight days; needless to say, this was not a traditional portage. Towing a canoe by bike is hard work, but it is possible and is a wonderful challenge either in expedition use or for shuttling to your local play spot.

No matter what the conveyance, if you are on a road, you should be on the shoulder, brightly lit or colored, and should avoid times of darkness or low light. Being on the side of the road, even with a giant plastic boat, can be more dangerous than running whitewater.

APPENDIX C | CAREERS IN CANOEING

Canoe expeditions are expensive both for their prime cost and deferred cost—that is to say, the money that supports them and the money you aren't making while you are on them. One way to reduce or eliminate the former and minimize the latter is to engage in work in which your job is to support or participate in a canoe expedition. In most cases, this work will be incredibly meaningful for you as well as the participants, and although you will not get rich doing it, at least not in monetary wealth, it can be life changing for a variety of reasons.

If you decide to pursue a career in canoeing, you need to have sufficient experience and be competent in both technical skills and leadership.

The primary career options for canoeists are in summer camps or youth programs, guiding companies, or teaching youth and adults.

CAMP ROUTE: TRIP LEADER

Summer camps can be a great way for young people to build experience on real expeditions. Many camps will hire mature eighteen-year-olds with previous experience, especially if it was at that camp. Camps with more professional wilderness programs will sometimes hire only those who are twenty-one years or older, or require that the senior leader on a trip be at least twenty-one years old. Some camps have a large discrepancy between the skill or experience of their leaders and the amount of responsibility that is placed on them; novices may be tasked with leading first-time canoeists, occasionally with bad results. Be careful and research the program.

Summer programs for youth that focus on travel and outdoor adventure are numerous and very popular, and can be fantastic ways of gaining experience in a number of different skill types.

Whether you will be working at a camp or with a program, you will be required to take a Wilderness First Aid and CPR course, and a Wilderness First Responder course is often required or highly recommended.

GUIDING ROUTE: GUIDE

The vast majority of guiding jobs are in day and half-day whitewater rafting, though there is a subset of multiday rafting as well. Multiday canoe guiding is at the sharp end of the pyramid; few such jobs are available, though the pay is better than for any other option here. You have to put in some time before choice assignments will become available to you, but with charm, skill, and time, guides can eventually get flown around North America and the world to incredible locations to eat well and paddle with interesting clients. Guides work extremely hard; they sometimes have to set up tents and organize and portage much of the gear, and they usually have to cook and clean for the entire group. Finding off-season or migratory work is also a big part of making the guide lifestyle work.

TEACHING ROUTE: INSTRUCTOR

While there are elements of education in both camp trip leading and guiding, those jobs focus more on managing the experience of the participants than teaching them. The educator emerges as a role in working for NOLS or other organizations, instructing frontcountry courses for a paddling school or organizing body, or serving as a coach. The real difference is that as an instructor, you seek to eventually make yourself unnecessary.

SCALE OF RIVER DIFFICULTY

The International Scale of River Difficulty is a system of classification for moving water with six levels that describe general stages of challenge. The scale runs from Class I to VI and is helpful in communicating information about a river through guidebooks, trip reports, or orally when getting details on a new route.

Rivers change drastically both in flow and obstacles present through the seasons and over time: Class III rapids at one flow might not even exist during a high-water event, and in spring the stretch might be so choked with woody debris that it is unrunnable. Factors of water temperature, group skill and experience, downstream consequences, and equipment all play into real and perceived difficulty, as does how remote, continuous, or inaccessible that section of river is.

Whether paddling a river for the first or the twentieth time, treat it as an exploratory run. Rapids may have shifted in floods; new features may have been exposed by changing water levels; new man-made or natural hazards like ropes, boats, or trees may be present. Relying on a guidebook description or your often fuzzy memories of a previous experience can be a recipe for disaster. The river is different every time.

For reference, the scale, with notes for expedition canoeing, is as follows:

Class I. No significant obstacles or waves. Lines are clear and water is not pushy. Canoes can float through with little direction or skill.

Class II. Significant obstacles and waves are present but are easily avoidable with some skill and proper equipment. Lines are mostly clear, and water can be pushy near rocks, on eddy lines, or on steep pitches. Can require scouting.

Class III. Significant obstacles and large waves are present and must be aggressively avoided; this is usually possible only with good equipment and significant experience. Lines must be carefully chosen and stuck to. Water is pushy nearly everywhere. Requires scouting and a detailed safety plan. This is the limit of navigability for loaded expedition canoes.

Class IV. Significant obstacles and large waves dominate most or all of the set of rapids. These are frequently steep, rocky, and continuous big-water rapids of noticeable complexity. Lines are present but must be analyzed through mandatory scouting and the formation of a safety plan. This class is beyond the limits of navigability for loaded expedition canoes, save for select short, big-water rapids with clear passages, clean run-outs, or obvious moves being run by highly trained and equipped experts.

Class V. Significant obstacles and large waves dominate the rapids and are impossible to avoid; steep, rocky, and continuous rapids of excessive violence and complexity. Few or no good lines exist. Often cannot be scouted adequately or at all. Can be run in front- or sidecountry settings by expert canoeists in professional teams and with dedicated equipment and safety precautions.

Class VI. Steep, rocky, continuous, and possibly big-water rapids where small mistakes will result in death. This class is also used for large and dramatic unexplored rivers that have not been adequately scouted and figured out by professional whitewater kayakers. Until recently, this has been the limit of navigability for all craft, but a few descents by the best kayakers in the world have changed that.

Note: These ratings are often modified with a + or − sign (e.g., Class II+) to designate slightly easier or harder rapids. Sometimes modifiers like steep, continuous, rocky, or big-water might be applied to a given set of rapids in a guidebook or trip report.

Index

Page numbers in italics indicates illustrations and sidebars.

The Leader in Wilderness Education

NOLS

The National Outdoor Leadership School is the leading educational organization for outdoor skills and leadership and offers courses ranging from ten days to a full academic year in the world's most spectacular wilderness classrooms. Founded in 1965, this nonprofit school based in Lander, Wyoming, teaches a wide variety of outdoor skills, including backpacking, mountaineering, sea kayaking, canoeing, skiing, caving, horsepacking, and rock climbing.

NOLS operates primarily in the Rocky Mountains (Wyoming and Idaho), the Pacific Northwest (Washington), the Southwest United States, Alaska, Mexico, Canada (Yukon Territory and British Columbia), Patagonia (Chile), India, Australia, New Zealand, and the Amazon. In addition to field courses, the NOLS Wilderness Medicine Institute gives students the tools to handle difficult medical decisions in remote locations, and NOLS Professional Training offers customized training for outdoor programs, educational organizations, and corporations. NOLS has graduated close to 200,000 students.

PHOTO: JEFF STEIN, NOLS INSTRUCTOR

On a NOLS course, students learn to live and travel in the wilderness. They benefit from the best instructors in the business, well-trained educators and leaders with a passion for teaching. The school's hands-on, learn-by-doing approach to education means that students come away ready to lead others on their own wilderness expeditions. In addition to outdoor instruction, NOLS teaches leadership lessons in decision-making, problem-solving, teamwork, and judgment that transfer to life at school, in sports, and at work.

The NOLS method of instruction provides an excellent counterpart to the traditional classroom setting, and each year the school attracts thousands of students who want to complement their conventional learning with a NOLS education. Just like other schools, NOLS offers scholarships as well as college and graduate-level credit in a range of areas, from environmental ethics and leadership techniques to natural history.

For more information call 800-710-NOLS, or visit us at www.nols.edu.

NOLS and Stackpole
Partners in Wilderness Education